Guillaume Apollinaire

Revised Edition

Twayne's World Authors Series

French Literature

David O'Connell, Editor

Georgia State University

TWAS 14

Group of Artists, 1908 by Marie Laurencin. Left to right: Pablo Picasso, Marie Laurencin, Guillaume Apollinaire, and Fernande Olivier. *(Baltimore Museum of Art)*

Guillaume Apollinaire

Revised Edition

By Scott Bates

University of the South

Twayne Publishers
A Division of G. K. Hall & Co. • *Boston*

PQ
2601
.P6
Z55
1989

Guillaume Apollinaire, Revised Edition
Scott Bates

Copyright 1989 by G. K. Hall & Co.
All rights reserved.
Published by Twayne Publishers
A Division of G. K. Hall & Co.
70 Lincoln Street
Boston, Massachusetts 02111

Copyediting supervised by Barbara Sutton.
Book production by Gabrielle B. McDonald.
Book design by Barbara Anderson.

Typeset in 11 pt. Garamond
by Modern Graphics, Inc., Weymouth, Massachusetts.

Printed on permanent/durable acid-free paper
and bound in the United States of America.

Library of Congress Cataloging-in-Publication Data

Bates, Scott.
    Guillaume Apollinaire / by Scott Bates. — Rev. ed.
        p.   cm. — (Twayne's world authors series ; TWAS 14. French literature.)
    Bibliography: p.
    Includes index.
    ISBN 0-8057-8246-X
    1. Apollinaire, Guillaume, 1880–1918—Criticism and interpretation.
I. Title.   II. Series: Twayne's world authors series ; TWAS 14.   III. Series:
Twayne's world authors series. French literature.
PQ2601.P6Z55   1989
841'.912—dc19
                                                                88-24828
                                                                CIP

To Phoebe

Contents

About the Author

Scott Bates received his B.A. from Carleton College and his M.A. and Ph.D. in French studies at the University of Wisconsin. He served in France and Germany with the Military Government Division of the U.S. Army during World War II and spent two years in France after the war on a Fulbright scholarship studying modern French poetry. Since 1954 he has been teaching French language and literature and film study at the University of the South at Sewanee, Tennessee. He has edited a volume of antiwar poetry, *Poems of War Resistance, from 2300 B.C. to the Present* (Grossman), as well as three calendars of antiwar material for the War Resisters League. His poems and translations have appeared, among other places, in *Furioso*, the *New Yorker*, the *Partisan Review*, the *Sewanee Review*, the *New Republic*, the *Carleton Miscellany*, and *Delos*, and he has published two books of poetry, *The ABC of Radical Ecology* (for Highlander Center) and *Lupo's Fables*. His many articles on Apollinaire have been appearing since 1956, and he is currently working on a major study dealing with Apollinaire's eroticism.

Preface

J'ai bâti une maison au milieu de l'Océan.

—"Océan de terre"

Like Christians of the first or tenth centuries we live in an eschatological age; it is no more news to anyone who reads the newspapers that the world could end today from nuclear destruction than it is that he or she could die in an automobile accident tonight or from cancer next year. It is therefore pertinent to recall that certain poets, novelists, cranks, priests, and scholars have been concerned with the arrival of the ultimate catastrophe for more than a hundred years now. In their analyses and prophecies our present situation has been anticipated and even oriented; so that a serious study of modern literature and art today cannot any more ignore "the end of the world theme" than it can ignore, say, myth, Freud, entropy, semiotics, or deconstruction theory.

In secular literature the theme has been with us since Grainville and Mary Shelley wrote works on "the last man" in 1805 and 1826, respectively, and since Poe and Baudelaire gave currency to an accelerating wave of science fiction known to the trade as "the anti-utopia (dystopia) theme." During the same years the theme continued to be a prominent one in religious works and utterances, with, however, a romantic intensification: as Paul Vulliaud notes in his comprehensive study of its course from ancient India to the present, "The nineteenth century was one of the ages most fraught with predictions of the end of the world, which constitute, it might be said, a specialty of its [religious] literature" (*La Fin du monde,* 1952). In poetry, we are familiar with multiple apocalyptic prognostications ranging from Baudelaire's "the world is going to end" (in *Fusées*) and Rimbaud's "the earth is melting" to Yeats's rough beast and Eliot's final whimper.

Before 6 August 1945, however, there was a major difference between secular and religious visions of Armageddon. While various fundamentalist sects and heretics saw it as immediate and called upon the world to repent before it was too late, secular prophets, literati, scientists, and socialists either postponed an ultimate scientific calamity to a vague distant date when the comet would strike, the sun explode or burn out, and the world ignite or freeze, or they foresaw a relative human ending in which the yellow horde would sweep in from the East ("over the new Trans-Siberian railway," ironized Apollinaire), nations would exterminate each other, or the downtrodden Occidental masses would rise and wash the earth with the blood of their oppressors. In these last predictions, particularly numerous in the last half of the nineteenth century, the imminent catastrophe was only occasionally seen as absolute; usually some millennium—aesthetic, socialist, and/or scientific—would rise from the smoking ruins to establish itself as the Crystal City, the eternal New Jerusalem.

The idea of revolutionary death and rebirth, a kind of poetico-religio-socialist phoenix theme, will be the one that will concern us most in the works of the poet Guillaume Apollinaire and his friend the painter Pablo Picasso. The two artists chanced on the globe during the turn-of-the-century apogee of all these eschatological currents and made a specialty of bringing them to the attention of the twentieth century. In the case of Apollinaire, fundamentalist Catholic dogma concerning the biblical prophets, the Antichrist, and the Messiah played a major role in orienting his secular thought—and thereafter the thought of his numerous heirs.

When he wrote in the first decade of the century, for example, "I used to hope for the end of the world" ("Les Fiançailles" ["The Betrothal"]), he was probably referring to his earlier utopian anarchist leanings; yet the plot of his first novel, *La Gloire de l'olive* (The glory of the olive)—or at least what may be perceived of it in the remaining fragments of the book—follows more or less traditional religious beliefs in its description of the Antichrist's attempt to avert the end of the world by preventing the accession to the Roman See of the last pope, called "la Gloire de l'olive." In his most violent anticlericalism he believed in the inevitable death and resurrection cycles of nations and masses, as did his mentors of anarchist thought, the writers Sébastien Faure, Laurent Tailhade, Octave Mirbeau, Saint-Georges de Bouhélier, and Mécislas Golberg, several of whom had undergone a similar Catholic upbringing. Out of this witches' brew of the sacred and profane came much of our modern art and literature, including that, for example, of Picasso, Yeats, Rilke, Kafka, Gide, Lawrence, Joyce, and Sartre. Also the new gods of the century, Mussolini (a revolutionary anarchist), Hitler (Mussolini's disciple), Lenin, and Mao Tse-tung. "The more carefully one compares the outbreaks of militant social chiliasm during the later Middle Ages with modern totalitarian movements the more remarkable the similarities appear," writes Norman Cohn in *The Pursuit of the Millennium*.

An eschatological age, therefore, is our age, with its anxiety and its desperate search for religious and secular solutions, for gods, for mere survival. An age similar to that approaching the year 1000, wrote Apollinaire in 1915: "If we aren't in an early medieval age of mental licence, of lyrical irony, of the *danse macabre* and the terrors of the year 1000, we are in an age roughly equivalent to it, today is the time of Anguish *{le temps de l'Angoisse}*" (letter to Lou, 2 February 1915).

An age in which, thought both he and Picasso, God was dead and the artist was obliged either to assert his prerogative as a microcosm of the universe, to become the macrocosm and save the world for beauty, or else to perish miserably with the anonymous masses. In short, an age in which at least two of our leaders of modern taste were early acquainted with existential anguish, the terrible responsibility of re-creating the world in one's own image before it died in natural or supernatural agony. It is a tribute to them and perhaps a lesson to us that they were able to formulate and impose their image in Dionysian energy and joy ("the anguish of my delight," wrote Apollinaire) with full Apollonian awareness of the proximity of the danger.

For thirty years after his death in 1918, this picture of a committed Apollinaire dedicated to the task of bringing light to chaos and, if not to replace God in person, at least to become a sort of illegitimate Christ saving the world through the Verb, was not taken seriously by many admirers of the poet. Given the surface dilletantism, the cultivated mystery, the charm and fantasy of the person Apollinaire, this attitude is completely understandable. By friends and enemies alike, he was variously described as the delightful impresario of the avant-garde (whose ideas were overly poetic), the pontiff of cubism (who really knew very little about painting), the continuator of France's lyrical traditions from Villon through Verlaine (whose poems were intuitively created almost in spite of himself), the inventor of the word *surréalisme* who used it without full knowledge of its implications, the man who would embrace anything if it were new, who was a slave to love, who bridged the gap between two centuries of great literature and art by a miraculous combination of luck, ubiquitousness, enthusiasm, audacity, and lyrical intoxication.

Some of this is partly true; but it is superficial truth at best. As in the earlier case of Rimbaud, much influence was here united to much misunderstanding, as some of Apollinaire's closest friends, followers, and critics failed to catch the largest import of his communication and to understand what he was saying—what his works "meant." In the 1950s, the picture substantially changed. The large number of manuscripts and other documents that became available for the first time following World War II rendered possible a close look at Apollinaire's aesthetics and philosophy and brought clarity to many obscure passages. The first accurate biography in 1952 and the first Sorbonne course on him in 1953 only reinforced what many critics, scholars, and writers by this time recognized, our awareness of the major contributions made to art and literature by one of the most learned, innovative and universal creators of a seminal age; and it came as no surprise in the 1970s that the editors of the Cabeen bibliography should select Apollinaire along with Proust, Gide, Valéry, Malraux, Mauriac, Camus, and Sartre as one of the twenty most important French authors of the century.

This study, the first comprehensive survey of Apollinaire's symbolism and ideas, is especially indebted to the earlier works of Michel Décaudin, Marcel Adéma, L.C. Breunig, and Pierre Caizergues. Michel Décaudin's careful *Dossier d'Alcools* (1960) and his two Pléiade editions of the poetry and prose, L. C. Breunig's *Chroniques d'art* (1960) and annotated edition with J.-C. Chevalier of *Les Peintres cubistes* (1965), and Pierre Caizergues's *Apollinaire journaliste* (1979) have provided essential documents and information; and Marcel Adéma's *Guillaume Apollinaire le mal-aimé* (1952) and *Guillaume Apollinaire* (1968), the first biographies to penetrate through the enormous quantity of legendary material accumulated about the poet to the truths of his existence, have provided basic facts and valuable insights. Finally, special thanks are due to the many Apollinaire scholars who have personally helped me with my research, particularly Willard Bohn, Madeleine Boisson, L. C. Breunig, Pierre Caizergues, J.-C. Chevalier, Claude Debon, Michel Décaudin, Lionel Follet, Anne Hyde Greet, Ian Lockerbie, Victor Martin-Schmets, Marc Poupon, and Georges Schmits. Also those now deceased: Jacqueline Apollinaire, Françoise Dininman, Armand Huysmans, and Pascal Pia.

In my study I have endeavored to help the reader arrive at an understanding of the meaning of the major works of Apollinaire by 1) considering in a schematic way principal themes and symbols; 2) analyzing key works of poetry, fiction, and criticism; 3) surveying chronologically the philosophical and aesthetic ideas of the poet in relation to the facts of his life and the ideas of his time; and 4) listing in glossary form the sources and meanings that have been discovered to date concerning the poet's obscurer references. Inevitably, because of the complexity of symbolism, breadth of cultural reference, and extreme subjectivity of Apollinaire's work, many of my interpretations are partial and conjectural; intensive research into literary sources and the deciphering of manuscripts proceeds apace, and we can expect major discoveries in the near future. In all, I hope this study will serve as a guide and reference work to an important, very concerned body of literature that traces at least one possible path for the twentieth century to follow along its by now all-too-familiar precipice.

Scott Bates

University of the South

Acknowledgments

For permission to quote from Guillaume Apollinaire's works not yet in the public domain, I am grateful to Editions Gallimard for "Peu de chose," "Endurcis-toi vieux coeur," and "Le Quatrième Poème secret" *(Oeuvres poétiques).* The extract from "Ispahan" is reprinted from *Il y a,* Editions Messein. The frontispiece, *Group of Artists, 1908,* is reproduced by permission of the Baltimore Museum of Art: The Cone Collection, formed by Dr. Claribel Cone and Miss Etta Cone of Baltimore, Maryland.

Chronology

1880   16 August, born Wilhelm Albert Wladimir Alexandre Apollinaris de Kostrowitzky, biological son of Angelica Alexandrina de Kostrowitzky and Francesco-Costantino-Camillo Flugi d'Aspermont (?), in Rome.

1887   Moves to Monaco with mother and brother Albert (b. 1882).

1888   Enters Catholic parochial school at Monaco.

1892   8 May, first communion; fall, writes first poetry.

1895   First love affair; enters Catholic parochial school at Cannes.

1897   February, enters public high school at Nice; June, fails oral part of graduation examination (*le baccalauréat*); leaves school without receiving diploma.

1898   Is a strong partisan of Dreyfus.

1899   April, arrives in Paris with mother and brother; July, takes lodgings at Stavelot, Belgium, in the Ardennes; falls in love with Maria Dubois. 5 October, leaves lodgings secretly to avoid payment of rent; returns to Paris.

1900   Spring, collaborates anonymously on serialized novel *Que faire?* (What to do?). Difficult existence in Paris. In love with Linda Molina da Sylva; helps her father write dance manual.

1901   August, employed as tutor for the eight-year-old daughter of the Viscountess de Milhau; Anna Maria Playden (Annie) employed as girl's companion and maid; leaves for the properties of the Viscountess in the Rhineland; falls in love with Annie.

1902   Travels extensively in Germany, Austria, and Czechoslovakia. August, terminates employment with the Viscountess; September, becomes bank clerk in Paris; adopts pseudonym, Guillaume Apollinaire.

1903   Active in leftist literary circles. November, travels to London to see Annie Playden; edits small review *Le Festin d'Esope* (Aesop's feast).

1904   Works on financial paper. May, second trip to London; meets André Derain, Pablo Picasso, Max Jacob. Discontinues *Le Festin d'Esope*.

1905   Spring, edits *La Revue Immoraliste* (two issues).

1906   Writes erotic novels.

1907   Meets Marie Laurencin; introduces Picasso to Braque; moves from mother's house in suburbs to apartment in Paris.

1908   Lectures on symbolist poets; collaborates with Jean Royère on symbolist review *La Phalange;* meets Jules Romains. Summer, travels to Belgium, Holland, visits Gustave Kahn, Théo Varlet.

1909   Publishes *L'Enchanteur pourrissant*. October, moves to Auteuil, to be near Marie Laurencin; begins editing classic erotic novels.

1910   Publishes *L'Hérésiarque et cie;* almost wins Prix Goncourt.

1911   Begins writing chronicle for the *Mercure de France;* publishes *Le Bestiaire ou Cortège d'Orphée*. 7–11 September, arrested, imprisoned for theft of *Mona Lisa* from Louvre, released as innocent.

1912   With friends, founds review *Les Soirées de Paris*. Summer, Marie leaves him; friendship with Robert Delaunay, Blaise Cendrars.

1913   January, moves from Auteuil to the Latin Quarter. Publishes *Alcools, Les Peintres cubistes, L'Antitradition futuriste.*

1914   August, war declared; tries in vain to enlist. September, leaves Paris for Nice; meets the Countess Louise de Coligny-Châtillon (Lou). 6 December, joins the artillery at Nîmes.

1915   2 January, meets briefly Madeleine Pagès on a train returning from a three-day leave with Lou at Nice; 23–29 January, week's leave with Lou; April, moves from Nîmes to front near Reims; August, becomes engaged to Madeleine; is made gunnery sergeant; November, joins infantry to become second lieutenant; December, two weeks leave in Oran with Madeleine.

1916   Becomes French citizen. 17 March, wounded in the head by shrapnel; 9 May, trepanned; fall, publishes *Le Poète assassiné.*

1917   24 June, produces *Les Mamelles de Tirésias;* 26 November, lectures on *l'esprit nouveau* (the new spirit).

1918   2 May, marries Jacqueline Kolb; summer, publishes *Calligrammes;* 9 November, dies of grippe.

Tentative Chronology of the Poems of *Alcools* (1913)

Pre-Rhineland to Post-Rhineland Period, 1898–1903

L'Ermite   Hôtels (?)
Le Larron   La Porte (?)
Merlin et la vieille femme   Signe
Clair de lune

Rhineland and Post-Rhineland Period, 1901–3

Nuit rhénane   Automne malade
Le Vent nocturne   Les Sapins
La Synagogue   Les Femmes
Marizibill (?)   La Blanche Neige
Automne   La Tzigane
L'Adieu   La Maison des morts
La Dame   Mai
Rhénane d'automne   Les Cloches
Les Colchiques   Schinderhannes
La Loreley

1903–7

Un soir (?)   Palais
L'Emigrant de Landor Road   Salomé
La Chanson du mal-aimé   Annie (?)
Lul de Faltenin

1908–10

Le Brasier   Poème lu au mariage d'André
Rosemonde (?)[1]   Salmon
Les Fiançailles   Cortège
1909   Vendémiaire

1910–12

Saltimbanques   Clotilde (?)[2]
Crépuscule (?)   Cors de chasse
A la Santé   Le Voyageur
Marie   Zone
Le Pont Mirabeau   Chantre

Chapter One
Christ and Antichrist

Patriarche, qui donc n'est pas un sauveur?
—L'Enchanteur pourrissant

Biography

An illegitimate child of a rebellious Polish woman and (probably) an Italian aristocrat, Apollinaire was raised by his gambling mother in Italy, in Monaco, on the French Riviera, and in Paris. The resulting cosmopolitanism of his outlook was to have a profound influence on the course of twentieth-century literature and art. Combining a Slavic with a Latin personality, he also brought together a range of social classes: his mother, Angelica de Kostrowitzky, was proud of her noble Polish inheritance and her revolutionary, anti-Russian ancestors, yet she led something of a marginal existence, and her two children "Wilhelm" and Albert (two years younger) seem to have been partially raised in their early years by Roman tradespeople. Up until his seventh year, therefore, Apollinaire must have had experiences in lower-class districts in Italy similar to those of his protagonist in the semiautobiographical story, "Giovanni Moroni," which gave him a lifetime interest in proletarian causes and in the picturesque, often violent life of big city slums. In 1887, his mother took the two boys to Monaco (the father had disappeared), where she became a rather shady *entraîneuse* (hostess) at the Casino; there she formed a lasting liaison with a Jewish gambler from Alsace, Jules Weil. Guillaume was a star pupil in religious boarding schools in Monaco and Cannes, with one last year of public high school in Nice. As a teenager, he was a precocious, literary boy, a leader in school and an instigator of devious extracurricular activities. By the time of his seventeenth year (1897), he had lost his Catholic faith, had experienced his first sexual encounters, and had acquired an extraordinary knowledge of fin-de-siècle esoteric, erotic, and revolutionary literature. He had also written a number of poems, short stories, and novel fragments. After short sojourns in Paris and Stavelot, Belgium, the Kostrowitskys and Weil settled in Paris in 1899, where they lived a life of genteel poverty in a succession of hotel rooms and cheap apartments. Guillaume worked at various low-paying jobs and did ghostwriting for small literary, political, and financial enterprises—and a dance manual! He did not neglect his own writing, however, which was brought quickly to an astonishing level of maturity by the romantic experiences of a year spent as a tutor for an aristocratic German family in the Rhineland, falling in love with the English governess, and traveling with the family through central Europe (1901–2). Almost half of the poems of his great collection *Alcools* (1913) and a number of his best short stories were written as a result of the events of that year.

Back in Paris, he finally found a stable job at a bank in 1902 and launched himself enthusiastically into the exciting literary world of *la belle époque*. He cultivated both intellectual anarchists like Alfred Jarry, André Salmon, Mécislas Golberg, and Remy de Gourmont and humanists like Fernand Gregh, Paul Fort, and Jean Moréas; he began a vanguard magazine, wrote for the socialist press, started publishing his poems and short stories, wandered indefatigably through his beloved Paris, drank all night in the bars of Montmartre and the Left Bank, and embarked countless young women on tempestuous, short-lived love affairs—while saving his stronger emotions (and better poems) for Annie Playden, the English governess. In a relatively short space of time, the five years between 1903 and 1908, he became a catalytic force in the avant-garde, a friend and defender of the young experimental artists Picasso, Braque, Matisse, and Derain, and a spokesman for symbolist poets and novelists; and he began a career in journalistic criticism that was to make him one of the major art critics of our time. He was a controversial catalyst for the cubist, orphist, futurist, dadaist, and surrealist movements, for primitivism, and for African art. A leading member of *la bande à Picasso* (Picasso's gang), he was instrumental in putting first Montmartre on the map of modern art and then, in the immediate prewar years, Montparnasse; to many he was the father of "the School of Paris." He became so confident of his writing potential, indeed, that he courageously abandoned both his mother's house and his regular job in finance—over the strong objections of Mme de Kostrowitzky, who found his poems idiotic and his friends low-class—for an apartment in Paris and a full-time literary career, a terrifying, joyous leap in the dark recorded in his two great poems of literary renewal, "Le Brasier" and "Les Fiançailles."

New love for the painter Marie Laurencin and fame from his first book of stories, *L'Hérésiarque et cie,* seemed to justify his optimism—until he was suddenly arrested and imprisoned for the theft of the *Mona Lisa* from the Louvre in 1911 (a friend of his had stolen some statuettes). He was quickly released as innocent, so the incident might appear on the surface to be a trivial one; but it gave his enemies a chance to increase their attacks against him and brought out a latent (Oedipal?) paranoia that took all the good will of his friends, the publication of his poems *(Alcools)* and a book of art criticism *(Les Peintres cubistes),* and the founding of a new review *(Les Soirées de Paris)* to alleviate. To top it all off, his mistress, Marie Laurencin, left him. In 1914 he wooed and won a new mistress, the Countess Louise de Coligny-Châtillon, by enlisting in the artillery, and he served for a year in the trenches in Champagne first as a gunnery sergeant and then as an infantry lieutenant. When his "Lou" left him in the spring of 1915, he quickly rebounded by falling in love with an Algerian correspondent, Madeleine Pagès, but he abandoned her after being wounded in the head by a shell fragment in March 1916. The wound and subsequent trepanation caused him periodic bouts of sickness during the next three years, and lowered his resistance to the flu from which he died in 1918. His stays at veterans' hospitals did not prevent him from having one of the most creative years of his life in 1917, however, or from retaining his leadership of the international avant-garde, from writing a large body of journalistic criticism, from publishing seminal new works of poetry *(Calligrammes),* short stories *(Le Poète assassiné),* and drama *(Les Mamelles de Tirésias),* and from holding down a fatiguing and time-consuming government job at the Colonial Office. In 1918 he married Jacqueline Kolb, the subject of one of his greatest poems, "La Jolie Rousse" ("The Pretty Redhead"). He died on 9 November 1918 and was buried in the military section of Père Lachaise Cemetery on Armistice Day; his funeral procession wound through celebrating crowds shouting "Conspuez Guillaume!" (Down with Guillaume! [Kaiser Wilhelm]). His mother, brother, and Jules Weil all died the following year.

"Un soir" ("One Evening")

Some of Apollinaire's primary themes and symbols are found in the following poem from his important collection *Alcools (Alcohol,* 1913).

Un soir

Un aigle descendit de ce ciel blanc d'archanges
    Et vous soutenez-moi
Laisserez-vous trembler longtemps toutes ces
               lampes
    Priez priez pour moi

La ville est métallique et c'est la seule étoile
    Noyée dans tes yeux bleus
Quand les tramways roulaient jaillissaient des
              feux pâles
    Sur des oiseaux galeux

Et tout ce qui tremblait dans tes yeux de mes
              songes
    Qu'un seul homme buvait
Sous les feux de gaz roux comme la fausse
              oronge
    O vêtue ton bras se lovait

Vois l'histrion tire la langue aux attentives
    Un fantôme s'est suicidé
L'apôtre au figuier pend et lentement salive
    Jouons donc cet amour aux dés

Des cloches aux sons clairs annonçaient ta
              naissance
    Vois
Les chemins sont fleuris et les palmes
              s'avancent
    Vers toi

(An eagle descended from the sky white with archangels / Help me to bear / Will you permit all these lamps to tremble for long / Pray pray for me // The city is metallic and the only star is drowned / In thy blue eyes / When the trolleys were rolling casting pale fires / On mangy birds // And all that was trembling in thine eyes of my dreams // Drunk by one man / Under the gaslights russet as the false agaric / O clothed-one thine arm coiled // See the mountebank sticks out his tongue at the women waiting / A phantom has committed suicide / The apostle on the fig tree hangs slowly salivating / Let us play for this love then with dice // Thy birth was proclaimed by the clear bells ringing / See / The ways are in flower and the palms are moving / Towards thee)

At first glance "Un soir" seems a jumbled résumé of New Testament history. The narrator is first present at the end of the world as he witnesses the eagle and the archangels of Revelation (8:13 in the Revised Standard Version) and as he prays (to Mary?). He spies the Star of Bethlehem in blue eyes, watches the suicide of the apostle Judas—apocryphally supposed to have hanged himself on a fig tree—and finally hails the birth and entrance into Jerusalem of the Messiah. On closer examination, however, the poem takes a diabolical turn. The feminine "clothed-one" *(vêtue)* and the pun *se lovait* at the end of the third stanza reveal the *thee* of the poem to be a woman, associated with a serpent and with "love," and thus a fallen Eve. Moreover, the *fausse oronge* is the demonic, phallic mushroom par excellence, an ancient shamanistic god, sometimes associated with Eden's forbidden tree; while *vêtue* is an adjective used in the thirteenth century for a female heretic.[1] Apollinaire's placing of the exclusive guiding star in her blue eyes would suggest that she is both his beloved and his new Messiah, a kind of a female Antichrist; she will reign transcendent only after the deaths of an impotent Judas hanged on a phallic-vulvic fig tree and of Christ Himself whose death turns love into a game of chance—just as Roman soldiers gambled for His robe.[2] The images at the beginning of the fourth stanza—mountebank, projected tongue, and attentive women *(attentives;* prostitutes?)—are used elsewhere by Apollinaire to symbolize the death of love; here the mountebank *(histrion* or Italian buffoon, as contrasted to the serious *saltimbanque* or artist) undergoes a phantom death like that of Judas and puts out his tongue like a fool or a hanged man at the female lovers. Indeed, the mountebank, Judas, and love may be one and the same phantom; this follows the thesis of Remy de Gourmont's novel *Le Fantôme* and anticipates Proust's similar ideas.

Certain biographical precisions clarify the poem's experience. Apollinaire's blue-eyed beloved was Anna Maria (!) Playden, "Annie," the frustrating young English governess he had met in Germany *(vêtue* because he presumably could not get her clothes off) who ultimately emigrated to America. Her love is described as poison in other poems—like the poisonous mushroom in this one, with its color of Christ's, Lucifer's, and Judas's red hair[3]—and he loved her sensual arms *(all* women's arms were sensual to him and to Remy de Gourmont). She was his divinity: before leaving the Catholic faith in school, he had celebrated a cult of hyperdulia for

the Virgin Mary, the nostalgia for which was to haunt him the rest
of his life and change his mistresses into Madonnas and goddesses;
as he later wrote to another fugitive mistress named Marie, "Christmas was the Passion." On the other hand, the influence exerted
upon him during his early years in Monaco by a gambling, passionate
mother caused him to associate the cycles of profane love, particularly
its downward trend of frustration, cruelty, and death, with the
wheel of fortune, defeat at the gaming table, and suicide. An illegitimate child who never knew his father, he took out his Oedipal
deprivations on a series of negative parent figures (not to mention
the Christian God) in many of his writings; for one typical example,
his protagonist's surrogate father, François des Ygrès, in the novella
"Le Poète assassiné" ("The Poet Assassinated") gambles his money
away at Monte Carlo, loses his love, and commits suicide—all on
Palm Sunday. On the other hand, he could also sublimate his illegitimacy and fashion for himself the "divine bastard" myths of
the sun gods Apollo, Dionysus, and Jesus.

"Un soir" serves as an introduction to Apollinaire's nature myths.
On a visual level, the eagle descending seems to represent the setting
sun, which in turn suggests the eclipse of Christ the sun god and
the Christian faith. In keeping with an ancient poetic tradition,
Apollinaire usually represented the death of love as taking place in
evening (and autumn) whereas dawn and spring were often his times
for creation and rebirth.

A great mastery of poetic technique is revealed in the poem. The
abrupt changes from the past tense to the present of the first and
fourth stanzas give a dramatic suddenness to the corresponding
changes of emotion. The second stanza retains the present tense
found in the formal prayer of the first, but then slips into the
imperfect and the intimate form of address to translate a depth of
nostalgia that remains contemporary through an adroit combination
of tenses ("the only star *is* drowned / . . . / When the trolley cars
were rolling"). In the last stanza, a less abrupt change of tense keeps
the emotion muted, and the soft monosyllables, "Vois" ("See") and
"Vers toi" ("Towards thee"), quietly indicate the poet's beloved.
The vocabulary is sharp and modern except for the symbolist *se lover,*
which finds new freshness in a striking image with its pun on the
English word "love"; and the romantic, elegiac line of the third
stanza, "Et tout ce qui tremblait dans tes yeux de mes songes," is
abruptly broken by the short line following it yet sets the tone for

the worshipful last stanza. The first and last stanzas contain the same basic vowel rimes, *anges—moi—lampes—moi;—ssance—vois—vancent—toi,* dissonant and assonant at the beginning, homophonous and resolved at the end. The images are direct and carefully linked: the movement from the present world to the beloved is kept in each stanza and between stanzas until the entire poem follows this rhythm directed at first toward the suffering poet—"pour moi"—and cumulating in his Love—"Vers toi." The lyrical techniques of repetition ("Priez priez") and exclamation ("O vêtue"), both often used to excess by Apollinaire, here do not force the power of the emotion and become part of it; and the two "Vois" transmit a sense of quiet urgency that corresponds to the suppressed excitement of the mood. Finally, the imagery, intentionally ambiguous, is directed toward a single, unique perspective in the mind's eye of the poet.

In summary, the main themes of "Un soir" are the end of the old world and Christian faith; the secular second coming with its divinization of beauty and love and its canonization of the poet-prophet-worshiper; and the presence of a marvelous iron pastoral of modern urbanity full of despair and hope, death and resurrection, and the legendary ghosts of the past. In a later poem, "Zone," Apollinaire will transfer his beloved's messiahship to a soaring twentieth century and send up an eagle and a phoenix to accompany it.

The End of the World

Apollinaire's interest in the end of the world very likely began on the Riviera at the age of six when he spent a month living in a tent because of a serious earthquake, a natural calamity that the panicked populace—including, probably, Mme de Kostrowitzky—immediately took to be the beginning of world destruction. It was symbolic of his future philosophy that he on the contrary enjoyed the shocks and was sorry when they were over.[4] Soon after, he was enrolled in a private religious school in Monaco run by Marianist nuns and priests who, judging by the amazing familiarity he showed in later life concerning hagiography and Church history and ritual, must have well indoctrinated him along the lines of the most orthodox Roman Catholic belief, much concerned with the final questions. During his school years more interest in the millennium was manifested throughout Western civilization than had been shown since the sixteenth century, and if his teachers were not acquainted with the numerous little pamphlets predicting the end of the world for 1900 or early in the next century, they must have known many of the summaries of orthodox belief in the Antichrist, popularizations and tracts that often cited the latest secular scholarship of Conway (1881), Huntingford (1891), Gunkel (1895), and particularly Bousset (1895). Apollinaire may have read them, too; in any event, his writings prove he knew the finer points in the legend of the Last Judgment, both from the writings of Church Fathers like Saint Jerome,[5] Saint Augustine, and Saint Thomas Aquinas, and from the archaeologists' rationalizations. When he lost his faith around 1894 at the age of fourteen, he was already well-versed in symbolist literature, full of eschatological speculation.

Poetically, Decadent writers like Léon Dierx, Catulle Mendès, Maurice Rollinat, Jean Lorrain, and Maurice Maeterlinck were suffocating in civilization's claustrophobic ennui and bloody dreams of self-destruction; politically, in the climactic years of French anarchism (1880–1900), poets like Laurent Tailhade, Félix Fénéon, Adolphe Retté, and Pierre Quillard were hailing the idealistic bombers Ravachol, Vaillant, and Henry, and anticipating a forthcoming purge of blood. In the novel, the apocalyptic Russians were all the rage, Dostoyevski and Tolstoy as well as those prophets of new Antichrists Soloviev and Merejkovski; Wagnerism and "the twilight of the gods" were everywhere; Nietzsche's denunciations were becoming popular; Ibsen translations abounded; Sar Péladan was describing the decline and fall of Latinity in an interminable flood of gnostic fiction; and Des Esseintes's weary "Oh, go ahead and die, old world!" in Huysmans's *A Rebours* (1884) was being echoed by many an aesthete, including Oscar Wilde's Dorian Gray:

> "*Fin de siècle*," murmured Lord Henry.
> "*Fin du globe*," answered his hostess.
> "I wish it were *fin du globe*," said Dorian with a sigh. "Life is a great disappointment."
>
> (*The Picture of Dorian Gray*, 1890)

Aesthetic Byzantinism was the order of the day: "The period of antiquity with which these artists of the fin de siècle liked best to compare their own," writes Mario Praz, "was the long Byzantine twilight . . . a period of anonymous corruption with none of the heroic about it" (*The Romantic Agony*, 1956). "I dream of the Byzantine Emperors," wrote Apollinaire in one of his earliest poems.

In scientific, historical, and sociological writings things were not much more hopeful. Camille Flammarion and the "Baron" de Novaye gave learned recapitulations of the prophecies of world's end, the first (1894) with an added description of the arrival of the comet in the twenty-fifth century after anarchist revolution and world war; the second (1896) with a vivid account of the Apocalypse in the twentieth century. Apollinaire had Flammarion's more benign picture of the end of the world, *Uranie* (1896), in his library; he printed predictions similar to those of the Baron de Norvaye in 1905 and 1912. This is the first great period of science fiction, with J.–H. Rosny in *Le Cataclysme* (1896) and Wells in *The Time Machine* (1894) discussing terrestrial finality and dominating a host of minor writers whose works bore titles like *The Crack of Doom, The Yellow Horde,* and *The Violent Flame.* Apollinaire ghosted part of a novel on a scientist-superman in 1900, *Que Faire?* (What to do?), and made scientists his Antichrists in *La Gloire de l'olive,* "Le Poète assassiné," and a story, "Le Toucher à distance" ("Touch at a distance"). In fin de siècle short stories Poe's macabre fantasy merged with Wells's and Verne's scientism to create a tone of learned detachment in violence characteristic of Villiers de l'Isle-Adam, Marcel Schwob, and Alfred Jarry, all influences on Apollinaire. All of them exploited the end of the world theme. "Even now," Wells wrote in 1894, "for all we can tell, the coming terror may be crouching for its spring and the fall of humanity be at hand" ("The Extinction of Man").

In philosophy and sociology the movement upward of the world toward a materialist or idealist heaven was being exhaustively analyzed by anarchist disciples of Max Stirner, Proudhon, Hegel, and Marx, who coupled their utopianism with predictions of bourgeois decadence and extinction. Perhaps no one was listened to more attentively than the Hungarian sociologist Max Nordau, whose monumental *Dégénérescence* (1894) ponderously attempted to diagnose the French malady and thus the world's—France's culture being the highest—by citing the symbolist poets' and painters' esoteric cults for Wagner, Nietzsche, the *Mona Lisa,* the Virgin Mary, Salome, the Wandering Jew, the Pre-Raphaelites, Mallarmé, hashish, the Cabala, King Ludwig of Bavaria, Aretino, de Sade and Nerciat, Dostoyevski, Ibsen, and suicide as symptoms of "the twilight of nations." Apollinaire became well acquainted with all of these, with the possible exception of hashish (his drugs were alcohol and opium).

Nordau's book was an immediate sensation in England and France and remained a topic of discussion in French literary circles up until World War I; Apollinaire reported on Nordau's change of opinion in 1904.

The effect these influences had on an impressionable adolescent who from the beginning was an authority among his schoolmates on current intellectual trends cannot be overestimated. They explain the pessimism of his earliest poems and their obsession with the finality of death ("Tell me, did you know my soul was mortal?") with all its ambivalence ("—For we are afraid of dying— / We want to die" ["Un son de cor" (A sound of hunting horn)]). And of course the crepuscular futility of the universe:

> Notre machine ronde elle tourne et m'endort
> Où la vie est mortelle et vit après la mort
> En latin c'est terra l'Allemand l'appelle Erde
> Un clair echo peut-être a su répondre Merde
> ("Le Ciel se couvre un matin de mai" [The sky
> becomes cloudy one morning in May])

(Our spherical machine turns and lulls me to sleep / Where life is mortal and lives after death / In Latin it's terra the German calls it Erde / A clear echo perhaps has succeeded in answering Merde)

> Il ne faut pas sonder les devenirs
> Il vaut mieux vivre et jouir de la fraîcheur des soirs
> Où l'on s'endort en rêvant aux delà sans espoir
> ("Il me revient quelquefois" [It comes to me sometimes])

(One must not plumb the future / It is better to live and enjoy the freshness of evening / Where one falls asleep dreaming hopelessly of the beyond)

and the desire for flight:

> Et je me voudrais fuir
> Je voudrais l'inconnu de ce pays du soir
> Je serais comme un aigle puisqu'il n'y aurait
>   pas
> De soleil à fixer
> ("Il me revient quelquefois" [It comes to me sometimes])

(And I'd like to flee / I'd like the unknown of this evening country / I'd be like an eagle since there wouldn't be / Any sun to stare at)

They also partly explain recurrent returns to a latent pessimism at unguarded moments of future enthusiasm over the new city to rise out of the ruins of the old:

> . . . Il me semble que la paix
> Sera aussi monstrueuse que la guerre
>
> O temps de la tyrannie
> Démocratique
> ("Orphée" [Orpheus])

(It seems to me that peace / Will be as monstrous as war // O time of democratic / Tyranny)

> Prends en pitié les Dieux
> Les Dieux qui vont mourir
> Si l'humanité meurt
> (*Couleur du temps* [Color of the weather])

(Take pity on the Gods / The Gods who will die / If humanity dies)

As a subject, the end of the world is found throughout his work. He lost most of the manuscript of his first novel *La Gloire de l'olive*[6] (*The Glory of the Olive*) on a train; a remaining fragment shows Enoch as a bellboy in a Marseilles hotel denouncing the Antichrist, an Australian agronomist (in prophecy he will come from the East) named Apollonius Zabath who has arrived in Europe in 2107 to prevent the election of *De gloria olivae,* the last pope. As predicted, he defeats Enoch, just as the fragment ends; this scene is later incorporated into "Le Poète assassiné" where Enoch becomes the poet's spokesman Croniamantal, denouncing the cultural mediocrity of world democracy in the same divinely inspired terms.

In another fragment of *La Gloire de l'olive,* Apollinaire describes Enoch falling from the sky in the company of Elijah, a professional dishwasher, and meeting Isaac Laquedem, the Wandering Jew, doomed to die shortly at the Last Judgment. Isaac's connection with the Antichrist forms the framework for *L'Hérésiarque et cie* (*The Her-*

esiarch and Company, 1910), Apollinaire's first collection of short stories. In the first story, "Le Passant de Prague" (The passerby of Prague) he describes his own meeting with the Wandering Jew in Prague in 1902 and again hints that the latter's wandering days may soon be terminated; and in the last story, "Le Toucher à distance" (Touch at a distance), he casts himself in the role of an avenging Christ destroying with a revolver on Easter Day a presumptuous former friend who has discovered the scientific secret of ubiquity and the polygamous art of playing the Messiah in all the major cities of the world.

In his second collection of stories grouped with the title novella "Le Poète assassiné," a like outline is followed. Introduced by the anti-intellectual Armageddon denounced by a Christ-like Croniamantal, the book ends on a triumphant picture of *The Poet Resuscitated* at the beginning of World War I, preceded by a story about the return of King Arthur in 2105, an event scheduled for 2108 in *La Gloire de l'olive.* Similarly, his major collection of poetry, *Alcools,* is framed by the poet's spiritual death in the poem-preface "Zone," and his poetic ascension in the epilogic "Vendémiaire." In addition, there are several apocalyptic visions in between: "La Synagogue" with its Leviathan and its final citation from the Psalms concerning God's vengeance over Christian heretics; "La Maison des morts" ("The House of the Dead") with its lively resurrection scene; "Cortège" with its revelation of the poet's divine gift of resurrecting others; "Un soir" with its eagle and archangels; "Les Fiançailles" ("The Betrothal") with its description of the end of the poet's world and his second coming: "Le Brasier" ("The Brazier") with its celestial beasts; and "Vendémiaire" itself with its death of kings (Rev. 19) and new Eucharist in a Parisian millennium.

In a mysterious prose poem of 1907–8, *Onirocritique* (Dream-criticism), there is a marvelous panorama of world's end—much resembling the end of the world in the Apocalypse—with the poet as *the last man* (Mary Shelley's term) wandering over depopulated lands left full of song, empty cities, and the crowns of kings. And in his last play, the work produced posthumously, *Couleur du temps* (Color of the weather), allegorical figures representing the wealth of the past, contemporary science, and prophetic poetry destroy each other for the sake of a beautiful phantom in an Antarctic world of absolute cold. Humanity falls victim to its illusions as a final chorus of the quick and the dead chant, "Farewell farewell everything must die."

The First and Second Coming: "Le Larron" and "Merlin et la vieille femme"

The nihilism of *Couleur du temps* is unusual in Apollinaire's work. More often his idealism and Nietzschean energy led him to revel in the more picturesque aspects of world decadence—the dance on the edge of the abyss—rather than to allow it to become an ultimate destructive force. The Dreyfus affair with its sudden illumination of the depths of bourgeois corruption and its call to action gave the lie to the case for the death wish and latent melancholy; and the socialist newspapers that Apollinaire read at the time[7] lived literally in weekly headlined expectation of the Revolution. "Destinies are dreamers," he wrote in a school notebook, "present-day society is dying of uncertainty; let us spread more confusion: it is good that it die." He and other poets wondered who would be the blond Superman, the new Christ, to lead the fray: "The poets go singing Noël on the ways / Celebrating Justice and attendant upon tomorrow" ("Les Poètes").

"Ravochol–Jesus" and Vaillant had been crucified on the guillotine, but new saviors were everywhere coming out of the suburbs. In 1898 Ernest La Jeunesse, a quixotic admirer of Napoleon, wrote a serious introduction to a new gospel by a cousin who believed he was the Messiah. In 1900, Nietzsche, dying insane, wrote to a friend that he was the Christ who had saved the world a second time (Remy de Gourmont, in reporting this, remarked that it was probably true). In 1901, the avant-garde play of the year in Paris was Saint-Georges de Bouhélier's *La Tragédie du nouveau Christ* (The tragedy of the new Christ), "the great revolutionary drama" in which Jesus returned to contemporary workers "menacing with his prophetic parables the outworn hierarchies of a dying society" (I am quoting from a lecture on the work that Apollinaire may well have attended).[8] Bouhélier's Messiah ended by giving himself up to a second martyrdom for the crimes of his well-meaning but overzealous anarchist disciples. This poet-playwright, incidentally, had been heralding the rebirth of the Poet-King-God-Christ-Prometheus-Hero-Savior and his attendant pantheon for ten years before *La*

Tragédie du nouveau Christ; Apollinaire listened to his metaphorical lectures in 1901 and may have profited by them in his later eulogies of Picasso and his friends (1905–8).

The solitary, prophetic anarchist-savior, a descendant of Manfred and Julien Sorel and influenced by Kropotkin, Ivan Karamazov, and Zarathustra, became so popular by the end of the century that Alfred Jarry, reviewing Fernand Hauser's *Le Ressuscité* (The Resurrected One) in 1901, could act quite bored by the subject (he had already set several burlesque Christs and Supermen in motion himself). It was probably about this time that Apollinaire was putting the finishing touches on two anarchist allegories that became important poems, "Le Larron" ("The Thief") and "Merlin et la vieille femme" ("Merlin and the Old Woman") *(Alcools).*

While anticipating a new savior he attempted to destroy the old one, turning in "Le Larron" to Christ's *first* coming. Christ "comes like a thief" in the Apocalypse. Apollinaire's thief seems at first a mysterious symbolist figure, strongly resembling—in physical appearance at least—the Christ anticipated in Henri de Régnier's "La Vigile des grèves" (The vigil of the beaches, 1890), until he turns out not to be mysterious or poetic at all. The two poems are similar enough to permit me to think that Apollinaire was intending to make a reference to his predecessor in "Le Larron"; just as the introduction of his protagonist into a Mediterranean orchard at the beginning of the poem, "Marauder stranger unfortunate unskillful / Thief thief," might be a conscious parody of a pagan orchard god's cries in a Parnassian poem by Hérédia; "Don't approach! Go away: sail on by, Stranger, / Insidious Pillager" *("Hortorum Deus,"* 1893). As Madeleine Boisson has pointed out, nineteenth-century comparative mythologists and symbolists saw a synchretistic Christ as the archetypal sun-hero in the line of Apollo, Hercules, Orpheus, Prometheus, Ulysses, and many others.[9] Apollinaire wrote to the Cologne cathedral in 1902, "Every sunset in your stained-glass windows / . . . / The sun-Christ and the good pelican bleed" ("Le Dôme de Cologne").

In Régnier's poem, exotic virgins waited in exile on pagan isles for the coming of the Beloved (also called the harvester, fisherman, shepherd, sweet knight, and victorious swimmer), his face pale and his brow wounded by thorns, who would be accompanied by a unicorn and a peacock, who would drink from their cups and be their King. This was the Bridegroom for the attendant Virgins.

But who arrives in Apollinaire's poem? A weak sneak thief, "unfortunate unskillful," covetous of the exotic-erotic fruits of paganism but too devious to ask for them outright and too impoverished in his own right to be able to offer any symbolic wealth in return.

"Le Larron" is the most direct and violent attack Apollinaire ever made on the orthodox, Catholic Christ, His fundamentalist followers, and Christianity's Jewish patrimony. It is a barbarous, clanging poem, full of dissonances and ambiguities, erotic puns, drunken verbalisms, and an extraordinary compendium of the pagan marvelous culled from the young poet's already considerable knowledge of ancient lore. For his setting, he chose the ancient world of the Middle East from Italy to Mesopotamia, extending in time from the Exodus to 29 A.D. and including—in the future—Spain under the Moors. In this setting he placed the narrative of Christ, the first Christian ("I am a Christian"), who comes to steal the pagan fruits of the earth without at first revealing His identity to the excited pagans, and without accepting the inherent conditions of their rich inheritance:

> Je confesse le vol des fruits doux des fruits
> mûrs
> Mais ce n'est pas l'exil que je viens simuler
> Et sachez que j'attends de moyennes tortures
> Injustes si je rends tout ce que j'ai volé
> (stanza 2)

(I confess the theft of the sweet ripe fruit / But it isn't exile I come to feign / And know that I expect the usual unjust / Tortures if I give back everything I stole)

These conditions are primarily those of profane love, the only possible love—which leads them to what is for Him an insulting misconception about His virgin birth, "Since they the maiden and the adult had in the final analysis / No pretext [for my birth] but that of nightly love" (stanza 4). They are in full possession of the talismans, cults, and rich magic of the past, which even includes much of early Christianity with its pagan roots ("The black bishops unknowingly adoring / By the isosceles triangles open at the morse of their copes / Pallas" [stanza 18]).

Love means sensuality. The wise men make Socratic (homosexual) gestures at the thief, the women have "Ligurian voices," and one woman finds him nobler than "the dolphin the male viper or the bull" and asks him hopefully if his sect worships an obscene sign. Moreover, the thief is not even aware of the erotic implications of his own religious symbolism: when the pagans discover his identity, they scoff, "So be it! the triad [the Trinity: a pun on the phallus and the testicles] is virile and you are virgin and cold" (stanza 31). Although attracted by the fruits of love, he naïvely discards them ("The birds with their beaks have wounded your grenades / And almost all your figs were split"). Instead of adoring an obscene sign, his only sign is the sign of the cross (stanza 31).

Back of these lines is the symbolist philosophy of the young poet. Apollinaire had been an authority on erotic literature since his early adolescence, and to him "obscene" love was the whole of love. He knew that *aller en orient,* "to go to the East," was a slang term for *fellatio,* and *aller en Ligure,* "to go to Liguria," a parallel expression for *cunnilingus.* The pagan Garden of Eden was one without either Yaveh or the threat of the Fall, with the phallic tree of life, a peach tree (*pêcher,* a pun on *péché,* "sin"), at its center. It included, besides the homosexual Socrates, Orpheus, the first pederast; a precious forest of homosexual poets; Florentine (anal) kisses; Tanagran aphrodisiacs; and the gods' solar and nocturnal incest in the clouds. It also contained the erotic beasts, sphinxes, dolphins, vipers, bulls, and cows of such ancient archetypes as Zeus, Apollo, Mithra, Zagreus, Osiris, Apis, and Marduk; these are the sun gods who rise from the bed of their mother, Night, every morning and return to it every evening (discussed in chapter 2).

Complementary to eroticism is exoticism. The ancients at first welcome the thief as a handsome, mysterious member of their own race who obviously has no need for their fruits; but after he spurns them, they nobly pardon him and hospitably offer him food their broth-drinking Spartans and bean-shunning Pythagoreans would not touch. Then as the watchers do in Régnier's poem, they pass in review the great invasions, migrations, and festivals of the past, dazzling the thief with their wealth of spectacle and inviting him to display his own wares. But "the fruit-thief cried I am a Christian"; and the poem pivots to a frontal attack on Christian dogma in a burlesque dialectic Apollinaire uses in another early blasphemous work, the novel *L'Enchanteur pourrissant* (The putrescent enchanter).

The chorus mockingly compares the "thief" to the real thieves, bad and good, Gestas and Dysmas, to be crucified on his left and right:

> Ah! Ah! le larron de gauche dans la bourrasque
> Rira de toi comme hennissent les chevaux . . .
> Si tu n'es pas de droite tu es sinistre
>
> (stanzas 22, 24)

(Ha! Ha! the thief on the left in the storm / Will laugh at you just as horses neigh / . . . / If you're not on the right you're sinister)

They compare his voice unfavorably with the semidivine voice of Orpheus; they scoff at his ideas of the Trinity and Virgin birth (stanza 25); they ridicule his two poor symbols, the reed and the cross; they tell him he should have accepted Abgar V's invitation to live with him at the marvelous court of Edessa. In a last stanza, dropped at the time of publication in *Alcools,* they mock the idea of hellfire as they return to the Eleatic school. Truly, everything is theirs ("Tout est à nous" [stanza 26]). In the scholarly articles of the 1890s that Apollinaire used for some of the poem's sources, one that seems to have particularly interested him attempted to prove the ascendancy of Babylonian over Hebrew and Christian myth. Because of recent archaeological findings, Babylon was as much à la mode as Byzantium.[10] Indeed, the two were synonymous in much of the occult literature of the fin du siècle; the "Chaldean" language that the pagans speak (stanza 9) was a syncretist formula for the languages of Egypt, Babylon, and Byzantium; and Remy de Gourmont wrote in his *Epilogues,* one of Apollinaire's favorite books, that the basket for the fruits of the moderns was made in Byzantium. Furthermore, if these "Chaldeans" return at the end of the poem to the Eleatic school, this is Apollinaire's way of saying that their philosophy, like his own, is based on that of the pre-Socratic philosophers so admired by Nietzsche and Gourmont, the ideas of Pythagorus, Heraclitus, and Empedocles. In 1900, in the novel *Que faire?* (What to do?), he had put a hint of this thought in the mouth of his protagonist: "Everything is in everything. Nothing can be isolated or specified unto itself" (chapter 10). Variations on this monistic, materialistic, and yet Orphic system of belief will appear in his writings for the rest of his life. They appear for example in the early poem "L'Ensemble seul est parfait" (Only the whole is perfect), in the later unanimist poems "Cortège" and "Vendémiaire," and even in the short story "L'Infirme divinisé" ("The Deified Invalid"), in which the protagonist, who loses half of his body in an accident, becomes this whole—and this nothing, this shadow and this light, this eternity in the moment. For Nietzsche the pre-Socratic universe was placed under the aegis of Dionysus; for Apollinaire, under Orpheus, Amphion, and Pan; and two years after the publication of "Le Larron," he includes in his Nietzschean philosophy the pantheism of Spinoza in the pages of his periodical *La Revue Immoraliste*. There, again like Nietzsche, he makes *volupté* (voluptuousness, sexuality) his *summum bonum,* the highest kind of love. In the pagans' descriptions, therefore, may be found a veritable compendium of the various postures *volupté* may take, the postures severely frowned upon by the Catholic Church of his childhood.

But his most serious charge leveled against a fundamentalist, puritanical Christ is His inhumanity, His inability to allow the flesh to play an equal role with the spirit in determining the whole man. A woman asks Christ, "Thief do you know the laws better in spite of mankind" (stanza 12). The equivocal shadow, symbol of magic, and, to the Christian, the evil inherent in things of the flesh ("the sorrow of your flesh"), is *human* and accepted by the ancients (stanza 27); it prevails against the fire of God (stanza 22).

I have paraphrased "Le Larron" at some length since there still remains much controversy about it and many conflicting interpretations of its meaning, mainly arising from the fact that the Jesus figure, seen from the point of view of the pagans, greatly resembles Apollinaire himself. The line "Your father was a sphinx and your mother a night" (stanza 4) has become famous as a reference to the exiled Pole's mysterious origins, especially since he arrived on a "Scythian" (Slavic?) wind (stanza 14), and since his parents could be thought of as "a maiden and an adult" (stanza 5)—although this better applies to Jesus than to Apollinaire, since Mme de Kostrowitsky was twenty-one when her first son was conceived. In addition, Apollinaire's mother had what might be vaguely termed a "Ligurian voice" (stanza 5) since she raised him at Monaco in Liguria. But it must be remembered that *these traits are only the conjectures of the pagans before they find out the identity of the thief.* After the fruit thief cries out indignantly, "I am a Christian!" (Nietzsche said that the only Christian was Jesus), they attack him both as Jesus himself and as his credulous, puritanical followers (Renan wrote that the only answer early Christians gave to their pagan tormentors was "I am a Christian"). Especially are they scornful of orthodox Christianity's paucity of picturesque symbolism and its antagonism to the joys of sensual love. In short, what the erotic and ambitious young poet was ingeniously doing was cultivating intentionally the ambiguity of the description of the syncretistic symbolist sun god in the first half of the poem so that it would include himself. As we shall see, he was to spend the greater part of his life in becoming a mysterious and poetic Savior.

In summary, Apollinaire in "Le Larron" is both the sensuous pagans and their ideal of an erotic solar god. In another major work probably written around the same time and later included in *Alcools,* "Merlin et la vieille femme" ("Merlin and the Old Woman") he gives a description of himself as a messiah and even prophesies his imminent advent.

In January 1899, just a year after Émile Zola had published *"J'accuse,"* his famous vindication of justice in the Dreyfus case, Apollinaire concluded a letter to school friend Toussaint-Luca with ". . . I leave you, hoping that Souvarine will come, the blond who will destroy cities and men. Let 1899 hear another voice like Zola's and the Revolution is in the fire."[11] Souvarine is the solitary, absolutely free Russian terrorist in Zola's *Germinal* who destroys a mine—with the miners in it—and whose ideas ("Anarchy, void, the earth washed by blood, purged by fire") are similar to those in Apollinaire's anarchist poems "Les Poètes," "Les Doukhobors," and "Avenir" (The future). He is blond like Émile Henry, the young anarchist Don Quixote who was guillotined in 1894 for throwing a bomb into a crowded café, and like "the blond beauty" of Apollinaire's heroes in "Avenir" whose torches "make a halo around every brow."

In "Merlin et la vieille femme," the son of the old couple will also be haloed with fire. He will be handsome and unhappy, marching alone looking at the sky with the dawning sun on his brow on the road to Rome—one of the two native cities (Babylon is the other) of the Antichrist. His mother is "Memory equal to Love" who is both the Greek goddess of memory, the mother of Poetry, and an allegorical recasting of the hundred-year-old woman Merlin loved in medieval romance. And Michel Décaudin has pointed out that Merlin and Viviane had a son in Edgar Quinet's *Merlin l'en-*

chanteur (1860) who had reddish-blond hair like his grandfather
Satan. In any event, Merlin's son is finally reminiscent of Apollinaire
himself, "son of light" (first stanza), with his ashy-blond hair, born
illegitimately at Rome. He was early aware of the many destinies
that conspired to make him the ideal candidate for the Antichrist—
or, better, a second, truly pagan Christ.

Antichrists: Isaac Laquedem, Simon Magus, Merlin the Magician, and Guillaume the Hermit

I mentioned above that Apollinaire was acquainted with the opinions of the Church fathers and nineteenth-century archaeologists
about the Antichrist. In addition, he knew such medieval and
sixteenth-century authorities on the subject as Nicéphore Calliste,
Malvenda, and John of Hildesheim and admired the prophetic works
of Nostradamus and the false Saint Malachy. Works of Edgar Quinet
and Léon Bloy showed up in his library, and he became personally
acquainted with Marcel Schwob and Alfred Jarry. Nietzsche's Antichrist was discussed in the circles he frequented, and he had occasion to refer to Paulus Cassel and M. D. Conway, both of whom
had treated the story of the Wandering Jew as a later development
of that of the Antichrist and a continuation of the Messianic Dream.
From his work with the radical press he knew that Dreyfus, the
Jews, Zola, Anatole France, and later, Prime Minister Combes were
termed Antichrists by the reaction. So it was not surprising that
besides creating his own scientific Antichrists in *Que faire?*, *La Gloire
de l'olive*, and "Toucher à distance," he should elaborate on such
traditional ones as Gestas, Isaac Laquedem, Simon Magus, and Merlin in other works.

We have already caught a glimpse of Gestas, the bad thief, one
of many apocryphal personalities regarded as the Antichrist in the
Middle Ages; in a minor poem of 1901, "Tierce Rime pour votre
âme" (Terza rima for your soul), this thief represents the amorous
poet. In the story "L'Hérésiarque" (The heresiarch) of the preceding
year, he becomes in the mind of an Italian arch-heretic none other
than the Holy Ghost made flesh, who has violated at one time in
his nefarious career a sleeping virgin! The epicurean, masochistic
heretic is naturally excommunicated (as Tolstoy would be the year
following); Apollinaire remarks that he is no different from other

men, who are all "both sinners and saints, when they aren't criminals and martyrs."

Isaac Laquedem, who had conducted Apollinaire on a guided tour of Prague in 1902, appearing there as a delightful sensualist who had flouted Christ and was enjoying his *superhuman* immortality (Apollinaire's emphasis) wanders through other works of the young writer eternally waiting for the fifteen Sibylline signs of the Last Judgment. In this he inherits the archetypal myth of Cain and Wotan, according to comparative mythologists M. D. Conway and Charles Schoebel, becoming in turn Moses (immortal in folklore), Enoch, Elijah, Tiresias, Laquedem, Arthur, Merlin, Christ, and Antichrist, among others. Our poet will add to this list Empedocles, Apollonius of Tyana, Pan, Orpheus, and the ubiquitous poet-wanderer, himself.

Vertical displacement in the legend of the Antichrist often accompanies horizontal and temporal peripatetics, a miraculous ascension having been interpreted as constituting a direct attack upon God by Saint Ambrose, Saint Jerome, and Saint Thomas, all of whom wrote that the Beast would try to rise in the air like Simon Magus. Secular scholars of the 1890s prosaically agreed with them by considering fourth-century legends of the magician's prowess to be variations on the Antichrist stories of the first century. In Simon's flight before Nero and his destruction by Saint Peter, they said, he followed the path of Satan—to be cast down at the end of time by either Saint Michael or Christ—and the Dragon of Revelation. In *La Gloire de l'olive,* the Australian Antichrist Apollonius Zabath had "planed above other men like an eagle." In "Simon Mage," a story in *L'Hérésiarque et cie,* Apollinaire follows the traditional legend for the most part, the biblical precedents of Luke and Acts and the apocryphal story in the Acts of Saint Peter, while adding the demonic angels of the Cabala to help Simon in his miraculous flight.[12] But after he has the magus shot down by Peter's prayer, Apollinaire adds a modern moral. He has given Peter's name to Simon and made the two figures resemble each other as closely as Castor and Pollux; he ends his story with a final victory of the immortal magician as he attempts to buy or win by gaming the dying body of his Christian rival (see also "Un soir"). Antipeter as well as Antichrist, the father of gnosticism and heresy thereby triumphs over the father of the Church. A curious postscript: the first French histories of aviation included Simon (Peter) Magus along with Icarus as a forerunner of the Wright brothers.[13] Appropriately enough, Apollinaire has him anticipate the flight of the twentieth century in "Zone."

Simon Magus also arrives, horizontally and temporally this time, in the company of Enoch, Elijah, Empedocles, Isaac Laquedem, and Apollonius of Tyana at the tomb of Merlin in *L'Enchanteur pourrissant* (The putrescent enchanter). More than any other Apollinaire character, Merlin is the antithesis of Christ. The son of a virgin and a devil, he is nonetheless baptized (like Jesus, Simon Magus, and Apollinaire) as he retains mastery over all the diabolical powers of the underworld. He takes after his father, Satan. He extols suicide and revolution before his six immortal visitors:

When the fruit is ripe, it drops and doesn't wait for the gardener to come and pick it. Let man, that fruit ripening freely on the tree of light, do the same. But you who did not die, who are six in the forest like the fingers of the hand and a dagger in the hand, why don't you close up, why don't you double up? O fingers that could ransack; O fist that could stab; O hand that could beat, that could indicate, that could scratch decay. . . .

He is buried underground by a sterile, ignorant love, in contrast to Saint Simeon Stylite's pillar "which leaps to the sky." His solitary nature as a poet leads him to hate crowds, while "God loves those who meet together." He places man higher than Christ. Yet he would be an angel were he not baptized, perhaps one of the marvelous host described in "Simon Mage."

As in "Le Larron," Apollinaire satirizes divine birth and resurrection in *L'Enchanteur pourrissant*, this time in scenes of a "funereal Christmas" and a "voluntary damnation." In the first of these, he seems to have taken his lead from a medieval Merlin prophecy that, at the end of the world, three descendants of the Magi will arrive in starless darkness at the desert birthplace of the Dragon with gifts of an olive branch, ashes, and a knife.[14] His Magi are the relics in the Cologne cathedral; their bodiless heads come guided by shadow and bring alchemical gifts to Merlin's tomb. In the second scene, that of the damnation, Ariosto's heroine Angelica, who has been converted to Christianity, thereby forgetting "all that is pagan, magic and even natural," is sodomized to death by an assembled company of demons and magicians while she is praying to the Virgin; a veritable Black Mass is consummated over her body "in an obscene and pious position." Her crucified form is borne aloft by choiring angels, until suddenly she is inexplicably precipitated from heaven by Saint Michael. Merlin explains that she has been damned in his place and remarks that if his body were living it would sweat blood. After the death of Love—*the funereal Christmas*—comes the diabolical redemption.

What has become of Merlin's savior son who was "looking at the sky" in "Merlin et la vieille femme"? No mention of him is made in *L'Enchanteur pourrissant,* and by the time Apollinaire wrote the final section of the book (probably during the summer of 1904) the death of love had in fact struck him down. A parallel decline in expectation of a revolution made the living death of unrequited love that Merlin's entombment principally symbolized especially dark. The hope implicit in the last stanza of "Un soir" and in earlier poems that the beloved would embody the resurrection had not been realized. One of these earlier poems bears witness to the deflation Apollinaire must have felt in his darkest moments: in "L'Ermite" ("The Hermit," *Alcools*) he carries his revolt from the Church to a summit of burlesque in the caricature of a lecherous old ascetic who, fleeing his self-inflicted sufferings for God, finds minor but satisfactory salvation outside the Lord.

When Enoch had asked Merlin in *L'Enchanteur pourrissant* if it were certain that a savior had arrived, Merlin had replied, "Why do you ask me, since you know me so well? Patriarch, who isn't a savior? Perhaps you will be the true savior yourself when you come back to die. . . ." The hermit is Apollinaire's most pathetic, bedraggled Antichrist; his problem is that he can be neither spiritual savior nor pagan lover. Like Saint Simeon Stylites in *L'Enchanteur pourrissant,* who was assailed by temptations according to the temperature, but as an antithesis of Christ, he suffers a new kind of fleshly Passion-in-reverse by *not* sweating the bloody sweat, the hematidrosis (in French, *hématidroses*); by *not* perceiving the comforting angel on his Mount of Olives; by *not* having his unleavened bread consecrated (a pun on his enforced sterility). Nor does a transcendent Magdalen, his mysterious *Unknown,* arrive. Half-crucified by his libidinous desires, his sole ascension that of his anxious flesh, he finds nothing but the cruel passion of owls nailed to impure peasants' huts. His salvation is achieved only when he abandons the desert for a counseling job in the city, as he discovers like Saint Jerome a kind of purity in the voyeurism, the vicarious sexual activity of the confessor.

If *le larron* is not Apollinaire, as I believe—the poet is rather the thief's pagan interrogators and their ideal of a sun-hero—I think that there can be little doubt that the hermit, like Merlin, is he. In 1915, during a period of mental and physical frustration, he wrote defiantly, "I can occasionally at the beginning of a decision have that confusion, that profound agony of Christ on the Mount of Olives who knew the bloody sweat, the hematidrosis, but I've finished being the hermit *(mais ermite c'est fini)* and I march straight ahead" (letter to Lou, 29 April). The first draft of "L'Ermite" probably only included stanzas 16, 17, 18, 5, 21, 22, 19, and 23, in that order, which contain lines based on the poet's Belgian frustrations in 1899.[15] Many of the erotic images in the remainder of the poem reflect adolescent attitudes and humor reminiscent of Jarry's "La Passion considérée comme course de côte" (The Passion considered as an uphill bicycle race). Probably no longer a virgin after the age of fifteen (he wrote Louise de Coligny on 8 April 1915 that he had experienced all the joys of love at that age), he was subject for the rest of his life to sudden attacks of masochistic, onanistic depression, at which times he hungered after the purity and security of the monastery or the grave. The final stanza of "The Hermit" may well reflect a similar moment of world-weariness:

> Car je ne veux plus rien sinon laisser se
> clore
> Mes yeux couple lassé au verger pantelant
> Plein du râle pompeux des groseilliers
> sanglants
> Et de la sainte cruauté des passiflores

(For all I desire is to close my eyes / Exhausted couple in the panting orchard / Full of the pompous death rattle of the bloody currant bushes / And the sainted cruelty of the passion flowers)

> Le grand Pan l'amour Jésus-Christ
> Sont bien morts et les chats miaulent
> Dans la cour je pleure à Paris

(Great Pan love Jesus Christ / Are definitely dead and the cats wail / In the courtyard in Paris I weep)

he wrote, probably in 1904. But, "who isn't a savior?" And Merlin had prophesied, "For a long time the earth will bear no more enchanters but the time of the enchanters will return. . . ." The Behemoth in the same book had told some wyverns, "man is closer to a metamorphosis than you. . . ." In the years 1903–5 Apollinaire met André Salmon, Max Jacob, Mécislas Golberg, and Pablo Picasso and set out with them on the tremendous artistic adventure of the twentieth century. On confronting Picasso's harlequin families in 1905 he cried, "Noël!"—and his own martyred face, along with those of his three new literary friends, in one of the best stories of *L'Hérésiarque et cie,* "La Serviette des poètes" (The napkin of the poets), spread out on the floor of Picasso's studio on the artist's solitary napkin transformed into a new veronica and a Christ-like sun. He was finally beginning to move in a company of saviors.

Chapter Two

The Death of the Sun

Le soleil et la forêt ce sont mes père et mère

—*Poèmes à Lou*

The Myth

Apollinaire like Rimbaud was a *fils du Soleil,* a son of the Sun; like both Rimbaud and Baudelaire he had a dominant mother and no father. The physical and mental attitudes that resulted in his case affected, as in the cases of his revolutionary predecessors, the course of modern poetry.

Here historical coincidence rises—as it usually does in the lives of mind-shapers—to the level of destiny and myth. Apollinaire was not responsible for his illegitimacy, his name "Apollinaris," or his birth in Rome of noble Slavic and Latin blood; nor did he plan his arrival in the steps of Baudelaire, Rimbaud, and Mallarmé during the autumnal last days of a romantic, autumnal century. He did profit by the concurrence and exploit the breadth of his myth; but, as often happens, it is exceedingly difficult to ascertain where the man stops and where the myth begins. Suffice it to say that both he and his friends like Picasso and Max Jacob had Rimbaud's precocious awareness of the gifted person arriving at the privileged moment of history, in addition to their having the example of Rimbaud's Promethean myth itself before them.

How conscious Apollinaire became of what Freudians would now term the Oedipal import of his inheritance is evident in many passages in his writings. As we have seen, in *L'Enchanteur pourrissant,* the forty-year-old heroine Angelica is raped to death and eternally damned. Apollinaire's mother, Angelica de Kostrowitsky, was in her forties at the time of writing; the whole passage thus becomes a kind of incestuous episode in which the entombed (wombed) Merlin-Apollinaire is redeemed. In his pornographic novel *Les Onze Mille Verges* (The eleven thousand rods [phalluses]—a pun relating the sainted *virgins* [*vierges*] supposedly massacred by the Huns at Cologne with the punishing rods of the Old Testament), the most sadistic ghoul-queen of a whole succession of lubricious women is a lovely Polish aristocrat, a "madonna," with a *face angélique*. In "Le Toucher à distance," on the other hand, the adventurous Antichrist shot by Apollinaire-Christ on Easter Day has a name that was originally based on that of his erstwhile father. In 1908 he wrote of the originality of modern art, "You can't carry your father around everywhere; you abandon him with the other dead." The problems involved in such an abandonment he implied in a 1914 review of Synge's *The Playboy of the Western World,* "Poets have always more or less tried to kill their fathers, but it's a very difficult thing to do, witness the Playboy," after discussing in a parallel article Freud, the subconscious, and father-and-son rivalries. In his fiction especially, he never could lose his father; if nothing else, his father's name kept turning up as Costantino, François, and Françoise in stories from *Le Poète assassiné,* and as la Chancesse (Françoise) in *L'Hérésiarque et cie.*[1] Incidentally, Synge's play was one of his favorites because of its realism, poetry, and bitter laughter. While he praised *Playboy,* however, he disliked Renard's *Poil-de-carotte* (Carrot-top) with its message of father-and-son harmony. He revolted against father authority when he left first the Church and then bourgeois society; he attempted to become his own father when he began to use the phoenix symbol for himself; and—again like Baudelaire and Rimbaud—he could never really leave his mother either, she whose "door" led to everything and nothing ("La Porte" ["The Door"], *Alcools*).

On the archetypal side of his myth, it is significant that he grew up during the golden age of comparative religion, folklore, and evolutionary anthropology study. If he did not know the animistic treatises of Cox, Tylor, Frazer, and Lang, he was acquainted with the ideas of their continental counterparts Angelo de Gubernatis, Mallarmé, Nietzsche, Remy de Gourmont, Edouard Schuré, Louis Ménard, Paulus Cassel, and Charles Schoebel, and with at least some of their ingenious unravelings of nature myths through history. To them as to him the solar cycle of incestuous creation, death, and regeneration was the universal, primordial myth, the guiding rhythm of life and religion. Mallarmé, for example, had written in his adaptation of George Cox's *Tales of the Gods and Heroes* that Oedipus' marriage with his mother came out of one of the oldest Indian myths, "from ancient phrases speaking of the sun uniting in the evening with her from whom he had issued that morning."

The scholars and poets split the Orphic universe between the masculine and feminine principles, Tammuz and Ishtar, Cybele and Atys, Venus and Adonis, the priests of the sun and the priestesses of the moon; and they traced the evolutionary rise of man toward spirit and the Oversoul from Krishna through Apollo, Orpheus, Dionysus, and Christ to man himself. To Apollinaire as to Gérard de Nerval and Mallarmé, the violent love-death between Sun (Christ, Eros, phallus, phoenix, poet) and Night (Mary, Psyche, womb, siren, beloved) was an accepted poetic truism.

This child of Apollo prided himself on being able to look the sun straight in the eye like the eagle of myths;[2] yet like other poets of his time he was symbolically slain every night—and every autumn. No theme was so popular in symbolist art and poetry of the 1880s and 1890s: one has only to glance through the works of Laforgue, Mallarmé, Régnier, Catulle Mendès, and Gustave Moreau, just to name some of the best-known figures, to be struck by the ever-present motifs—as was Ezra Pound, writing against "the crepuscular spirit in modern poetry"—of twilight gardens and bloody sunsets. To cite one well-known example: Rostand's Cyrano de Bergerac was pathetically yet heroically struck down in a convent garden in the autumn of 1898 amid growing darkness and falling leaves.

Night, on the other hand, with her inevitable extension *ombre* (shadow) and her association with the sea (the three words are feminine in French), was the familiar companion of an adolescent whose pen names were Guillaume Macabre and Nyctor and who watched many sunsets over the Mediterranean.

> Adieu jeunesse blanc Noël
> Quand la vie n'était qu'une étoile
> Dont je contemplais le reflet
> Dans la mer Méditerranée
> Plus nacrée que les météores
> ("Les Collines" ["The Hills"])

(Farewell youth white Noël / When life was but a star / Whose reflection I used to watch / In the Mediterranean Sea / More lustrous than the meteors)

I have mentioned the Virgin-Night-Jesus association in the line describing the sun-hero, "Your father was a sphinx and your mother a night," as well as the play of fire and shadow, Christ and the pagan world, in "Le Larron." At the end of the poem, Jesus leaves as the evening comes on (in "Un soir" the eagle descends as the beloved's nativity star comes into view). In another line of "Le Larron" there is a description of pagan frescoes figuring "solar and nocturnal incest in the clouds" (stanza 8), which parallels references in an early poem to the sun, "that circular and benevolent god," and to Night "his incestuous mother" ("L'Ignorance"). To evolutionary anthropologists, the Christian equivalent of Indian, Egyptian, and Chaldean creation myths was God's act of self-engendering through a virgin mother. In the words of the skeptical pagans, "Who doubles becomes triple before having been" (stanza 25).

The extent and importance of the Sun-Night relationship for Apollinaire and the extent of his fall from grace after "Le Larron" may be observed in a second dualism, the theme of *hyperdulia,* or spiritual adoration of the mother-deity, as opposed to the negative sexual idolatry, the *antidulia,* of the underworld mother Lilith.

The romantic Sylphide, the feminine ideal, had visited the little Wilhelm Kostrowitzsky when a dark, unknown woman appeared at the opening of the curtains around his bed, watched him quietly, and then disappeared. He never forgot her (letter to Madeleine, 20 October 1915). One of his first loves, the one recorded in chapter 9 of "Le Poète assassiné" for the peasant girl Mariette, shows an early stage of his quest for the pure ideal, the Rose of the World, the woman he was later to call Rosemonde. She was undoubtedly related to the *rosa mystica* of Apollinaire's cult of the Virgin at the Marianist school of Saint Charles; when he lost his faith, she remained for him as for many another symbolist poet an emotional ideal shining through the anarchism and materialism of his disbelief. In early love poems his loved ones were his "divinities" and his "Madonnas" deprived of corresponding metaphysical belief. In two poems, however, his faith in the divinity of the poet allowed him to deify his creations and to realize a kind of materialistic ladder of love in his imagination, raising "a madonna" to "Our Lady very real and necessary" ("Le Printemps" [Spring]), the mother of "a marvelous god / Created by man because man created the gods" ("Le Dôme de Cologne"). In "Un soir" his cries went out to her as both Madonna and Messiah. When he lost Annie Playden, a loss

made immortal through its telling in "La Chanson du mal-aimé"
("The Song of the Poorly Loved"), he translated the seven swords
traditionally placed in Mary's heart to his own (they are sometimes
placed in Jesus' heart); and, in a short story, "La Rose de Hildesheim," he described a death caused by the frustrated love of a
poor student in Germany for a blonde rose with the features of a
Raphael Madonna. It was not until he became divine again, his own
phoenix-son, and again betrothed to Mary—the artist Marie Laurencin—that he could move back under the sign of the Virgin, "the
pure sign of the third month" ("Les Fiançailles" ["The Betrothal"]).
He could aspire anew:

> Colombe, l'amour et l'esprit
> Qui engendrâtes Jésus-Christ,
> Comme vous j'aime une Marie.
> Qu'avec elle je me marie.
> ("La Colombe" ["The Dove"],
> Le Bestiaire)

(Dove, love and spirit / Who engendered Jesus Christ, / Like you I love
a Mary. / May I marry her.)

He then could add an epigraph to "La Chanson du mal-aimé":

> . . . mon amour à la semblance
> Du beau Phénix s'il meurt un soir
> Le matin voit sa renaissance.

(My love like / The fine Phoenix if it die one evening / Next morning
sees it reborn)

Throughout this personal death and ascension cycle, incest with
his mother, either positive (creative) or negative (masochistic) is a
hidden theme. It is usually most overt, as in the case of Angelica,
in his fiction: besides L'Enchanteur pourrissant, we find it in the story
"L'Histoire d'une famille vertueuse, d'une hotte et d'un calcul" (The
story of a virtuous family, a basket, and a gallstone) and in the
pornographic novel, Les Exploits d'un jeune Don Juan (The Exploits of
a Young Rakehell), in both of which—if we apply a Freudian interpretation—sisters are substituted for the mother. Having been an

apprentice Decadent, he well knew the importance of incest in literature: he admired Rousseau's *Confessions* and Rétif de la Bretonne's *Monsieur Nicolas,* campaigned in 1904 for Georges Polti's play *Cuirs de Boeuf* (Oxhides), a mystery play about blazing passion between a mother and son, and referred in his own writings to folk traditions of incest from medieval writers to Charles Perrault and the brothers Grimm.[3] In 1915, at the end of his semi-incestuous love affair with Louise de Coligny-Châtillon, he wrote her about his fellow soldiers' incestuous dreams, "It is curious to note how incest becomes dominant in troubled periods. History proves this. . . ." The Age of Anguish is an age of incest.

This incest is most openly found in Apollinaire as part of the sterile misogyny he felt during his poorly loved periods (a large percentage of the time). There it becomes a major theme connected with the myth of the impure demon-mother Lilith, antithesis of Mary, goddess of Night in Assyrian myth, child-killing bird of night to the Israelites, mother of Sodom and Gomorrah to Remy de Gourmont, a widely feared succubus with (in Apollinaire) an attendant train of vices including menstruation, lesbianism, flagellation, and sterility.

Lilith in Hebraic folklore was Adam's first wife, who, chased from Paradise for not obeying her husband, became the consort of the devil, the leading child-stealing demon. Apollinaire first turned her into a symbol of frustrated motherhood and sterility in *L'Enchanteur pourrissant.* He evidently knew the legend that she had lost a hundred children a day and had been pursued by angels to the Red Sea, for he made her an ingenious symbol of menstruation who had created the Red Sea "against the desires of men" before turning to deceive Beelzebub with female lovers ("Poème à Lou XLI"). A symbol of the impure roses of women, their *hematidroses,* as against Mary, the *rosa mystica,* she appears in three works commemorating the loss of a mistress, *L'Enchanteur pourrissant,* "Le Poète assassiné," and *Poèmes à Lou,* as well as in the misogynist posthumous novel *La Femme assise* (The seated woman). Menstruation unaccompanied by Lilith, on the other hand, characterized women—"twelve times impure," wrote Vigny—in several poems of *Alcools* from "Merlin et la vieille femme" and "La Chanson du mal-aimé" to "Annie" and "Zone." In *L'Enchanteur pourrissant,* Viviane leaves Merlin at the end of the work as "the red tears of perdition flowed along her legs." In *Les Exploits d'un jeune Don Juan,* the protagonist, Roger (an English

slang term for the phallus), deflowers his sister during her menstrual
period.

After the loss of Annie, love became bad, Apollinaire hinted in
1908; besides "La Chanson du mal-aimé," another poem to com-
memorate this loss was "L'Emigrant de Landor Road," in which
Lilith again appeared as the wife of the devil, beating her lover on
rainy days and Fridays. In the last chapter of *L'Enchanteur pourrissant*,
Viviane explained that, to the contrary, *he* beat *her* when he caught
her with her lesbian lover, a dragonfly. As for herself, she continued,
instead of resembling her teacher Merlin, she resembled the infernal
dragonfly—or else obscenely dancing houseflies consecrated to Beelzebub, to Lesbos (see "Tourbillon de mouches" ["Swirl of Flies"]
in *Calligrammes*), and to death. Beelzebub, the Lord of the Flies,
became a beautiful temptress in Cazotte's *Le Diable amoureux* (The
amorous devil), Apollinaire noted in 1915; he often commented on
the insects' grim dance on the Western front when he was losing
Lou; and when he lost Marie he met millions of them in the company
of a phallic Thanatos-Pan-Dionysus figure piping the prostitutes of
Saint Merry off to their own unmasculine ideal in the stars ("Le
Musicien de Saint-Merry" ["The Musician of Saint-Merry"]). His
final comment on women concerned the main character of his novel
La Femme assise, the lesbian Elvire: like a certain Swiss coin of his
childhood with a seated woman on it, he said, and like all women,
she was false and did not pass.

With flagellation and other forms of brutality, Apollinaire's misogyny coupled with incest in his most exacerbated pages. His mother,
according to many reports, had the nineteenth-century Polish aristocrat's freedom with the whip; her son's interest in the same can
be traced through his poems and letters to Lou and Madeleine and
in his violent, blackly humorous, anti-Russian novel, *Les Onze Mille
Verges,* a work whose bloody, tragicomic episodes are "punctuated
by the dead sound of birches on robust or over-ripe flesh" (Robert
Desnos, *De l'érotisme*).

When he met Lou in 1914, he was immediately attracted to that
red-haired aristocrat, a convent-bred *révoltée* like his mother and a
narcissistic flagellant to boot; he quickly became her twenty-fourth
lover and cruel tyrant-slave, calling her "his little boy" as he whipped
her, and pointing out to her that hers was "the major vice, that of
Eve listening to the serpent whistling like a whip." Their mythic
flagellation, he continued, was comparable to that of Xerxes taming

the treacherous sea (letter of 3 March 1915). Another letter in which he imagined trampling her naked breast with his artillery boots seems to parallel a passage in the semi-autobiographical short story "Giovanni Moroni," where a similar beating is administered to the protagonist's mother (Margaret Davies points out that this woman was probably Apollinaire's Roman foster mother). It is also similar to the beating of Françoise by Costantino (note the names) in "La Favorite." It is undoubtedly significant that the young Don Juan's first sexual relationship in *Les Exploits d'un jeune Don Juan*, like that of François des Ygrès in "Le Poète assassiné," is with a pregnant woman, and that Croniamantal in the latter book causes the death of his mother—in a good romantic tradition stemming from Tristan and Rousseau—by the simple act of being born. When Croniamantal comes into the world the midwives are conversing on the sterile love of Sodom as his mother dies "uttering a howl like the one the eternal first wife of Adam makes when she crosses the Red Sea."

Violence, usually misogynic and masochistic, is the keynote of Apollinaire's fiction. Here we meet in the young author a premature awareness of the ongoing process of "deconstruction" in the folk tale and fairy story that has been occurring since the early days of romanticism: he brings the ironic, satirical traditions of such pioneers as Mérimée, Poe, and Villiers de l'Isle-Adam into our contemporary modes of nihilism and black humor. Basing his tales on the traditional *conte merveilleux* (the fantasy tale) with its basic structure of the initiation, the quest, the battle with the dragon (the doppelgänger or the dark double), the spiritual marriage, and the transcendent ending, Apollinaire turns the tales upside down: instead of the dragon, the hero is defeated; instead of the happy ending, there is murder and mayhem; instead of marriage and children, the death of love.[4] For example, after Apollinaire lost the English girl Annie in the Rhineland and in London, he had an unfaithful English peeress shot in "Le Matelot d'Amsterdam" (The sailor of Amsterdam), a Rhenish countess driven away for the same reason in "La Comtesse d'Eisenberg," and he wiped out a whole English fleet— on Christmas!—in "La Noël des milords." He had one of his heroes carry off the Slavic girl Mara (Mary) in "L'Otmika" and another eat the legs of a dead German mistress, Marizibill (Mary-Sibyl) in "Cox City." His jealous castration impulses toward male lovers are equally severe; as Françoise Dininman points out, instead of the heroes of

legend and fable, they are the shadow doubles, the "false heroes,"
for the author's frustrated and masochistic inner selves; he, on the
other hand, often plays the avenging narrator figure.[5] One is brutally
murdered for the sake of a documentary film sequence in "Un beau
film" (A fine film)—this must be the first appearance of a "snuff
movie" in literature—after which the murderer coolly leaves to win
at the gaming table; one suffers a heart attack when he discovers
that his mistress has thrown out his treasured gallstone ("Histoire
d'une famille vertueuse . . ."); one is shot by a jealous husband
after he has learned to camouflage himself like an insect for protection ("La Disparition d'Honoré Subrac" [The disappearance of
Honoré Subrac]); and two carve themselves up in a knife fight over
a blowsy barmaid ("Que vlo-ve?" [What do you want?]). In this
last, very Oedipal story, one of the brawlers, dying, falls on his
derrière, "bloody, you might say, as if by menstruation."
    He often associates gambling, the passion of his mother, with
violent love-deaths. In "La Favorite," a story that begins with a
setting sun bleeding in the West, the passionate former mistress-
for-a-night of King Victor Emmanuel of Italy, lying on the dead
body of a workman, is trampled on by her latest lover who has just
lost at lotto. In "Le Départ de l'ombre" ("The Departure of the
Shadow"), the hero—Nyctor in the manuscript—gratuitously wills
the death of his mistress amid a pawnbroker's memories of drawing
lotto numbers in Rome, an event followed by scenes of suicide and
a mother's transgressions. Finally, in a kind of apotheosis of frustration and sterility that he wrote as Marie Laurencin was leaving
him, a Dutch millionaire, a great lover of women and gaming, loses
his fortune and is killed by the dying hand of a male transvestite
he has picked up in the gambling den ("La Rencontre au cercle
mixte" ["The Meeting at the Mixed Club"]). Apollinaire's gamblers
rarely win.
    Castration and purity (sublimation) motifs, finally, like those in
"L'Ermite," are found everywhere in his work. In 1912 and again
in 1916 a world-weary, loveless Apollinaire contemplated retiring
to a monastery; in "Les Pèlerins piémontais" (The Piedmont pil-
grims, 1903) he vicariously did so in a hot southern countryside
full of dust and swirls of flies. In La Gloire de l'olive, young Nyctor
was a virgin and prayed to remain so; at the front in 1915 after Lou
had left him, Sergeant Kostrowitsky resolutely kept a vow of "godlike chastity" for at least seven months. The pull and counterpull

of Eros and Anteros, desire and the death wish, are beautifully portrayed in chapter 12 of "Le Poète assassiné," where Croniamantal leaves his love momentarily "to die of thirst by the spring"; in "Les Femmes" ("The Women") where cozy indoor comfort is contrasted with the cold German winter; and in the festive, apocalyptic poem "La Maison des morts" ("The House of the Dead") where the poet finds a refuge from love in his glaciers of memory and in the past. The legend of a monk falling asleep for centuries upon hearing the bird of eternity, a picturesque symbol of Nirvana desire (or, to M. D. Conway, of the desire to be the Messiah) recurrently turns up in his works. Other variations on this theme are the sun-suicide motif of "Un soir" and *L'Enchanteur pourrissant,* which he returns to in the poems "La Chanson du mal-aimé," "L'Emigrant de Landor Road," and "La Loreley" (compare Mallarmé's "Victoriously fled the beautiful suicide / Firebrand of glory, frothing blood, storm and gold" and Baudelaire's "The sun has drowned itself in its coagulating blood"). Frequently this suicide is vicarious, when the narrator violently does away with the various picturesque protagonists who play out the roles of his shadow selves, his dragons, his doppelgängers. Finally, romantic madness caused by the death of love, a sort of mental suicide, is ambivalently feared and willed by the author of "Le Passant de Prague" and "La Rose de Hildesheim."

Both the suicide and madness themes are related to the theme of masturbation, of inflicting *la petite mort* upon oneself; and all three combine in the overriding theme of the Superman (Apollinaire knew Lombroso's and Nietzsche's theories on the affinity of genius and madness) who is at the same time master of and slave to his destiny. The tormented sun could set heroically: Merlin praised cremation as well as suicide in *L'Enchanteur pourrissant,* and Apollinaire discussed the nobility of beheading in his first version of "La Danseuse" (The dancing girl) in 1902.

A glance through the poems of *Alcools* that were conceived before 1908 reveals the importance of this masochistic, incestuous, and ultimately angelic sun-night theme, as in the Rhenish scene of "Le Vent nocturne" ("Night Wind"), cited here in full:

> Oh! les cimes des pins grincent en se heurtant
> Et l'on entend aussi se lamenter l'autan
> Et du fleuve prochain à grand'voix triomphales
> Les elfes rire au vent ou corner aux rafales

Attys Attys Attys charmant et débraillé
C'est ton nom qu'en la nuit les elfes ont
                    raillé
Parce qu'un de tes pins s'abat au vent
                    gothique
La forêt fuit au loin comme une armée
                    antique
Dont les lances ô pins s'agitent au tournant
Les villages éteints méditent maintenant
Comme les vierges les vieillards et les poètes
Et ne s'éveilleront au pas de nul venant
Ni quand sur leurs pigeons fondront les
                    gypaètes

(O the pine tops creak as they knock together / You can also hear the
south wind cry / In triumphant voice from the nearby river / Elves laugh
or trumpet as the blasts go by / Atys Atys Atys charming and half-
undressed / It's your name mocked by the elves tonight / For a pine has
fallen in the gothic wind / The forest resembles an army in flight / Whose
lances O pine trees wave at the turn / The villages dark now meditate /
Like virgins old people and poets / And wake to the step of no passerby /
When down on the pigeons the vultures fly)

Here the dramatic emasculation of Atys, son and lover of Cybele
the Mother Goddess, in one of his emblematic pines is mockingly
contrasted to the creative meditations of the physically sterile, virgins, old folks, and poets, after the sun has set and the lights have
gone out. The virile armies have fled; and the contrast between
creativity and sterility and flight and fall is pointed up by the
Manichaean whiteness and darkness of the last line (the European
vulture is a heavy, dark bird, the largest European bird of prey).
At the time the poem was written the founder of psychoanalysis
was singling out birds (later, airplanes) as important dream symbols
of erection and castration; he also wrote that his ideas were scooped
by the poets. Apollinaire's last line echoes two very Freudian lines
from "Merlin et la vieille femme": "And their hands rose up like a
flight of doves / Brightness on which night swooped like a vulture."
    Some of the same symbols are found with attenuated force in
"Automne malade" ("Sickly Autumn," *Alcools*), another poem from
the Rhineland about the melancholy, creative enjoyment of sterility.
There the descent of the birds of prey is accompanied by that of
the year, snow (purity-sterility), and fruit. The meditating old peo-

ple are absent (Apollinaire wrote in 1905, "old people wait without meditating, for only children meditate"), and the nightlike vultures have turned into falcons of the day; but the virgins are present as loveless water sprites, and the elves and armies have become mating stags:

> Pauvre automne
> Meurs en blancheur et en richesse
> De neige et de fruits mûrs
> Au fond du ciel
> Des éperviers planent
> Sur les nixes nicettes aux cheveux verts et
> > naines
> Qui n'ont jamais aimé
>
> Aux lisières lointaines
> Les cerfs ont bramé

(Poor autumn / Die in whiteness and in wealth / Of snow and ripe fruit / At the top of the sky / Falcons soar / On [or "above"] naïve little green-haired nixies / Who have never loved // At the distant edge of the forest / The stags have bugled)

When he wrote "Automne malade" Apollinaire may well have known that the falcon *(épervier)* was the bird of sun gods Ra, Horus, and Apollo, and was associated with undines in European folklore. Elsewhere in *Alcools* the phallic setting sun is more overtly connected with water, in "Lul de Faltenin," for instance, where the solar ship and beheaded Medusa (jelly fish) play roles, or in "L'Emigrant de Landor Road," where the sea swells toward night after the emigrant's suicide by drowning.

Other poems from this first period in which sunsets are associated with the death of love in autumn are "La Chanson du mal-aimé," "Les Colchiques," "Le Larron," "Automne," "Rhénane d'automne," "Signe," "Adieu," and "La Dame." The contrast between flight and darkness is made in "L'Emigrant de Landor Road," "Un soir" (in reverse), "Signe" ("The doves this evening make their final flight"), and "Merlin et la vieille femme." Finally, poems in which some kind of mutilation, castration, or crucifixion accompanies the death of love include "La Chanson du mal-aimé" (vampirism), "L'Emigrant de Landor Road" (decapitation, flagellation), "Palais" (crucifixion, and in the manuscript, decapitation), "Lul de Faltenin" (wounding, decapitation), and "L'Ermite" (mortification, nose-bleed). I shall presently examine some of these poems in more detail; for now let me close this section with three beautiful lines from a later poem in which the errant poet, searching for himself, comes upon a memory haunted by his main theme:

> Qui donc reconnais-tu sur ces vieilles
>   photographies
> Te souviens-tu du jour où une abeille tomba
>   dans le feu
> C'était tu t'en souviens à la fin de l'été
>   ("Le Voyageur" ["The Traveler"])

(Whom do you recognize in these old photographs / Do you remember the day a bee fell in the fire / It was you remember at the end of summer)

"La Chanson du mal-aimé"

Cain the wanderer, having killed his God and looking for a wife, appeared in London in the fall of 1903 and again in the spring of 1904 in the person of Guillaume Apollinaire, walking through the foggy streets at twilight in the company of a juvenile delinquent who turned out not to be Eros after all—the poet reports that Eros is dead like Christ and Pan—but Anteros, the bad twin brother of love, who is another version of the mountebank-Judas of "Un soir."[6] This lad was to take him to his beloved:

> Un soir de demi-brume à Londres
> Un voyou qui ressemblait à
> Mon amour vient à ma rencontre
> Et le regard qu'il me jeta
> Me fit baisser les yeux de honte
>   (stanza 1)

(One foggy night in London / A thug who resembled / My love came to meet me / And the glance he threw me / Made me lower my eyes in shame)

When his love appears, we find that it is she who resembles the thug, she is the prostitute to his pimp, the victim of his vampirism ("the scar on her naked neck"), as she staggers, drunk, out of a pub. The poet recognizes "the falseness of love it[him]self" (stanza 5).

So begins "La Chanson du mal-aimé" ("The Song of the Poorly Loved"), one of literature's most beautiful complaints, a modern elegy to rank with the love lyrics of Catullus, Ronsard, Keats, and Verlaine, "Rhyming out love's despair / To flatter beauty's ignorant ear" (Yeats). Yet this terribly twentieth-century poem, chronologically the first in *Alcools* to describe the "heap of broken images" (Apollinaire's "water bad to drink") the lost contemporary poet struggles through, and the first to set a tone for the most recent poetic cries of amorous distress, owes almost entirely its imagery, prosody, vocabulary, and references to the medieval and symbolist literature Apollinaire absorbed in his adolescence. In thus successfully bringing old themes in an old garb to a modern ethos and a modern urban setting, Apollinaire reveals himself for the first time as one of the world's great poets.

This miracle he accomplished mainly, I think, by his faith in his myth, his transcendent belief that he was in no way inferior to the tragic poets and heroes of history. Like T. S. Eliot, he hungered for cultural unity and significance; but unlike Eliot, he felt no personal inadequacy before the great shades of the past lost in the sterile wasteland of the present. *Au contraire!* He was one of the enchanters foretold by Merlin; he literally knew

> . . . des lais pour les reines
> Des complaintes de mes années
> Des hymnes d'esclave aux murènes
> La romance du mal aimé
> Et des chansons pour les sirènes
> (repeated stanza 19, 59)

(. . . lays for queens / Laments for my years / Slave hymns for Muraena eels / The romance of the poorly beloved / And for the sirens songs)

Although he found himself at the moment powerless to win his own siren-queen or to create a new kingdom of love on earth, he was able to turn a doomed quest into a courtly romance and himself into a knight-errant doing battle with the demons of destiny by the immortal power of the word; for this knight-errant was also a troubadour with an astonishing repertory of lays, hymns, complaints, and curses at his command. He was ready and eager to transport his listeners from London to the Red Sea and from cosmopolitan, twentieth-century Paris to fourth-century Asia Minor and Kalidasa's India.

As in "Le Larron" and *L'Enchanteur pourrissant* the past in "La Chanson du mal-aimé" is made contemporary: a seventeenth-century Cossacks' curse against the Turkish Sultan becomes the frustrated lover's imprecation; the goal of Columbus becomes the beloved; and the mythology of the ancient world mixes with medieval demons and unicorns to bring another fabulous cortege to life. But no longer is this literary framework a symbolic, enchanted world of its own, replacing a pale, lifeless Christianity, as in "Le Larron"; rather, it is determined by a powerful psychological line running through the poem, the poet's chaotic yet logical emotions of hope, despair, desire, madness, melancholy, jealousy, and hatred caused by the death of love.

L. C. Breunig in his excellent critical studies of the poem[7] stresses how closely Apollinaire keeps to the timetable of his love, from his stay in Munich with Annie in the spring of 1902 ("Aubade," stanzas 15–17), through the first visit to London in November 1903 (beginning), the Paris winter and spring of 1903–4 (stanzas 10, 38–40), to June 1904 (stanza 55) when he is back in Paris after the definitive second visit to London and Annie in May. All of this chronology transmits a consistent pattern of life to the work. On and through this pattern, he weaves a series of shorter narratives taken from the lives and legends of kings in which his life theme is supported or contrasted for associational depth; such are the narratives with the Egyptian Pharoah, Ulysses, King Dushyanta (the lover of Shakuntala), the Turkish Sultan, and mad King Ludwig of Bavaria. Finally, an imagined interlude describing seven swords in his heart proves his vaunted ability to create his own legend and make it a psychological truth—part of the whole psychological truth of the poem.

Two examples will serve to illustrate Apollinaire's skill in converting inherited poetic imagery into personal experience. Following in the footsteps of his evil cockney cupid at the beginning, he relates how

> . . . Nous semblions entre les maisons
> Onde ouverte de la mer Rouge

> Lui les Hébreux moi Pharaon
> (stanza 2)

(We seemed between the houses / The Red Sea's open wave / He the Hebrews I Pharoah)

He seizes upon the metaphor from a purely visual scene of fog and red brick walls. On further examination, however, the image falls apart: the Promised Land of the beloved is not sought by the ruffian but by the poet; the boy is not being pursued but followed; and Jehovah would punish the wrong party should he follow his biblical precedent. But the fallacy of this image is used by its author to establish the emotional truth of the next, personal image: in the following stanza, knowing well that the solid waves will not tumble, he invokes Jehovah himself to attest to the sincerity of his love: "Let these brick walls fall down / If you were not well loved."

Then exaggerating the false analogy between himself and Pharoah, he demonstrates his point in a magnificent hyperbole:

> Je suis le souverain d'Egypte
> Sa soeur-épouse son armée
> Si tu n'es pas l'amour unique

(I am the King of Egypt / His sister-spouse his army / If you are not my only love)

A sardonic, disconsolate attitude has broken through the fancy and the mixed metaphors, shattering them in their own terms and transferring depth and power to the underlying feeling; and the later image of love aspiring toward "the white streams of Canaan" (stanzas 13, 27, 49) is given added meaning.

In a contrasting example, the image is remarkably precise:

> J'ai hiverné dans mon passé
> Revienne le soleil de Pâques
> Pour chauffer un coeur plus glacé
> Que les quarante de Sébaste
> Moins que ma vie martyrisés
> (stanza 10)

(I have hibernated in my past / Let the Easter sun return / To warm a heart more icy / Than the forty of Sebastus / Less martyred than my life)

The Forty of Sebastus were Roman soldiers convicted of Christian belief in the Roman garrison at Sebastus in Asia Minor (now Turkey) during the fourth century; forced to spend the night on a frozen lake, they were burned to death in the morning. Their saints' day comes during Lent (March 9). Apollinaire brings the mystery surrounding the little event from an obscure place and age outside of the great lines of history into the ageless yet individual soul of the poem.

The narrative and images thus ebb and flow with the rhythms of the poet's torment. The ballad-like beginning in a London autumn with its slum exoticism, hope, and doubt is brought to a sudden conclusion by the realization that Love is as false as the beloved. The poet's doleful state is immediately contrasted with the joyful unions of Ulysses and Dushyanta with their loves, and the principal conflict in his mind begins: the desire for forgetfulness with its accompanying aspiration after new love (the white streams of Canaan) as against the impossibility of forgetfulness because of the beloved's desirability. Having hibernated through the cold winter's loss in the past—in his memory—he aspires to life in the spring and calls upon the Easter sun to compensate for a loveless present, which reminds him of an earlier spring and a holy Lenten Sunday when he sang his pagan happiness, at dawn, to his beloved ("Aubade"). Back to an empty reality in Paris, a reality in which both sacred and profane love are dead, he ironically considers his powers as an enchanter ("I who know lays for queens . . .") subject to painful memory. But in spite of all, he remains faithful, just as the womenless, Christian Zaporogian Cossacks stayed faithful to their steppes and their Decalogue. In a sudden burst of liberty, he momentarily regains dominance by phrasing his despair and rage in the Cossacks' brutal invective against the Moslem Turk (Annie was a protestant). Then reality again, with its pattern of future hope dissolved in the torment of desire alternating with recollections of beauty, until again his frustration centers on his grief's holocaust, which moves from a martyr's pyre to the sacrificial altar of the god of misfortune to the empty shadow of death—the only god remaining. Meanwhile, spring has returned to Paris, again in ironic contrast to the poet's suffering, a contrast first summarized by a wry, humorous image announcing the coming dislocation of insanity ("And I my heart is as heavy [gros] / As a Damascan woman's derrière [cul d'une dame damascène]"), and then bursting forth in the incoherency of frustrated eroticism

with the seven phallic swords. His madness next is metamorphosed
into the ill-fated life of mad King Ludwig of Bavaria, the Moon
King, and the haunted Starnberger See where the royal Wagner-
lover had himself pulled around in gondolas by swans and where
he was reputed to have committed suicide:

> Près d'un château sans châtelaine
> La barque aux barcarols chantants
> Sur un lac blanc et sous l'haleine
> Des vents qui tremblent au printemps
> Voguait cygne mourant sirène
>
> Un jour le roi dans l'eau d'argent
> Se noya puis la bouche ouverte
> Il s'en revint en surnageant
> Sur la rive dormir inerte
> Face tournée au ciel changeant
> (stanzas 53, 54)

(By a mistressless chateau / The bark with singing gondoliers / On a white
lake under breath / Of trembling winds in spring / Sailed siren dying
swan // One day the king in the silver water / Drowned himself then
openmouthed / Returned floating on the wave / To sleep inertly on the
bank / Face turned to the changing sky)

With this final metamorphosis, his last and gravest crisis of despair
has spent itself, and a passive melancholy takes its place, precluding
the possibility of his own suicide: "I wander through my lovely
Paris / Without the heart (courage) to die in it" (stanza 55). The
modern days and nights of Paris take over his life with their Barbary
organs, their trolley cars, their cafés crying out to the beloved,
"Towards thee thee I so dearly loved." He is left singing sadly to
himself, "I who know lays for queens . . ." (stanzas 58, 59).

Even after the varied experience in poetic creation revealed by the
large body of Apollinaire's earlier work, it is easy to wonder how
such a young poet could arrive at such a rich tapestry and such a
mature synthesis of form and subject matter. In regard to the latter,
I have already mentioned its debt to the past; in fact, symbolist
poetry and art (Apollinaire, like his friend Picasso, was an admirer
of English Pre-Raphaelites and French symbolists like Walter Crane,
Burne-Jones, Gustave Moreau, Odilon Redon, Eugène Carrière,

Maurice Denis, and Puvis de Chavannes) were teeming with the
same swans, sirens, vampires, unicorns, Rhenish scenes, cypresses,
weeping willows, will-o'-the-wisps, aegypans, Argyraspides, au-
bades, and *danses macabres* of men led by destiny through shadowy
lands that we find here.

Verlaine and Rimbaud before Apollinaire evoked the god *Malheur*
(Misfortune; stanza 35), while Alfred Jarry, Marcel Schwob, and
Remy de Gourmont were experts in hagiography, often inventing
their own saints—many of them erotic—like Sainte-Fabeau (stanza
46). Even the sainted Forty of Sebastus were discussed at length in
many of their common source books.[8] The seven swords in the Virgin
Mary's heart were cited by Baudelaire, Laforgue, Lecomte de Lisle,
Pierre Quillard, Remy de Gourmont, Alfred Jarry, and Henri de
Régnier among many others; and *Shakuntala* had been a popular
play among romantics and symbolists (including King Ludwig) all
through the nineteenth century. Men danced to the violins of Destiny in Albert Samain, were led by Evil ˙Chance in Saint-Georges
de Bouhélier's *La Vie héroïque des aventuriers, des poètes, des rois et des
artisans* (The heroic life of adventurers, poets, kings, and artisans,
1895)—which also celebrated the death of the gods and the birth
of heroes—and sailed through sidereal zones toward the ideal in
Henri de Régnier's poems. Rodin's famous statue of the Bourgeois
of Calais had brought the inevitable alliteration "corde au cou [neck]
à Calais" to literature (Remy de Gourmont also used it); and Ludwig
of Bavaria as a Decadent myth-in-the-flesh of aesthetic madness
driven to suicide was idealized by Wagner lovers. The slaves fed to
Muraena eels by the Roman gourmet Vedius Pollon were poetized
by Victor Hugo, moralized over by Karl Marx, and painted by
Gustave Moreau; and the old apocryphal (and very profane) text of
the Cossacks reviling the Sultan was still circulating secretly in the
Ukraine at the end of the nineteenth century.[9] In an aubade by
Victor Hugo Venus and Mars are mentioned among roses and naked,
dancing figures.[10]

The English woman was the vampirish femme fatale *par excellence*
in many a gruesome tale ("The exotic perversions which were the
vogue of the fin-de-siècle were *sadisme à l'anglaise* and the Slav soul,"
wrote Mario Praz in *The Romantic Agony*), and all the readers of
popular novels of the time were well acquainted with the murky,
vice-ridden streets of London.[11] Perhaps the erotic seven swords
sequence is the most original section of the poem in terms of subject

matter; but there, too, we find the Mount Gibel *(gibeline),* Carabosse, Rhenish landscapes, and castrated Herma (Hermes) of fin de siècle poetry.

As for form and theme, Villon and—surprisingly—Shakespeare could lead the list of influences. The critic Henri Ghéon in 1913 called attention to the similarity between the "Chanson" and Villon's *Grand testament* with the latter's narrative yet profoundly personal form interspersed with ballad interludes illustrating the author's thought—including "The Ballad of the Lords of Yesteryear." Apollinaire probably listened to Marcel Schwob's popular public lectures on the fifteenth-century poet in 1904; like Villon, he wove poem fragments written at various times and places into his basic narrative fabric: in the first, punctuated version of 1909, which he had been assembling over a period of four or five years, he employed no less than eight ellipses to compensate for its fragmentary appearance. His aristocratic origins and Nietzschean philosophy made royal names and titles come naturally to him as symbols, especially since as a republican anarchist he believed that he had arrived at the historical moment of the end of kings. A few kings had been assassinated by anarchists during his youth, and he had seen and even met some living royalty in his travels with the Viscountess de Milhau in Germany. This interest, constantly nourished by reading in history and legend, plus his admiration for Shakespeare—partly inspired like that for Villon by Léon Cahun, the librarian at the Mazarine Library—had caused him to see *Richard II* in London and to buy a copy of the play, which, L. C. Breunig suggests, may have given him the inspiration for his identification of himself with the kings of the "Chanson" ("For God's sake, let us sit upon the ground / And tell sad stories of the death of kings / . . ."; "Thus play I, in one person many people . . ."). I add to Professor Breunig's remarks only that the scene from the play that he liked the most ("the greatest in the theater") was the tragic act 4 in which the betrayed Richard compares his fate to that of Jesus fallen from glory into *shadow* among Judases and Pilates.

But all the popular sources and the most careful construction cannot account for the poem's rich self-sufficiency and personal music. Apollinaire's vaulting egoism combined all that he had learned poetically with the acuity of his feelings—whether remembered in tranquillity or not—to place him not only at the summit of contemporary French lyricism but in the ranks of the kings and heroes

of the past. The main myth of "La Chanson du mal-aimé"—and of
all the poetry of which it forms a part, in the final analysis—is his
own.

"L'Emigrant de Landor Road," "Lul de Faltenin," and "Palais"

Unlike "La Chanson du mal-aimé," "L'Emigrant de Landor
Road" ("The Emigrant of Landor Road") begins on a fairly cheerful
note, even though decapitation is involved: again a tourist in London, the traveler this time is preparing to emigrate to America like
Annie, former resident of Landor Road on the outskirts of London,
and is getting dressed up for the occasion:

> Le chapeau à la main il entra du pied droit
> Chez un tailleur très chic et fournisseur du
> roi
> Ce commerçant venait de couper quelques têtes
> De mannequins vêtus comme il faut qu'on se
> vête

(Hat in hand he entered right foot forward / The chic shop of a tailor
caterer to the king / The merchant had just cut off a few heads / Of
mannequins decked out very comme il faut)

Is this tailor again Anteros? Or, better, Thanatos? The mannequins
were corpses in "La Maison des Morts" ("The House of the Dead").
In any case, the headless forms dress our emigrant up like a millionaire in the suit of a dead lord, and he sails away for good:

> Car revenir c'est bon pour un soldat des Indes
> Les boursiers ont vendu tous mes crachats d'or
> fin
> Mais habillé de neuf je veux dormir enfin
> Sous des arbres pleins d'oiseaux muets et de
> singes
>
> (stanza 4)

(For returning is fine for a soldier of the Indies / The brokers have sold
all my medals [pun: spit] of gold / But dressed in new clothes I want
finally to sleep / Under trees full of monkeys and mute birds)

Surprisingly, the "soldier of the Indies" is probably Kipling's Tommy Atkins back from Mandalay (the "flying fishes" later become dolphins),[12] whereas the "medals" may be the poet's unappreciated poems. As he boards the ship in a port of autumn and it sails away into the future and the unknown, in two beautiful images the past seems to disappear: "For a long time he watched the coastline die / Only children's boats were trembling on the horizon," and beauty to be born: "A tiny little bouquet floating at random / Covered the ocean with an immense bloom." But creative desires awakened by this vision are crowded out by his past, now inescapable and interior, weaving a tapestry in his brain. Unable to escape back into an urban world of the present as in "La Chanson du mal-aimé," this time he unites with the sea to the cries of a familiar siren (*sirène* means also "boat whistle" and "prostitute"):

> Mais pour noyer changées en poux
> Ces tisseuses têtues qui sans cesse
> > interrogent
> Il se maria comme un doge
> Aux cris d'une sirène moderne sans époux
> > (stanza 12)

(To drown changed into lice / Those stubborn weavers questioning endlessly / He married like a doge [the sea] / To the cries of a modern siren without a spouse)[13]

Like the Rimbaud of "Le Bateau ivre" ("The Drunken Boat") he has cried, "Let me go to the sea!"—but he does not return to Europe and the "puddle / Dark and cold" of childhood like the poet of Charleville. He has chosen instead the death by drowning of the sun: in the final stanza, after his suicide, the Western sea swells into ravenous night.

"Lul de Faltenin" was the most priapic of the seven swords planted in the poet's heart in "La Chanson du mal-aimé"; it would appear indeed that the name means bluntly "phallus," "Lul" being a Flemish slang term for a pipe or a penis and "Faltenin" probably deriving from *phallum tenens*.[14] The name seems to have been one of Apollinaire's pseudonyms: he signed the name "Lul" to the card that became the poem "Carte postale" (*Calligrammes*) in 1915, and was amazed to hear of the death of a certain Guillaume Faltenin during the war. The manuscript of "Lul de Faltenin" leaves no doubt that it was intended among other things to describe a sunset in the sea,[15] so we can divide it into three levels: the narrative description of some sailor, perhaps Ulysses or Butes the Argonaut,[16] descending into the Sirens' grottoes; the self-defeating solar *liebestot*, which represents the mythic immolation of the poet-phallus-Christ caught between two personifications of the Mother, the Night-Sea (*mer-mère*) and the Sirens; and, on a more quotidian level, Apollinaire's masochistic abandon of self to onanism, prostitution, and sterility. Two symbols of aspiration are present: the stars, used to represent the amorous ideal in "La Chanson du mal-aimé," here found at the opposite pole from the erotic grottoes; and the swimmer, a favorite symbol of Apollinaire, with implications that are literary (he somewhat resembles Baudelaire's sidereal swimmer in the poem "Elévation"), biographical (Apollinaire was a good solitary swimmer), mythological (Remy de Gourmont had pointed out that the aspiring swimmer was one of the most common folk archetypes), and, naturally, Freudian. In "La Chanson du mal-aimé," the two symbols were united:

> Voie lactée ô soeur lumineuse
> Des blancs ruisseaux de Chanaan
> Et des corps blancs des amoureuses
> Nageurs morts suivrons-nous d'ahan
> Ton cours vers d'autres nébuleuses
> (repeated stanza 13, 27, 49)

(Milky Way O luminous sister / Of the milk-white Canaan streams / And our white lovers' forms / Dead swimmers shall we struggle on / Your path towards other nebulae)

Here, too, the poet at one point finds himself among the stars, this time with a godlike self-sufficiency we shall meet again:

> . . . ma sagesse égale
> Celle des constellations
> Car c'est moi seul nuit qui t'étoile
> (stanza 5)

(. . . my wisdom equals / That of the constellations / For I alone night give you stars)

But the spasm is short-lived; he sinks back mutilated (crucified? castrated?) into the Sirens' nests at the end of the poem as the sun and the stars go their opposite ways:

> Oiseaux tiriez aux mers la langue
> Le soleil d'hier m'a rejoint
> Les otelles nous ensanglantent
> Dans le nid des Sirènes loin
> Du troupeau d'étoiles oblongues
> (final stanza)

(Birds you put out your tongues at the seas [pun on "mothers"] / Yesterday's sun has rejoined me / The otelles cover us with blood / In the nests of the Sirens far / From the flock of oblong stars)

"Palais" ("Palace") is another erotic allegory. Where "Lul de Faltenin" describes a physical decline and fall, however, "Palais" reveals more of a mental one, the failure of the mind's spiritual quest for the *rosa mystica*. To Apollinaire as to English Pre-Raphaelites, Rosamond Clifford, the *rose of the world,* beloved of Henry II and mistress of a fabulous palace and labyrinth at Woodstock, was a favorite symbol of a kind of labyrinthine pursuit of love reminiscent of the one in Guillaume de Lorris's *Romance of the Rose*—or, in a negative way, Boccaccio's *Laberinto d'amore,* which Apollinaire had planned to translate in 1899. In his notes for *Le Bestiaire* (*The Bestiary,* 1911) he translated a verse from a celebrated sixteenth-century ballad about Miss Clifford's rivalry with Henry's jealous queen, Eleanor of Aquitaine:

> The king therefore, for her defence,
> Against the furious queene,
> At Woodstocke builded such a bower
> The like was never seene. [17]

He also made her the main object of his quest for beauty in a delightful little occasional poem in *Alcools* called "Rosemonde." In "Palais," however, she is far from the courtly ideal: she is "Madame Rosemonde," mysteriously rolling her little German eyes as she sits on her royal lover's pointed knees. In short, she has joined the ranks of Helen, Angelica, Viviane, and Salome, femmes fatales all who have fallen low from their romantic idealization under our poet's scabrous pen. Her fall is accompanied by a corresponding cynicism in language.

The poem is constructed on five main puns. The title also means "palet" in French; the pilgrim thoughts *(pensées)* are also flowers, "pansies"; *the tongues of fire* of the poet's burlesque Pentecost are nothing but tough meat (a play on words which Apollinaire inherited from Aesop and used in 1904 for the title of his first periodical, *Le Festin d'Esope* [Aesop's feast]); *Rosemonde* in German is a pun on *rosy mouth* and *rosy moon;* and the *orient* has at least four main meanings: the region where all religions were born, a symbolist metaphor for the inner life, an erotic action (see Glossary), and the orient of a pearl, a word perhaps taken from the line "Her sparkling eyes, like Orient pearls" in the old ballad (1.11) and applied here to another, more exotic part of her anatomy. Lesser puns, many of them erotic, are rampant throughout the poem, and the palace already becomes a phallus in the first stanza, raised, significantly enough, out of the flagellated roses of a crucified sun.

All this word play has naturally led critics to regard "Palais" as a Jarry- or Jacob-like satire directed against symbolist preoccupations. André Salmon has written that he and Max Jacob used to tease Apollinaire about his symbolist leanings ("Still too symbolist!" they would cry after he had read his latest creations aloud to them), and the poem in *Alcools* is dedicated to Max Jacob. It is true that crepuscular dream-gardens and haunted palaces abounded in the works of the older generation Apollinaire admired. Three examples close to "Palais" include a novel by Remy de Gourmont in which a phantom woman lover discovers that eternal beauty was found only in an invisible "palace of symbols" surrounded by sterile ponds with dead *pensées* the only flowers (*Le Fantôme,* 1893); a nude English vampire sits on her lover's knees in an Oriental garden in Octave Mirbeau's *Le Jardin des supplices* (*Torture Garden,* 1899); and roses "whipped by the brutal wind" nostalgically shed their petals toward the Orient in Pierre Quillard's *La Lyre héroïque et dolente* (The grieving and heroic lyre, 1897).

But if Apollinaire is satirizing his former masters in "Palais," he is also satirizing his own obsessions. Among other signs of love's demise, he finds that Cypress wine (from *Cypri botrus,* a medieval symbol for Christ in the Song of Songs, Lionel Follet points out) is bitter to him when he tastes it at agapes of the white lamb; his

"Last Supper" is decidedly scatological; and he waits in vain for the Pentecostal ascension of his thoughts en route to the Orient. Still-born, his brain turns into prehistoric meat; he can only rage when no Holy Ghost descends at his own agapes:

> Ah! nom de Dieu! qu'ont donc crié ces
> entrecôtes
> Ces grands pâtés ces os à moelle et mirotons
> Langues de feu où sont-elles mes pentecôtes
> Pour mes pensées de tous pays de tous les
> temps
>
> (final stanza)

(God damn it what did those cutlets cry / Those great pâtés those marrow bones and stews / Tongues of fire where are they my pentecosts / For my thoughts of all the lands of all the years)

Thus "Palais" is as frustrated as "Lul de Faltenin"; it is a Rabelaisian orgy of onanistic cannibalism in which the mystic rose palace becomes another dead-end grotto. Most critics consider the poem to be primarily an erotic and scatological dream in which the palace-palet is that of women's nether mouths.[18] The wide range of Apollinaire's fancy plus his use of similar erotic symbolism in other works makes this interpretation plausible (see the Glossary of References).

In a part of the manuscript of "Le Poète assassiné" probably dating from 1907, Apollinaire wrote of his main character, a stand-in for himself, "Claude Auray who had loved and was no longer in love believed that he could love no more."[19] The previous year he had announced publicly, after praising the thought of Pascal, Racine, Goethe, Baudelaire, and Rimbaud, "I possess no significant composition, and I regret it."[20] He published nothing new besides his pornographic works from January 1906 to August 1907. This was the time of a sort of Passion for him; an important manuscript of "Les Fiançailles" ("The Betrothal") gives us an insight into it:

> [J'ai rêvé] des poèmes si grandioses que j'ai
> dû les laisser inachevés . . .
> Parce que mon souci de perfection

Dépassait [mon goût] mon goût même et les
    forces d'un seul homme
[Puis j'ai reconnu que chaque moment porte
    en soi sa propre perfection]
Mais j'ai eu cette force ce goût et cette
    science
Et je me suis endormi
Un ange a exterminé pendant mon sommeil
Les agneaux, les pasteurs des tristes
    bergeries.
De faux centurions emportaient le vinaigre
Les gueux mal blessés par l'épurge dansaient
Puis après la fuite et la mort de mes vérités
    poétiques
Je m'éveillai au bout de cinq ans [et suivit]
    une nuit citadine . . .
La ville aux lueurs nocturnes semblait un
    archipel
Des femmes demandaient l'amour et la dulie
Et sombre éveil si faible je me rappelle
Les passantes ce soir n'étaient jamais jolies

([I have dreamed] poems so grandiose that I have had to leave them
unfinished . . . / Because my desire for perfection / Surpassed [my taste]
my very taste and the powers of one man / [Then I realized that each
moment carries in it its own perfection] / But I had that ability that taste
that science / And I fell asleep / An angel exterminated during my slum-
ber / The lambs the shepherds of the sad sheepfolds / False centurions were
removing the vinegar / Beggars badly wounded by spurge were dancing
. . . / Then after the flight and death of my poetic truths / I awoke after
five years [and followed] one city night / The city seemed an archipelago
with its nocturnal lights / Women were asking for love and dulia / And
dark awakening so feeble I remember / The passing women that evening
were never pretty)[21]

The version published in 1908 has this cry:

Pardonnez-moi mon ignorance;
Pardonnez-moi de ne plus connaître l'ancien
    jeu des vers.
Je ne sais plus rien et j'aime uniquement;
Mais les fleurs, à mes yeux, redeviennent des

flammes.
Je médite divinement. . . .

(Forgive me my ignorance / Forgive me for not knowing any more the ancient game of verse / I know nothing any longer and I love uniquely . . . / But flowers, in my eyes, turn back to flames. / I meditate divinely. . . .)[22]

It was not a coincidence that his spiritual death and resurrection paralleled the great crisis in modern poetry and art, during which the moribund symbolist sun finally set, leaving room for a host of new stars in the aesthetic Empyrean. In chapter 3 I describe Apollinaire's transfiguration in the period 1908–10 and the long and winding road that led him to his Mount Tabor.

Chapter Three
The Phoenix

Je suffis pour l'éternité à entretenir le feu de mes délices
—"Le Brasier"

The Death of God

In the second issue of his little magazine *Le Festin d'Esope* Apollinaire printed an article by his friend Jean de Gourmont which began, "The death of God which Zarathustra proclaims signifies the divinization of man and perhaps the culminating point of our civilization" (December 1903). Another close acquaintance, the Polish anarchist Mécislas Golberg, wrote a few months later, "the whole work of Renan can be summed up in a few words: the divinization of man and the hope of human perfection." He also cited Nietzsche's phrase, "We have killed God, we must become gods ourselves" *(Europe Artiste)*. Apollinaire wrote admiringly of Remy de Gourmont, "[If he] did not adore any god [the god he adored was Nietzsche], he would be our Renan" (*Le Festin d'Esope,* August 1904). His own godhead was in eclipse at this time, but when he finally began to realize his divine potential three years later it was toward the artist-divinity of Renan, Nietzsche, and Gourmont that he moved rather than toward the socialist-divinity of his youth, that of his mentors Kropotkin, Souvarine, and Sébastien Faure.

Five admirable long poems and a *Bestiaire* of short ones embody Apollinaire's angelism of 1908–10: "Le Brasier," "Les Fiançailles," "Cortège," "Vendémiaire," the prose poem *Onirocritique,* and the quatrains illustrated by Raoul Dufy in *Le Bestiaire ou Cortège d'Orphée.* Apollinaire later called the first two of these his most profound poems. They are certainly among his most hermetic. I shall attempt their exegesis below; but since they cannot be fully understood outside of the context of Apollinaire's life and times, I must trace the poet's political and critical thought through the period covered by chapters 1 and 2 in order to show how ideas prepared the way for the rise of a fallen god out of his own ashes.

Influences: Rimbaud and Picasso, 1901–5

If British and American readers should get the impression that the theme of man trying to play Prometheus and replace God is uniquely a continental literary phenomenon exemplified in writers from de Sade through Rimbaud and Nietzsche to Sartre and Genet, let them meditate on their own classics: The Ancient Mariner, Childe Harold, Arthur Gordon Pym, Captain Ahab, the Connecticut Yankee, Mr. Kurtz, and Willie Stark were equally caught up in the romantic "spiritual hunt" *(la chasse spirituelle)* for some kind of secular transcendency. Walt Whitman was particularly close to French symbolist thought in his remarkable "Song of Myself," a mid-nineteenth-century epic that filtered into the French poetic scene at the end of the century and very likely influenced Apollinaire's "Cortège" and "Vendémiaire." Whitman's discovery of Christ and Superman in himself was American literature's main contribution to the potent intellectual energy released to the Western world by the romantic movement and by such postromantic powers as Wagner, Rimbaud, Nietzsche, Gauguin, Gide, and Bergson.

Arthur Rimbaud (1854–91) the "adolescent satan" (Victor Hugo's term) who reoriented the course of French literature before leaving it in his twenties for the sterility of the African desert, had already become a legend before his death at the age of thirty-seven. Charles Maurras wrote that in the minds of young poets of 1890 "the man with the soles of wind" (Paul Verlaine's term) was "a magnificent navigator and sea-adventurer, perhaps a prisoner like Ulysses and like Merlin in the pearly grottoes of an Oriental fairy. We imagined him as another Orpheus devoured by black bacchantes. And he was the symbol of modern poetry itself, vagabond, exiled, far from laws, customs, civilizations."[1] By 1901, the year of Apollinaire's first published reference to Rimbaud—he put lines 75–76 from "Le Bateau ivre" into Molina da Silva's dance manual *La Grâce et le maintien français* (French grace and manners)—Rimbaud's countercultural tastes had become practically canons, a whole program of study for the budding writer:

> I loved idiot paintings, tops of doors,
> décors, saltimbanque canvases, signboards,
> popular engravings; obsolete literature,
> church Latin, badly-spelled pornographic

> works, novels by our grandmothers, fairy
> tales, little children's books, old operas,
> folk refrains, popular rhythms.
> *(Une saison en enfer {A Season in Hell})*

Apollinaire later proved himself an authority on all these items—
and many more (street signs, vendors' calls, graffiti, dreams, writings and drawings of the insane, religious prophecies, old dictionaries, anarchist tracts, etc.). He was undoubtedly first attracted to them by their picturesque side, the background of the poet-wanderer; as he matured, however, he came to understand their Promethean import, until he showed by 1910 that he considered such works to be essential steps in the artist's return to godlike primitivism and mystical illumination. The same could be said of Picasso. Both the poet and the painter, born within a year of each other and growing up under the same signs of the symbolists' materialistic mysticism and semireligious anarchism, admired the poet of Charleville. Like him, they found the bourgeois "so respectable they deserved to be boiled" *(Une saison en enfer);* like him, in Apollinaire's felicitous phrase, they lived "on the limit of life at the confines of art" ("La Serviette des poètes").

Apollinaire's 1905 essay on Picasso, the first major critical study of the painter, is astonishing for its prophetic delineation of the paths along which the Catalan's demiurge was subsequently to lead him; and it even anticipates in a precise way Jung's article of the 1920s on his archetypal descent into the Egyptian blue. Indeed, the essay was probably in large part responsible for Picasso's own search for occult powers in his vision when he progressed from the rose period to cubism from 1905 to 1908. In it there is the important idea of the artist as *voyant* or seer, an idea found everywhere in nineteenth-century literature and made particularly dramatic by Rimbaud's absolute conviction of its truth—and willingness to base his life and art upon it.

Formerly, Apollinaire had written that man created the gods in his imagination ("Le Printemps," "Le Dôme de Cologne"); now he would modify "create" to "find": he has met an artist who has only to *see,* to let himself be penetrated by his depths and the depths of others, to discover human divinity:

If we knew, all the gods would wake. Born of the profound knowledge humanity had of itself, the idolized pantheisms resembling it have slumbered. But in spite of eternal sleeps *(sommeils)* there are eyes reflecting humanities like divine and joyous phantoms. . . .

Picasso has watched human images floating in the azure of our memories and which participate in divinity to damn metaphysicians. How pious are his skies . . .

(*La Plume,* May 1905 *{Chroniques}*)

Picasso's externalized, naturalistic vessels for this divinity were subjects always loved by Apollinaire, by artists, and, at the time, by anarchists and socialists: the saltimbanques. Embellishing the Pagliacci theme of the *passionate clown* with its analogies to life, especially antiestablishment life—the clown as isolated traveler, masked illusionist, serious player of absurdity, mocker of respectability, tragic mime of human error—he like Rimbaud, Verlaine, Baudelaire, and many a symbolist and romantic back to the Shakespeare of *Hamlet* and the Ronsard of "The world is the theatre and the men actors," had capitalized on a classic symbol of the romantic personality. Now, however, with Picasso, the saltimbanques no longer imitate life but create religious art: "You can't compare these saltimbanques with buffoons *(histrions)*. Their spectator must be pious, for they celebrate mute rites. . . ." Thus is the archetype extended to the Middle Ages to include the "Holy Fool" of Saint Francis. The saltimbanques are the first-born of immaculate women in strange stables: "Noël: they gave birth to future acrobats among familar monkeys, white horses and bear-like dogs." They at last become demigods, cosmic creators: "The adolescent sisters . . . order spheres into the radiating movement of the worlds. . . ." Innocent, hypersensitive, androgynous, and rootless, the adolescents have infinite inner depths and distances which bring them close to the primitive springs of being and to animals (". . . animals teach them religious mystery . . .") until they become inseparable from the spiritual animality of nature:

. . . Placed on the limit of life, animals are humans and the sexes indecisive.
Hybrid beasts are conscious of Egyptian demigods; the cheeks and foreheads of taciturn harlequins are blighted by morbid sensitivity.

The saltimbanques are also associated with the poor and downtrodden of the world, Picasso's principal subject matter of his previous style, that of the blue period. In a parallel article, Apollinaire compares the saltimbanque boys to the young men of the people and their mothers to the young mothers of the working class (*Revue Immoraliste*, April 1905). Among these lonely ones, the old women are atheists, devoted to memories, innocent and good; the old men are animated by distant lands; the children are wise and wander without having learned their catechism; the youth is old; and the crippled beggars, mad as kings with too many elephants bearing little pavilions, encompass the universe in their gaze: "There are travelers who confuse flowers with stars" (*La Plume*).

Thus in the rituals of the fairgrounds, the whole of humanity participates in a primitivistic reversal of evolution, from civilized man to his pariahs, to his Christ-like saltimbanques on the limit of life, to animals, to the demigods, to the gods themselves, to, finally, the humid depths of the abyss—with the parallel movement from old age to youth to the instinctive profundities of children. This is the traditional voyage of the seer who descends into "the dark night of the soul" (Saint John of the Cross) before he or she ascends, an *illuminatus*, to the stars.[2] Rimbaud had traced out the same voyage in "Le Bateau ivre" and in his mythic life, recorded in advance in *Une saison en enfer*, passing beyond pariah and saltimbanque down through the history of Western man to the religious East to finally a godlike—or bestial—end in the desert. Gauguin had pursued his demigods, his Madonnas and Eves, as far as the Caribbean and the South Seas. And Picasso, the *voyant* whose eyes passively reflected the rhythms of the universe ("Those eyes are attentive as flowers always trying to gaze on the sun") was very soon to take five more occidental pariahs and turn them into the primitive fetishes and bitch-goddesses of his celebrated *Demoiselles d'Avignon*, the *opus initians* of modern art.

From the People-Christ to the Divine Poet, 1899–1908

Even as an adolescent Apollinaire was caught in the typical intellectual dilemma of his time between positivism and idealism. In politics, this dilemma was translated into his admiration for the working masses and their strong leaders along with his realistic awareness of mediocrity and demagoguery in both. He was an artistic individualist like Rimbaud, appalled by human misery and obsessed with the desire to change the world; he must have been disillusioned by the failure of his fellow revolutionaries to take power after the

Dreyfus affair just as Rimbaud had been disillusioned by the fall of the Commune. In short, he agreed with the poet of *Une saison en enfer* that scientific progress, while essentially desirable, was too slow. Like other literary revolutionaries about him and like many of the surrealists later, he was cursed with what the Marxists used to call the crime of anarchistic individualism. Believing in a pseudo-Christian blood-sacrifice to redeem the world, he distrusted political pragmatism. "I hold that politics is detestable, deceitful, sterile, and injurious," he wrote to an editor of the socialist *Plume,* refusing at the same time to comment on the detested Franco-Russian alliance and mentioning that the Russian people would need religious props for some time to come. He wrote in an early manuscript, later incorporated into chapter 12 of "Le Poète assassiné," that human equality was impossible, and he pointed out to the Royalist Charles Maurras in one of his notebooks that "the tyranny of unity [under a king] would not do away with unity of number, it would merely make two tyrannies instead of one. . . ."

The anarchist newspaper, *Le Journal du Peuple,* which he read in 1899 and which was edited by former Jesuit seminarian Sébastien Faure, was also averse to political solutions. In its first issue Faure spelled out his credo: *"The Journal of the People* will scrupulously avoid that horrible and repulsive thing which always and fatally soils and sterilizes: Politics" (6 February 1899). Faure went on to list his paper's other main enemies: nationalism, anti-Semitism, clericalism, militarism, and capitalism; a front-page article by Laurent Tailhade in the same issue stigmatized the "old agonizing society" with its throne of excrement raised to Fear by Religion, Patriotism, Family, and Property. In a later number, Faure in a typical burst of rhetoric predicted that a new city "animated by the wind of liberty, full of songs of life after the complaints of death," would rise out of "the ruins of cities sterilized by the pestilential wind of repression" (1 April 1899).

Apollinaire's early anarchist poems reflected some of these ideas (as did his later *Onirocritique*), and he published one of them as late as 1903. But by that time he was writing for the serious, intelligent, and political *Européen,* a pacifist, socialist weekly with a cosmopolitan outlook, and echoing in pleasantly detached little articles its anti-clericalism and antipathy to Russian and Turkish tyranny. He had even gone so far as to support actively two socialist politicians himself, Francisque Michaux in 1902 and Pierre Baudin in 1903.

His old bourgeois anarchism was never very far below the surface, however, and his would-be internationalism was often tainted by a latent germanophobia and anglophobia and by the French intellectual's prejudice—shared by many other nationals, however, including H. G. Wells—that French ideas and especially the French language were destined to save the world for civilization. It was ever difficult for him to take a moderate position: his Catholic-nurtured anticlericalism was restrained for the *Européen* but burst forth in the stories of *L'Hérésiarque et cie.* There he ridiculed the practices of baptism, communion, and canonization ("Le Sacrilège," "Le Juif latin"), the doctrine of the holy trinity ("L'Hérésiarque"), salvation through repentance ("Le Juif latin"), papal infallibility ("L'Infaillibilité"), divine retribution ("Trois histoires de châtiments divins"), relics ("Histoire d'une famille vertueuse, d'une hotte et d'un calcul," "La Serviette des poètes"), and Christ's coming kingdom ("Le Passant de Prague," "Le Toucher à distance"). "There is not a branch of science which does not contradict by irrefutable facts the so-called truths of religion," one of his spokesmen told the pope ("L'Infaillibilité"). He later said that he was one of the few writers to grasp the profound implications of the division of church and state in France in 1905.

In spite of his dogmatic stand for "the tree of science where revolution ripens" ("Les Poètes"), however, the demands of idealism were never absent. As an amateur anthropologist and a neo-Freudian before the letter, he could transfer his early love for the Christian trinity into a belief in the cyclical myth of incestuous creation and sublimation with its symbolic death of the Father. In one of his notebooks he did the same for science, perceiving it as a trinity, with History, the science of the past, representing the Father; Mathematics and "other exact sciences" of the present representing the Holy Ghost; and Philosophy, the science of the future, representing the Son. Mathematics with its "indisputable facts" he saw as the most important of the three, because it symbolized love and was the unifying force between past, present, and future (note how he feminizes the traditionally masculine Holy Ghost). As he came to expend more of his energies on artistic creation, he passed through stages in which first the Father (the past—sometimes the feminine "Memory") and then the Son (the revolutionary, prophetic vision) came to dominate, stages reflected in poems like "Merlin et la vieille femme," "La Maison des morts" ["The House of the Dead"], "La

Chanson du mal-aimé," and "Les Fiançailles." By 1908 he realized that a dialectical process was at work in his philosophy: he saw the Poet-Father historically uniting with the inner reality, the Mother-Muse, in an act of love (creation) to produce the Son-Future, the work of art. The work of art in turn became a new historical reality, the masculine *prototype,* which, acting upon the female, the author's brain, produced a new creation, and so on.[3] In short, he came to believe that the socialist facts of his adolescence could produce nothing but facts, and that an intervening artist was essential to "ennoble" them and to activate thereby the upward cycle or spiral toward the New City of the future.

In 1908 he saw scientific truth as no less true than artistic truth but important only as an adjunct to it; in an article of 1905 he had systematically composed his *vale* to positivistic doctrines of humanistic anarchism *by themselves* as possible social patterns for progress. As the one analytical, inductive excursion into his basic philosophy of life, this article, "Gouvernement," from his little magazine *La Revue Immoraliste* of April 1905, deserves our close attention here. The following is the way I summarize and interpret its main arguments:

Egoism, the basic human instinct, seeks its own fulfillment in power and pleasure, which, for the individual, constitute happiness: "Man to follow his instinct must only seek his happiness." Virtue, then, is passion accompanied by action (Spinoza) that creates collective and individual happiness, as when the individual helps himself or others; any other action is vice, a sin against the species. This includes the sin of vegetarianism (it was typical of Apollinaire to combine French cuisine with higher thought!). The supreme pleasure of the ego in which both power and pleasure are joined is *volupté* (voluptuousness, sensuality), found in the generative act, which is also the greatest sign of love the individual can make to the species. This act creates unity between individuals, the vicarious sympathy for fellow members of the same species, which can in turn cause the pain of commiseration when another individual suffers. As this pain will naturally seek relief in virtuous (egoistic) action, individual charity that carries love to the level of the species is born. But certain actions are individually virtuous and collectively sinful such as charity itself (since it collectively and impersonally salves the conscience of the rich and thus opposes the happiness of the poor) and especially politics (since collective laws cannot include the happiness of all). And because *power* is the other main drive of the ego for its own fulfillment, human society is built on inevitable conflicts: a social solution to the opposing drives of individual egos is impossible.

. . . If the laws of politicians are sins their conduct is reasonable and virtuous. They obey natural instincts which cry to every man the words of Macbeth's witches, "Thou shalt be king." They obey natural egotism which invites every man to take the first place on earth among his fellow men.

If Spinoza with his views on the pleasure principle, charity, compassion, and relative organic virtue is at the source of this thought, an attitude emerges that is remarkably close to Freud (as is Spinoza) with his two instincts of sex and power (death); and closest of all to Nietzsche and Remy de Gourmont. The latter, indeed, wrote in the *Européen* of 1 November 1902, that Nietzsche did away with doctrines of rationalized Christianity like Kant's categorical imperative and replaced them by a principle of liberty and individual royalty. Nietzsche's egoistic power drive, defense of voluptuousness, distrust of the Hegelian belief in government, and, above all, his faith in the privileged individual, are all near Apollinaire's thought. Only does Apollinaire omit the Nietzschean idea that some egos should exist at the expense of others. That is to say, he omits it here; but the doctrine of the superman is implicit in the essay, as well as occult and pre-Socratic beliefs in the microcosm-macrocosm embodied in every man, his potential to become a king and a god— and an animal and a devil. Apollinaire points out that a *social* utopia is impossible but makes no mention of an *aesthetic* utopia at this time; yet it is significant that his key article on Picasso will appear the next month. The direct opposite of "Gouvernement" in style, discursive, impressionistic, and poetic, the latter article rather than its predecessor sets the pattern for Apollinaire's future critical writing, as it describes a powerful *aesthetic* ego's ability to become a superman and give the gods back to mankind.

Thus did the artistic side of Apollinaire's anarchism gradually assume dominance over the political. Much nostalgia for the old militarism remained, of course, and traces of proletarian sympathies and revolutionary fervor are found in the last works of his life;[4] but more and more he placed himself on the side of the poetic kings

and heroes he had identified with in "La Chanson du mal-aimé."
He still attended anarchist meetings after 1911[5] and wrote for the
socialist press as late as 1910 (in *La Démocratie Sociale*); but his
change of outlook—and his nostalgia for his former ideas—had
been recorded in two poems of 1909, "1909" and "Poème lu au
mariage d'André Salmon" ("Poem read at the marriage of André
Salmon," *Alcools*). Both of them, it is true, do deal with the decline
and fall of the French Republican flag and its colors of red, white,
and blue; but neither of them puts the black flag of anarchy in its
place.

"1909" may be seen as something of an updating of his old
revolutionary poem "Au prolétaire" (To the proletariat), a view of
his adopted country, France, as seen from the side of the "divine
alcoves" instead of from the bottom of the mines. From a rough
beauty fashioned by the hands of workers, France has become a very
chic Marianne indeed with her elegant Ottoman gown and her "blue
eyes white teeth and very red lips." But she makes the poet uneasy;
he remembers his old love for "the atrocious women of the enormous
suburbs" and wonders when the midnight hour (perhaps the *nov-
issima hora* of medieval millennarians, introduced here to suggest
the hour of the workers' uprising) will strike. "Poème lu au mariage
d'André Salmon," on the other hand, is a brilliantly conceived
résumé of the changes that have taken place since the two anarchist
poets first met at the revolutionary sessions of *La Plume* at the café
Le Départ in 1903. They were deceived at that time, he says; no
one is going to retake the Bastille and renew the world politically
in this timid democracy. He knows now that only "those founded
in poetry" can renew it, and that they in turn are under the direction
of cosmic, Dantesque love: "Director of fire and poets / Love . . .
like light / Fills all the solid space between the stars and the planets."
It may not have been long after this that Apollinaire changed the
"courageous, thrice-powerful anarchists" in the manuscript of "Vendémiaire" to their victims the "courageous, thrice-powerful kings"
who appear in the final version of the poem in *Alcools*.

Literary influences played a dominant role in this evolution. A
survey of his reading before 1908 shows that from a solid background
in literary classics and an eclectic interest in all fin de siècle tastes,
he became increasingly aware of a special significance in the works
of Baudelaire, Rimbaud, and Mallarmé, and their idealogical
ancestors.

Besides the works of Rimbaud's canons, we know from letters
and internal evidence in his writings that his early reading covered
much of the same material that was given to Croniamantal in "Le
Poète assassiné," chapter 9: Virgil's *Eclogues,* Theocritus, Villon,
Ronsard, Racine, La Fontaine, Shakespeare, Goethe, and Cervantes.
He wrote in answer to a Spanish inquiry in 1915 that he had read
Don Quixote several times in his childhood and that it "gave me the
curiosity to read the Chivalric Romances which I devoured later at
twenty, so Cervantes's goal was not attained." He even read "with
inexpressible pleasure" Avellaneda's plagiarizing continuation of the
novel.[6] He knew Dante, Petrarch, and Boccaccio, and used characters from Ariosto, Tasso, and Ovid in *L'Enchanteur pourrissant* along
with the knights, fairies, and enchantresses out of Don Quixote's
library. He liked dime novels, Nick Carter and Buffalo Bill, Robin-
son Crusoe, popular serials, detective stories, the novels of Paul
Féval, Pierre Prudent Legay, Emile Gaboriau, and many others. In
his late adolescence and early twenties, he read widely in scholarly
reviews, medical journals, books of natural history, encyclopedias
like Migne's, Bayle's, Larousse's, Moreri's, and the Dictionary of
Trévoux; also ancient grammars, dictionaries of Old French, books
on blasonry, the occult, erotic folklore and gastronomy, dance manuals, medieval travel books, the Golden Legend, and saints' lives.
His first education in sex may well have been out of books like
those read by his young Don Juan or the books found in his Heresiarch's library (and the library of his ecclesiastical uncle?) by Or-
ibasius, Galenus, Fracastor, and Bandello.

His first writing is full of imitations of symbolists, Parnassians,
and naturists with a few conscientious copies of Shakespeare and
Ronsard. The great fervor for life that swept through the literary
chapels at the beginning of the century and that coincided with his
period of travels in the Rhineland and love for Annie Playden shook
him free from a fin de siècle muse, and his wind-blown Rhineland
poems, some of the most beautiful of the genre in French, brought
German romantics like Brentano and Heine into a Latin view of the
Rhenish landscape (touristic travel poetry was beginning to be popular at the time). He returned to Paris in 1902 full of everyone
else's ideas about the "healthy, vigorous, true, cosmopolitan" and
humanistic literature that was rising out of the defunct little symbolist and Parnassian circles of the 1890s and creating a new harmonious and classical age of reason in the new century.[7] He praised

in his articles Decadents and romantics, Moréas and Verhaeren, Verlaine and Raoul Ponchon, Robert Randau and the *vers libristes,* René Ghil, and the neonaturalists. He translated a long article from the German for the *Grande France* on Rimbaud, Mallarmé, Baudelaire, and the Parnassians, and slanted it along the lines of his admiration for the humanistic verse of Fernand Gregh.[8] As always, he celebrated the French classic writers Racine, La Fontaine, and Molière. He liked proletarian songs, "the pure gold of Mallarmé," the prophecies of Ezekiel, the classicism of Ernest Raynaud and the decadence of Catulle Mendès, and the fantasy of his special friends Alfred Jarry, Charles-Henry Hirsch, Félix Fénéon, and André Salmon—which resembled his own. He began to take his manuscripts to Remy de Gourmont for criticism.

By 1905 he, like Picasso, was admiring Saint Teresa, Pascal, and Goethe, and he began referring to the latter's *Conversations with Eckermann* as if it were his bedside book (it was a favorite of Nietzsche's, too). In his essay on Picasso, as we have seen, he sketched out a visionary's way, and in a tribute to the Polish anarchist Mécislas Golberg he praised that poet's lynx eyes, casting their own light ("more intelligent when the obscurity is greater") and placed himself and his friends under the sign of Golberg's post-Dreyfus treatise *Prométhée repenti* (Prometheus repentent). This was the year that he, perhaps through Golberg's influence, showed his scorn for metaphysicians, those "mellifluous liars." In 1906 he said he was for an art of "fantasy, feeling, and thought," the art of Racine, Baudelaire, and Rimbaud. He also wrote his proto-Sadean pornographic novel *Les Onze Mille Verges,* in which he not only gave vent in savagely black humor to his amorous frustrations and his love-hate relationship with his mother but relieved some of his pent-up hatred toward Russia (and toward popular French sympathy for Russia) by documenting various czarist atrocities in the Russo-Japanese war.[9] In 1907 came silence. Finally by 1908 the time of his Promethean resurrection had arrived, he was traveling with Jean Royère and his review *La Phalange* (The phalanx) in Mallarmé's symbolist wake, and the revolutionary end of the world he had foreseen had become his own end, the one suffered by seers:

> Jadis les morts sont revenus pour m'adorer
> Car ma vie avait le pouvoir de faire renaître
> tout l'univers

> Et j'espérais la fin du monde
> Mais la mienne [arrive] [s'avance]
> arrive [comm] en sifflant
> pareille à l'ouragon glacé
> (manuscript of "Les Fiançailles")

(Formerly the dead returned to worship me / For my life had the power of renewing the whole universe / And I was hoping for the end of the world / But mine [arrives] [is advancing] / arrives [like] whistling / like an icy hurricane)

Like Picasso, he was one of those travelers confusing flowers and stars: "Flowers, in my eyes, turn back to flames" ("Les Fiançailles"). He was the prophet of an aesthetic new order:

. . . We know that our breath has had no commencement and will not cease, but we conceive before everything else the creation and the end of the world.

(*Chroniques*, June 1908).

. . . Each work becomes a new universe with its particular laws.

(*Chroniques*, November 1908).

Every day, perhaps, a powerful will changes the order of things . . . and wipes out the memory and even the truth of what existed the evening before.

(*La Phalange*, 15 August 1908).

Orpheus, Amphion, and Ixion: Ideas of 1908–9

Apollinaire in 1908 and 1909 suddenly found himself in the forefront of avant-garde literary and art movements. A friend of the Mallarméan Jean Royère, he became the novel critic for the latter's *La Phalange* from March 1908 to April 1909; he was chosen for the delicate office of presenting poems by young contemporary poets in a lecture on symbolism in April 1908; he published an article in June 1908 on the fauvist painters that was to become the first chapter of *Les Peintres cubistes* (*The Cubist Painters*) in 1913; and he wrote perspicacious essays on the painters and poets Matisse, Royère, Salmon, Braque, Théo Varlet (a disciple of Rimbaud), Paul Fort, Jarry, and a galaxy of women writers including Colette and Mme

Catulle Mendès. In most of these writings he expressed ideas that related to a new symbolist crusade on the part of the magazine *La Phalange,* which he called "that young review which almost alone in France defends the cause of lyricism" *(La Poésie symboliste).* These ideas expressed in essence the philosophy he was to advocate during the remainder of his life for both poetry and painting.

A parenthesis is necessary here. Apollinaire, who became after 1908 one of the leading apologists in Western culture for the modern art movements—fauvism, cubism, orphism, primitive art, abstract art, African art, and the beginnings of dadaism and surrealism— the man who actually invented the two terms "Orphisme" and "Surréalisme," has been called ignorant and incompetent in matters of painting by no lesser authorities than Picasso, Braque, Duchamp, Villon, and Vlaminck, as well as by his first publisher, art dealer Henri Kahnweiler, his friend Max Jacob, and art historians Gustave Pimenta, Adolph Basler, and Pierre Cabanne. His influence on modern painting has been ignored by such important critics as Jacques Rivière, Herbert Read, André Richard, Pierre Marois, and François de Herain among many others.[10] On the other hand, artists Derain and Delaunay, poets Roch Grey and André Salmon, and critics Maurice Raynal, Georges Lemaître, Stanislas Fumet, Jean Cassou, Robert Motherwell, Christopher Gray, Michel Ragon, Lionello Venturi, John Golding, Jean-Claude Chevalier, L. C. Breunig, and Katiä Samaltanos have praised his profundity, perceptiveness, universality, critical acumen, and incredible ability to pick the major artists of our time out of the thousands of paintings and sculptures he was obliged to discuss in his more than five years of writing for leading Parisian newspapers (1910–14).[11]

Yet in all this difference of opinion, the following points have been generally overlooked, largely because of the tendency of art critics up until only recently to concentrate on the plastic values of modern art works to the detriment of their literary, psychological, political, and mythic significance: 1) Apollinaire's art criticism was based on the same philosophy of revolutionary aestheticism that his 1908–10 poetry embodied; 2) this philosophy, instead of deriving from the painters' ideas as has been claimed, was a logical development out of the ideas of such nineteenth-century writers as Gérard de Nerval, Lamennais, Michelet, Quinet, Hugo, Rimbaud, Mallarmé, Jarry, and such writer-inspired art critics as Baudelaire, Albert Aurier, Maurice Denis, Paul Sérusier and Paul Gauguin; 3)

Apollinaire thus brought to his critical articles a philosophy that, as Professor Breunig writes, "although it existed in poetry after Baudelaire, was revolutionary in painting,"[12] and that Apollinaire also applied in his criticism of poets André Salmon, Jean Royère, Théo Varlet, and—himself; 4) he devoted the last ten years of his life, from 1908 to 1918, to an extraordinary effort to impose this philosophy on the world in a synthesis of literature and art that would include and transcend the principal new movements cubism, futurism, imagism, dramatism, simultaneism, surrealism, and dadaism in a kind of "popular front" of art he called *l'esprit nouveau* (the new spirit) and that he claimed would revolutionize twentieth-century society from top to bottom and bring forth a new golden age; and 5) such a synthesis required a great deal of subterfuge, overpraise, and rationalization of what he thought were impure and imperfect works of art; it was often based more on promise than on actual performance. Those artists among his friends who found him critically incompetent were either too close to their own goals, too embroiled in factional disputes, or too mystified by the subtleties of his poetic and mythic vocabulary to see the overall picture and understand what he was doing. In addition, he was often obliged to conceal the ulterior motives of his criticism, as is revealed by the following letter to the futurist Ardengo Soffici in 1912:

. . . Don't you think that, for a new artistic conception to impose itself, second-rate things must appear at the same time as those which are sublime? In this way one can judge the extent of their new beauty. It is for this reason and for the sake of great artists such as Picasso, for example, that I support Braque and the Cubists in my writings, for to subscribe to the general condemnation of some would entail personal criticism of a talent which deserves only encouragement.[13]

"It is time to become the masters," he wrote at the same period.

What, then, were his main critical ideas? Ideas that, since they were at the very basis of modern art, assume an extraordinary importance for the study of the development of twentieth-century aesthetics. Inevitably, they were the result of the revolutionary rise of his thought into a new dimension of his Promethean conception of the universe. His new vision fell into a new neo-Joächimite trinity, a further extension of his earliest ones of God-Mary-Christ, Sun-

Night-Poet, and History-Mathematics-Philosophy. This philosophy contained three different kinds of reality: the external reality of nature, science, and the cosmopolitan picturesque; the hereditary inner reality of imagination, instinct, dream, and intuition; and the final reality of art. The last reality, created out of the other two and externalized, becomes a new part of material reality, thereby changing it into something else for new artistic intuitions to make into new art in the spiral dialectic upward toward utopia already described.

He never denies the truths of science in this period, science "[which] makes and unmakes that which exists";[14] he merely considers scientific questions analogous to questions of religion, philosophy, and psychology, that is, questions dealing with the minor, incomplete realities of nature, which become dull and commonplace when used by their greatest exponents the naturalists, writers like Zola, Maupassant, and Huysmans.[15] Art based exclusively on them must necessarily be relatively transient, this side of eternity, impure, and imperfect, and subject to the laws of cause and effect and relative truth.[16] Only when these realities are infused with the modern picturesque or marvelous—for example, twentieth-century Paris with its dazzling electrical illumination (recently installed), its smoke-filled cafés, its prostitutes, its bohemians—will they become the subject matter for the writer, into which he dips his pen as a painter dips his brush into his colors. "The marvelous should be the first care of the novelist," he counsels, adding that he should be conscious of reality.[17]

The second reality, the greatest reality next to the work of art itself, is in the artist. In the poet's inner night "divine cadavers float in the brightnesses," and Psyche, the only living being, sings her eternal song. André Salmon's memory contains the mysterious folk songs, "the most ancient monuments of poetic thought." All of civilization's great cultural achievements of the past, although forgotten or disregarded by the artist at work, are contained in him. Pursuit of knowledge, discovery of instinct and intuition, are the ways here toward shaping the artistic self, in which the ageless popular instinct will play a great role.[18] In one of his book reviews Apollinaire praises Mécislas Golberg's book, *La Moralité des lignes* (The morality of lines) in which that curious philosopher reduces all art and life to *a point,* which he then demonstrates to be the beginning and end of art:

The soul of life is the personality, individualization, the search for a
constant, immutable form across varieties and clumsily experimental multiple divergences. . . . The individual: a point.[19]

Matisse having told Apollinaire that he had found a personality
constant for himself, the writer comments, "Instinct was discovered.
You [Matisse] finally submitted your human consciousness to the
natural unconscious. . . . What an image for an artist: the omniscient gods, all-powerful, but submitted to destiny!" ("Henri
Matisse").

The artist, therefore, creates the third reality, and in so doing
becomes the absolute creator, the supreme master of the universe.
A privileged term Apollinaire uses at this time in speaking of the
artist is *divinité:* the painter "must, before all, give himself the
spectacle of his own divinity, and the canvases he offers up to man's
admiration confer upon them the glory of likewise exercising momentarily their own divinity." He is like Gauguin, "the most religious of painters . . . who turns to the limits of humanity to
surprise the pure divinity of art." The poet likewise has divinity.
"He knows that in his creation truth is infallible. He admires his
work." Their creations will not be limited to the false appearances
of the past, to the unknown future, or to the temporary fashions of
the present; rather, they will incorporate past, present, and future
in one essential, ecstatic unity, a higher reality of truth constantly
renewed that belongs only to eternity.[20]

The truth of this final reality of the work of art will naturally
seem *false* at first (he will later say *surprising*) compared to the more
readily apprehensible truths of nature and science; the poet "knows
the error which animates his creation, false to our visions but presenting to momentary powers an eternal truth."[21] This is the doctrine of the willful lie, advocated by Nietzsche ("a man must be a
liar in his heart, but he must above all be an artist"[22]) and summed
up in Picasso's famous statement that art is a lie the artist makes
into a truth. The artist's individual vision can only be true to him
alone until he succeeds in imposing it upon humanity—or until
humanity succeeds in acquiring it. The end of a world is thus
implicit in each masterpiece: the poet's discoveries "give the lie to
former truth. Such is the poetic work: the falseness of an obliterated
reality. And even the memory of it has disappeared. Comparison is
impossible. Life and truth are undeniable." In art, the famous
"painting-object," so sought-after by the cubists, is born: "The

painting will exist inescapably. The vision will be entire, complete, and its infinity instead of denoting an imperfection, will bring out only the relationship between a new creator and a new creation and nothing else."[23] And for this false, yet divine creation out of self that gives birth to a new reality, Apollinaire finds a striking new celestial trinity, another solar myth, that of King Ixion who had intercourse with a cloud believing it to be Hera, the Mother Goddess, from which union the centaurs were born (Mallarmé in his French adaptation of Cox's myths had related the Ixion legend to the solar cycle). The vision of the goddess is in the creator; whether Hera, Psyche, Muse, or the illusory nude sister of Narcissus pursued by her twin brother in the fountain, she is the breeder of art. "Every divinity creates in his own image; in the same way, the painters. And only photographers fabricate the reproduction of nature."[24]

Nevertheless, external, scientific nature at the base of the pyramid of art must still be considered as a verifying factor. Apollinaire's pragmatic knowledge of art techniques led him to concede a certain amount of relativity to absolute creation. "Reality verifies what the writer imagines. . . . It animates a work which without it would only have the impersonal existence of cadavers." In painting, works of Derain are "samples of that noble discipline which purifies reality 'and grants authenticity to nature' (Mallarmé)."[25] But for the most part, a great work of art actually *transforms the external reality of nature into its own reality.* Picasso by lending us his eyes has enabled us to find the gods again and to use them to change the world. The poet re-creates the old world into the new image he has of it: "Founded in poetry we have rights over words which create and destroy the universe." The rule of Merlin the Enchanter is over; in Apollinaire's new classicism, two Greek artists who hold all nature in the power of their song take his place. He cries out, "New Amphions, new Orpheuses, young poets . . . will soon . . . make wild animals and the stones themselves susceptible to their accents" *(La Poésie symboliste).*[26] Later, in 1912, in perhaps his supreme statements of Orphic anthropomorphism, he writes:

Everything we experience is nothing but illusion and the role of artists is to orient the illusions of the public in the direction of their creative arts.
(*Soirées de Paris,* April)

Without poets, without artists, man would quickly [grow] weary of the monotony of nature. The sublime conception he has of the universe

would come crashing down with dizzying rapidity. Order, which appears
in nature and which is only an effect of art, would vanish. Everything
would return to chaos. No more seasons, no more civilization, no more
thought, no more humanity—indeed, no more life, sterile semi-obscurity
would reign forever.

(Les Peintres cubistes)

He then gives a striking example of this anthropomorphism in a
demonstration of how Auguste Renoir's creation of a *type,* a social
illusion out of his vision, actually caused society to model itself
upon it and thus resemble it for future ages. Considered false and
even ridiculous at the moment of its conception, Renoir's vision is
now accepted as the true expression of his time. In this way the
artist is a true *prophet:* his vision will shape future visions.

Other terminology of Apollinarian criticism becomes clear when
placed against this ideological backdrop, *obscurity* and *simplicity,*
inhumanity and *humanism,* and harmonious *order* as opposed to adventurous *chance.*

In the eyes of the profane, artistic truth in its pure simplicity is
as obscure as it is inhuman—like a lily, for example. Jean Royère's
tongue is as clear (pun: "bright") as the flames of Pentecost; Gérard
de Nerval knows another purity from the one of mathematicians
and grammarians who are continually asking what it *proves;* Max
Jacob is a simple poet and appears a strange one.[27] One is reminded
of Saint Paul's statement that "The wisdom of this world is fool-
ishness with God."

What about Apollinaire's prophecy of a new humanism to arise
out of twentieth-century art? How can this be reconciled with the
essential *inhumanity* of the work of art? In reality, he says, this
inhumanity is "the highest manifestation of the human spirit," the
highest sublimation of our animal nature; it is "beyond all natures
which try to keep us back in the fatal order where we are nothing
but animals." It is actually the ultimate humanism: "To consider
purity is to baptize instinct, humanize art, and divinize personality."[28]

Being an absolute, moreover, the poem or the painting is a perfect
unity like its creator, at the same time a complete organism and a
chance product of nature's chaos. Both order and chance are essential
to the creative process. Adventurous chance without order leads to
the "hazardous ingenuousness" of Henri Rousseau's canvases (an
opinion Apollinaire will soon change); to the "ignorant frenzy" of

impressionism, an art ruled by chance; or to the unrestrained cult of the personality of expressionism.[29] Order without adventure leads to the dull realism and psychology of the contemporary naturalistic novel (Apollinaire campaigned for three years in *La Phalange* and *Les Marges* for the *realistic* novel of fantasy). Adventure and order are reconciled by the talent of a Jean de Gourmont with his restrained audacity; by an André Salmon with his necessary, concrete, and marvelous vision; by the poems of a Jean Royère with their harmonious and joyful mystery; and by the reasonable, ordered explorations into personality of a Matisse or a Braque.[30]

Perhaps the best symbol Apollinaire finds to represent his duality into unity of life and art is one always favored by symbolists and illuminists, the flame. In this one image he summarizes the three plastic virtues of the new (fauvist!) painting, virtues we have seen him apply also to poetry:

The flame has purity which tolerates nothing foreign to its nature and cruelly transforms into itself whatever it attains.

It has that magical unity, whereby each little flame when it is divided is like the single one.

Finally it has the sublime and undeniable truth of its light.

(*Chroniques,* 1908, 47–49)[31]

It is clear from this synopsis why Apollinaire's art criticism has created so much difference of opinion among painters and critics: it is highly poetic, metaphoric, and abstract, not to mention rhetorical (Marcel Duchamp found it incomprehensible); and many of the paintings did not seem to jibe with the theories. These ideas of 1908–9 are in essence the same as those of 1910–12, which he published along with them in *Les Peintres cubistes.* There, Picasso is the supreme example of the divine creator. He is the leader of the *scientific cubists* (the term *analytical cubists* is used today) who rearrange subjects taken from chaotic nature along the lines of science (geometry) and their own intuition until the new construction—of a violin, say—has its own new order, grandeur, and harmonies of light and truth. The *orphic cubists* (orphists), on the other hand, take mainly color forms from external reality and arrange them more instinctively and with fewer external references than the analytical artists into plastic harmonies. Both groups have as their common denominator *light,* the origin of fire's truth and the greatest gift of external nature. The futurists, finally, although basically instinctive artists like the orphists, are too impressionistic, too involved in painting subjects outside themselves—like "the speed and the dynamism of the machine age"—to arrive at perfection.

If any one artist or art critic formulated these ideas in a coherent, universal way before Apollinaire's articles of 1908–9, the evidence has not been forthcoming. The ideas were in the air and hotly discussed on the terrasses of Montmartre cafés, and the scattered and rather vague symbolist writings of Gauguin, Maurice Denis, Albert Aurier, and Mécislas Golberg undoubtedly played a large role in these discussions; but overall cubist theory owed a great part of its profundity and comprehensiveness to its championing by the poets and literary critics like Apollinaire, the disciples of Baudelaire, Rimbaud, Mallarmé, and Nietzsche, who had long been applying these ideas to literature.[32] Although Picasso, also an admirer of Rimbaud and Mallarmé, did not usually communicate his ideas other than through his painting, André Derain, whom Apollinaire believed to be the main influence both on Matisse's fauvism and on Picasso's epoch-making move to cubism,[33] was a vocal source of symbolist ideas, having been a former intellectual anarchist turned aesthetic revolutionary like Apollinaire, with as much interest in Nietzsche's literary iconoclasm as in Cézanne's cones, cubes, and spheres.[34] Apollinaire's great role was to put these poetic ideas into action, first by enthusiastically espousing them himself, and secondly, by convincing others of their truth. Being totally convinced and remarkably persuasive, he played the role of polemicist with great success; yet he could not but be disappointed by art works which, he thought, did not come up to his standards of perfection. Anyone reading closely *Les Peintres cubistes* and *Chroniques d'art* can sense immediately an aberration between theorizing and reviewing, the reserve Apollinaire must have felt before many of the cubists' tangible productions. How could it have been otherwise when Braque and Picasso—to name only the best—chose dull monochromatic subject matter from nature rather than the poetic marvelous he advocated (and which they had formerly used) and then decomposed and reordered it by the lesser truths of mathematics?

It is obvious that he more highly esteemed the more *truthful* and instinctive works of Matisse, Derain, Dufy, Marie Laurencin, Rousseau, and Chagall, the enigmas of Chirico, the "divinely drunken" color poems of Picabia and Delaunay, the archetypal, mystical sculpture of Archipenko, the fauvist works of Braque, and the blue and rose paintings of Picasso; and he repeatedly asserted that Renoir was the greatest living painter. The semi-abstract paintings of the orphists particularly, which he considered to have derived from fauvism (*Chroniques,* February 1913), more accurately fitted his theories of autonomous, poetic art, and he was rarely reserved in his fervent admiration of them. On the other hand, he frequently referred to works of the analytical cubists as "enumerations" and "experiments." Those artists were going through a stage, he said, and not even, originally, an essential one, with "less grace than crudity," toward ultimate masterpieces. He had waxed enthusiastic over Michelangelo's beliefs that religious art was the greatest art and that great art was essentially a religion, and he wrote an essay in 1912 on Picasso as a continuator of Michelangelo's tradition—in which he again used the blue and rose paintings as examples. Thus when he writes in *Les Peintres cubistes* that the great religious painter of the future has not yet arrived ("May he come one day . . . may God command him, force him, order him . . . he will be here, perhaps he is here already, near us all, I know his name, but I dare not say it. . . ."), it is plausible to think that he is referring to Picasso's failure to fulfill as yet his early promise. He often uses the future tense in the book: the drama *will* break forth, the painters "created in the image of God" *will* rest one day and "admire their work." But in the meantime—while waiting for the new Michelangelo to reveal himself—"what fatigue, imperfections, grotesqueness."

Thus did Apollinaire set as the highest goal for life its divine creation through art, and join the "life for art's sake" writers of the nineteenth century—Baudelaire, Flaubert, Rimbaud, and Mallarmé—to say nothing of contemporaries like Yeats, Rilke, and Proust, with whose writings he was not acquainted. Like many of the works of those authors, his two complementary Orphic poems "Le Brasier" and "Les Fiançailles" prove that the subject matter of the poem-object, that microcosm of the universe, can only be itself, its description of its own voyage to itself, its own creation of itself. It is thus an absolute, an eternal unity of form and matter, constantly renewed with each new reading, the most significant absolute the poet-explorer can discover. He creates Byzantium by sailing poetically to it.

"Le Brasier"

Apollinaire's own joyful voyage to the erotic godhead of pure
poetry in "Le Brasier" ("The Brazier," *Alcools*) is at the same time
mobile and immobile, horizontal and vertical, like the voyages of
Dante and Mallarmé's Igitur. He travels both upward toward the
Empyrean and outward toward the isle of Désirade—while remaining firmly pinned to a bank of the Seine. Dividing the poem into
the symbolic three parts, which I shall characterize generally as
Renunciation, Renewal, and Elevation, he relates both the poem's
and the poet's voluntary martyrdom and final ascension. In the
analysis of the poem that follows, the parenthetical quotations are
from the critical works I have just discussed.

In the first section, Renunciation, we find three principal images
of his criticism: the flame, Ixion, and Amphion. In the pyre of his
lyrical personality Apollinaire heroically—with the same leap in the
dark toward purity he took in other traumatic periods of his life—
sacrifices his past, consecrating it to the flames ("The flame which
transforms cruelly into itself what it attains"). This past consists
primarily of his beheaded past loves, sacred and profane. Divine
love has become as bad as any other, "Our hearts hang on the lemon
trees" (lemons, Mary's fruit, are symbols of the golden hearts, ex-
piational ex-votos that Apollinaire had once seen in a chapel dedicated to the Virgin[35]).

From the excessively human past, the poet turns to the divine
future and evokes the vegetable cries and whinnying centaurs (born
of Ixion's false embrace of a "phantom of clouds") of a world of
demigods proper to artistic creation. Back in the present he becomes
immobile, attached to Paris like the Seine "pinned" by its bridges,
ready, like the building stones in the Amphion legend, to undergo
passively the lyrical experience. He will build the city of art out of
his own transcendency.

In the second section, Renewal, the phoenix theme becomes overt
as the martyred poet joyously accepts the pain of losing love for the
fire of his delight ("Théo Varlet knows the anguish of delight"). In
a burst of self-sufficiency, he boasts that he who had stripped off
his soul to the sun in the first section ("[Picasso's] meditations strip
bare in silence") now requires the sun to need protection from his
brilliant face—luminous, incidentally, like the legendary faces of

Moses, Pan, and Christ. The past was a degeneration from the Tyndarides to these flames; but now the ancient swan-gods (Zeus was the swan-father of the Tyndarides) die singing in them (in Théo Varlet's psyche, "one would say that all the swans are going to die"). The poet's life is renewed out of them. Flaming in his own pyre, be boasts that he has nothing in common with those who are afraid of burns (in the last, suppressed stanza of "Le Larron," the pagans scoff at Christians' fear of hellfire). He flames, *emigrates,* and ascends all at once.

To describe the ultimate in experience, Apollinaire has chosen to portray visually physical elevation and horizontal extension at the same time by a heavenly theater and a marine city brought together by a pun on *places* (theater seats—city squares). The third section, Elevation, thus opens with a close-up of the world of outer space glimpsed in the first section, a world where light thinks, the future flames, and a city is built, Thebes-fashion, out of art. But Amphion's lyre has now changed to a favorite gnostic beast, Shamir, Solomon's traditional stone-cutting worm, which had constructed the celestial theater of the city ("The worm Shamir who could build the temple of Jerusalem without tools, what a striking image of the poet!"). Into this city, Apollinaire introduces two other symbols popular with French occultists of the turn of the century: Pan, the central figure of the zodiac, and the medieval astral pentacle. Again immobile, seated in one of the *places* before the divine spectacle like Taliesin in his legendary heavenly chair ("the artist must above all give himself the spectacle of his own divinity"), he becomes a star with five points (elbows, knees, head), a human pentacle, pinned like Ixion to the sky-wheel of himself (cabalistically, the five-sided figure is the symbol of Pan and the microcosm-macrocosm, while Panic puns may be found both in the verb *pense* [thinks] and the noun *pentacle*). His pentacle is called "vain" here because it does not prevent his ardent immolation; but it does not prevent him either from watching the *bright, inhuman* actors—"new beasts" like the centaurs—of this apocalypse of art triumph over lesser mankind. Pan himself, as a shepherd-god with a flock of female sphinxes, symbols of art and erotic knowledge,[36] has just passed through the poem. As the poet watches the tamed men on earth with his stellar eyes ("men will be astonished by the miracle of his stellar eyes admiring the world"), he ends the poem by musing that he would

prefer to their lot his own of being eternally devoured by knowledge
in the "sphinxeries"—where he, like the sphinxes, will hear Pan's
song for the rest of his life.

Thus does he reverse his old negative sun-night theme in "Le
Brasier." Beheaded and burned alive like the setting sun, no more
does he dive into the Western sea like the Emigrant or sink into
the twilight sterility of "Palais" or "Lul de Faltenin." Rather, he
replaces the gods Zeus, father of the Tyndarides, and Hera, the
phantom of clouds, to rise transfigured as his own solar myth,
outdazzling the sun. His ultimate flamelike unity is that of his
creation, the poem.

Finally, in this apotheosis there is the strong suggestion that a
new love will appear in the heavens, an actual physical incarnation
of Hera-Mary, the second member of the trinity. "Le Brasier" was
written in the first year of Apollinaire's affair with Marie Laurencin,
and, significantly enough, he chose for the title a word that was a
traditional metaphor for the vulva in erotic literature. Night was a
castrating murderess no longer. Changed into Aphrodite, she would
perhaps rise from the sea to be illuminated by a new poet-sun:
"Nous attendons ton bon plaisir ô mon amie / . . . / Quand bleuira
sur l'horizon la Désirade" (We await your good pleasure O my
beloved / . . . / When will Désirade [Columbus's island] become
blue on the horizon).

"Les Fiançailles"

Apollinaire took similar trips to the stars in other poems of this
period. In "Pipe," a poem on the experience of opium-smoking,
the ascension is again immobile and again involves nonhuman wisdom ("I was guided by the owl / And I didn't make a movement").
Onirocritique begins close to the coals of heaven and ends, after a
dreamlike spectacle of inhuman new beasts being shown off by a
shape-shifting poet-enchanter, with the end of the human world.
In "Cortège" *(Alcools)*, the poet becomes a kind of comet as he goes
off into space illuminating himself in an "oblong fire whose intensity
will go increasing / Until it will become one day the only light."
In "Les Fiançailles" ("The Betrothal"), "An Icarus tries to rise up
to each of my eyes / And sun-bearer I burn between two nebulae."

"Les Fiançailles" is more biographical than "Le Brasier" and re-
counts Apollinaire's passion in greater detail; but it offers the same

journey to the same divine, phallic-vulvic pyre of creation. It picks up the quest for a new love alluded to in the last section of its complementary poem, and carries a betrothal theme to its consummation on three levels: profane love, sacred love, and divine poetry. A similar ladder of love to that of "Le Printemps" is realized (the first section is taken from that poem), but here the Christian progression is followed—that of innocence-sin-renunciation-confession-hope-salvation—in the symbolic nine parts. Apollinaire's new Madonna, Marie Laurencin, to whom he was newly "betrothed" at the time of writing, is found throughout, but, as he later truthfully stated in 1915 to his first real fiancée, Madeleine Pagès, "no woman is the object of the poem" (30 June). It treats rather of all women—and all poetic creation. More of an *ars poetica* than "Le Brasier," it is also less unified, its fragmentary appearance (it was put together in at least four versions, with extracts from earlier poems attached to it) being justified, as in "La Chanson du mal-aimé," by a psychological, biographical logic reflecting a typically diffuse modern psyche.

It is less original in subject matter than "Le Brasier." Saint-Georges de Bouhélier and the naturists often celebrated the Poet-God's betrothal to Nature and the Virgin and the subsequent rebirth of the gods; and in his little magazine of the 1890s, *L'Annonciation,* Bouhélier had announced among other things that a poet-king was coming, that he would be Adam, Orpheus, Pan, and Jesus, that the theater would replace the cathedral, that the poet would sacrifice himself as the lamb in a love mass to the Maternal Virgin Fiancée, and that he would renew himself and mankind, re-create the universe, resuscitate the gods, etc. Jean Royère in 1908 called works of Verlaine, Mallarmé, Valéry, and Régnier along with the new poems of Apollinaire "Transfiguring Poetry." Apollinaire dedicated the final *Alcools* version of the poem to Picasso, whose blue "madonnas" especially appealed to him; and he also admired the religious painter Maurice Denis whose works bore titles like "Pâques" (Easter), "Fiançailles," and "Annonciation."

In 1905 he had compared Picasso's mysticism to that of Saint Teresa; that earlier Spanish visionary had described spiritual betrothal and marriage to God in *The Mansions.* Her master, Saint John of the Cross, had shown that the three steps leading to such a union were the Purgative, the Illuminative, and the Unitive—the very steps that were taken in "Le Brasier." The latter Spanish

mystic had also written that a joyful death in the flames of the spirit
was the only way to life ("The Flame"), and that spiritual resurrection was preceded by a voyage into the depths, into "the dark
night of the soul" (Apollinaire's "sleep"). Yet both "Le Brasier" and
"Les Fiançailles," closely related as they are (their fragments unite
on the manuscript), incorporate these ancient symbols so subjectively
that they become highly original. They justify the poet's claim to
Madeleine that they are the most profound poems in *Alcools* (30
June 1915).

The dedication to Picasso thus may have more significance than
many of the other dedications in *Alcools*, made often simply for
friendship, to pay back a favor, or for minor relevancy.[37] The seer-
painter's example was probably an inspiration to the poet; it is likely
that the reference of the *Alcools* version of the poem (1913), "Pro-
phétisons ensemble ô grand maître ["grands maîtres" in 1908] je
suis / Le désirable feu qui pour vous se dévoue" (Let us prophesy
together O grand master ["grand masters" in 1908] I am / The
desirable fire consecrating itself for you) was made more specific in
order to refer to him.

By 1908 the Spanish painter had passed beyond his aesthetic goals
of the blue and rose periods, and, after living for a time with classical
and primitive gods, was undertaking experiments based on more
conceptual formalizations of the universe: he was applying Cézanne's
plastic techniques to his art, attempting to make it as self-sufficient,
nonanecdotal, and inhuman as possible. How did this affect his
admiring poet-friend? Mutual acquaintances report that when first
confronted by the *Demoiselles d'Avignon*, Apollinaire found the painting excessively audacious[38] (my guess is that he found it grotesque).
But after the rose period, Apollinaire probably did not cull many
ideas from Picasso himself anyway; the artist was notoriously stingy
of theory, and André Derain who was not, and whom Apollinaire
considered to be the mentor of both Picasso and Matisse anyway,
was a good enough influence in his own right. We have seen that
Apollinaire applied Derain's (among others') symbolist ideas of autonomous art to both fauvist and cubist painting.

His fictional account of his first meeting with Picasso leaves no
doubt that symbolist paintings of the blue period were sufficient to
inspire the same ideas:

. . . He knocked on the door and cried out: "It is I, Croniamantal."
And behind the door the heavy steps of a weary man, or one who carries

a very heavy burden, arrived slowly and when the door opened there was
in the sharp light the creation of two beings and their immediate
marriage. . . .

Croniamantal . . . looked silently at the new painting on the easel.
Clothed in blue and barefoot, the painter was also looking at the canvas
where in a glacial mist two women were remembering.

There was also in the garret a fatal thing, that great piece of broken
mirror . . . It was a fathomless, vertical dead sea at the bottom of which
a false life was animating what doesn't exist. Thus, opposite Art, there is
its appearance, into which men put their trust and which lowers them
when Art has elevated them.

("Le Poète assassiné," chapter 10)

Nevertheless, the later example of Picasso's extraordinary change
from passive Dionysian reflector of the gods to active Apollonian
explorer of himself, seeking "traces of inhumanity found nowhere
in nature," must have been an additional shattering experience. At
least, here is his 1912 account of the Picasso revolution:

Then, severely, [Picasso] questioned the universe. He became accus-
tomed to the immense light of the depths. . . .

There is the poet whose muse dictates his works, there is the artist
whose hand is guided by an unknown being who uses him as an instrument. . . . Other poets, other artists . . . force themselves and turn
toward nature, they have no direct contact with it, they must draw everything out of themselves, and no demon, no muse inspires them. . . .
Men created in the image of God, they will rest one day and find their
work good. But what fatigue, imperfections, grotesqueness! Picasso was
the first kind of artist. Never has there been so fantastic a spectacle as the
metamorphosis he underwent when he became the second kind.

Picasso resolved to die. . . .

(Les Peintres cubistes)

"Les Fiançailles" celebrates *Apollinaire's* death and rebirth, new-
found ignorance, and gropings through instinct and intuition—
away from the evidence of the senses—toward his inhuman depths.
Part 1 presents his old poetic truths, a tender, symbolist dawn of
love with its King Charming, Madonna, and ex-voto hearts hanging
among the lemons. Suddenly, in part 2, the sun sets on his hopes.
Love dies, just as it did in his early poems, and an avenging angel
strikes. He is crucified by his "friends" (throughout his life he had
recurrent spells of paranoia) and falls into a sleep. He wakes to find
women decanonized and beauty fled, as it had formerly fallen in

L'Enchanteur pourrissant; the manuscript fragment quoted at the end of chapter 2 also mentions the death of his "poetic truths" and a five-year sleep (from 1902 to 1907?). Part 3 describes an ascension like that of "Le Brasier" and a different kind of martyrdom, a torment of silence (Théo Varlet, silent for two years, "could not speak and was grieved to be silent"). His end of the world has arrived. In part 4, sorrow and nostalgia for his lost past, including Italian churches and the lemon groves of part 1, sweep over him, and, like Picasso in the *Demoiselles,* he celebrates black art ("a mulatto girl who invented poetry"). In part 5, he has advanced to a stage where he can say, "I love divinely," and hope for powers of objective creation in a magnificent image taken both from Genesis and from his creative flame:

> Mais si le temps venait ou l'ombre enfin
> solide
> Se multipliait en réalisant la diversité
> formelle de mon amour
> J'admirerais mon ouvrage

(But if the time came when the finally solid shadow / Multiplied by realizing the formal diversity of my love / I would admire my work)

After his five days of creation, on Sunday he rests (part 6). There he finds himself facing the greatest martyrdom of all for a sensualist like himself, the sacrifice of his six senses (the sixth sense, first in order of appearance here, is the sexual sense). In "Cortège" he will boast that he knows "the five senses and several others." In "Lul de Faltenin," he had abandoned himself to his senses in erotic grottoes. His and Picasso's new austere aesthetics, however, demand a godlike detachment from empirical, illusory nature; and he will later rebuke futurists and expressionists for their slavish devotion to sensation. In part 6, therefore, he attempts to reduce the sensual awareness of sexuality, hearing, touch, sight, smell, and taste, in that order; and he especially regrets having to transcend the taste of Marie and poetic glory (with a pun on *laurel-Laurencin*[39]). I add as a postscript that he happily never succeeded in this purification process; in all his poems, including this one, he took his sensual nature to the stars with him.

In part 7, torment has turned to joy. No longer afraid of lies, he proceeds to tell a couple—thereby telling poetic truth—offers his divinely erotic passion flowers in ex-voto, and is off: the storm is over, angels are working *for* him, and the day is holy. In part 8, as in the second section of "Le Brasier," he sets sail after having stripped to the sun and moves under the constellation of the Virgin, the third sign of the summer solstice.

The important final section, that of his ultimate martyrdom and betrothal—death and resurrection—is one of the most obscure passages in Apollinaire. Here is the punctuated version from 1908:

> Templiers flamboyants, je brûle parmi vous.
> Prophétisons ensemble, ô grands maîtres, je
> suis
> Le désirable feu qui pour vous se dévoue,
> Et la girande tourne, ô belle, ô belle nuit.
>
> Liens déliés par une libre flamme, ardeur
> Que mon souffle éteindra, ô morts, à
> quarantaine.
> Je mire de ma mort la gloire et le malheur.
> Comme si je visais l'oiseau de la quintaine.
> * * *
> Incertitude, oiseau feint, peint, quand vous
> tombiez,
> Le soleil et l'amour dansaient dans le
> village.
> Et tes enfants galants, bien ou mal habillés,
> Ont bâti ce bûcher, le nid de mon courage.

(Flaming Templars, I burn among you. / Let us prophesy together, O grand masters, I am / The desirable fire consecrating itself for you, / And the fireworks turn / O lovely, lovely night. // Bonds loosed by a free flame, ardor / My breath will extinguish, O dead, at forty. / I aim at the glory and misfortune of my death [or, "I mirror glory and misfortune with my death"]. / As if I were aiming the bird of the quintain. / * * * / Uncertainty, feigned, painted bird, when you fell, / The sun and love danced in the village. / And your gallant children, well or badly dressed, / Built this stake, the nest of my courage.)

Some already-charted points of reference may help us to orient ourselves. In the last two stanzas of "Lul de Faltenin" the poet was flaming in defeat in the bird-sirens' nests; here the image is one of triumph, the sirens are gone, and the poet-phoenix is alone in the nest of his courage. That he will rise out of the nest is suggested by the second stanza (he sometimes uses *souffle,* "breath," for prophetic poetry) and by the image of the dancing sun in the last stanza, which replaces the setting sun of "Lul" and the other crepuscular poems. A sunlike bird does set or fall, but its name is "uncertainty"; it is feigned and artificial; and it is, perhaps, replaced by the courageous bird of the last line.

Since the poem is about a betrothal, some sort of flaming marriage ceremony is undoubtedly taking place. In "Le Brasier," Apollinaire used the builder of Solomon's Temple, the fabulous worm Shamir, to build the temple of art—also a celestial theater—for his New Jerusalem, his New City; here the poet is guardian of that temple, another Knight Templar, martyred like the Grand Masters of the Templars, Jacques de Molay and Geoffroi de Charnai, both burned at the stake in 1314. Apollinaire knew many of the works of occultists, Gnostics, Pythagoreans, Rosicrucians, and Freemasons that abounded at the end of the century, and he used some of their symbols, of which the main ones were fire, light, solar eyes, and temples (in the case of the Freemasons, Solomon's Temple). In the manuscript version of "Les Fiançailles" his five-year *sommeil* ("sleep") had perhaps the Freemason's connotation of "spiritual death" or "suspended animation," which he referred to in a letter to Lou in 1915 ("our loves are *en sommeil* as the Freemasons say"—29 March). To the occultists, the Templars represented purity, masculine abnegation, and devotion, especially since the knights swore allegiance to only one mistress, the Virgin Mary, Queen of Heaven. This is one of the betrothals here. Believers also credited the medieval legend of Jacques de Molay having correctly prophesied with his last breath the death of the evil pope in forty days. In any case, the Knights Templars make apt symbols for the small band of crusaders who set out with Royère, Matisse, and Picasso—as well as with various symbolist groups like the Nabis[40] and the Amphionians[41]— to defend the temple of art (an expression much used by symbolists), to serve Beauty, and to purify the world with their ardor.

The second stanza is particularly hermetic. *Quarantaine* means "Lent" in French as well as "quarantine" and "forty," so that the phrase *à quarantaine*—an unusual one, by the way—could mean "in Lent," "at the age of forty," "in forty days," "in a group (or in groups) of forty," and "in quarantine." Lent, of course, is the time of the Passion, and the two Grand Masters (as well as the Forty of Sebastus) were burned during Lent. Dancing around bonfires at this time (the last stanza) is an ancient European custom. And the sun is commonly believed to dance on Easter Day. But the expression still remains extremely equivocal, to say the least. And who or what is the "bird of the quintain"?

The 1908 version, unlike the one in *Alcools,* separates the last stanza from the rest of the poem, making it into part 9 (parts 4 and 5 are combined). The two birds, that of the quintain and that of "uncertainty," are thus separated. I have translated *viser* by its meaning "to aim" rather than "to aim at," for Apollinaire's erotic writings make it quite clear that if the *quintain,* the iron ring of the medieval jousting game, is one of his symbols for a female sexual organ, the bird besides being a phoenix is a phallus. Folklorists have noted many modern revivals of the jousting game in village festivals, which often involve knocking a cock off a pole. "To aim at" could still be used in its common meaning of "to emulate." The separation of the two stanzas, then, would suggest that the poet is *summarizing* in the last stanza what has preceded it. The second bird, that of uncertainty, may have been the first to fall, that is, the aged, artificial phoenix; and the quintain then would be the true pyre-phoenix nest for the victorious new phoenix, "the bird of the quintain," to die in and fly out of. From jousting knight, the poet would then become flaming Knight Templar, *rising* from his former fall.

Whatever the obscurities, I believe I can affirm with a reasonable amount of certainty that the last section of "Les Fiançailles" offers one more example of the erotic solar cycle. In it Apollinaire brings together Christian and occult symbols of death and resurrection to form another unified poem-star; his flame again represents purity, unity, and truth. With "Le Brasier" at the summit of his symbolism and at the most penetrating depth of his inner voyages, it reveals that he has been able, even more than Picasso, to place order in his universe. He has found it good.

Chapter Four
The Traveler

Ecoutez mes chants d'universelle ivrognerie
—"Vendémiaire"

Myths of 1909–13

Each work of fiction and poetry that Apollinaire published established a different myth for the poet. In *L'Enchanteur pourrissant* he was the Antichrist Merlin, buried alive by unrequited love but creating a marvelous world of enchantment out of the literary and historical dimensions of his experience. In *Le Bestiaire ou Cortège d'Orphée* (The bestiary or procession of Orpheus), another "divine" masterpiece like "Le Brasier" of the 1908–9 period, he was Orpheus, in command of nature, turning bird and beast into symbols of his poetic-erotic aspirations. In *L'Hérésiarque et cie,* that "Cortège d'Orfei," he was Benedetto Orfei himself, the epicurean Italian heresiarch of the title story with his mystical eroticism and his sainted vision of what true religion really is, that is, marvelous science fiction. He was also the heresiarch's company, the picturesque band of wanderers and Antichrists he knew so well from his travels through literature and Europe.

The favorable public reception given *L'Hérésiarque et cie*—the book narrowly missed winning the Prix Goncourt for 1910—helped to orient the creation of the composite myth of *Alcools,* his greatest achievement. He was enchanted by Thadée Natanson's review of his stories: the former editor of the prestigious *Revue Blanche* wrote of him, "He speaks with precision of the sites and inhabitants of so many countries in the world that no one knows exactly where he comes from, and everyone wonders where he *hasn't* been."[1] After the appearance of *Alcools* three years later, Apollinaire compared himself to a traveling spectator of the world, a sailor, adding on one occasion, "Each of my poems commemorates an event in my life."[2] In composing the book he had broken up the chronological

order of the poems to extend to his "song of himself" the widest—
and highest—range possible.

After the summits of the 1908 poems, it was inevitable that he
would turn to the more horizontal aspects of life, not only to play
Saint Paul to his own Messiah, but to bring more of the modern
marvelous into art. The publication of "Les Fiançailles" and the
article on Théo Varlet in November and December 1908 marked
the upper limit of his search for "purely poetic thought." It is
difficult for anyone to remain in the rarefied atmosphere of absolute
art for longer than privileged moments, and Apollinaire, now completely dependent upon his pen for a living (he had formerly scratched
out a livelihood in finance), was too busy with his rapidly ascending
literary career and his journalistic labors to continue climbing toward
perfection and its ultimate condition of ecstatic silence. Thus he
became linked with Jules Romains and the unanimists for a short
time, searching like them for the place of poetry in the collective
world soul, and extending the experience of "Le Brasier" back to
the beginning of time and to the ends of space. In "Cortège," for
example, he brought the second coming of himself—he who could
"resurrect others"—up from the depths of the past:

> Tous ceux qui survenaient et n'étaient pas
> > moi-même
> Amenaient un à un les morceaux de moi-
> > même
> On me bâtit peu à peu comme on élève une
> > tour
> Les peuples s'entassaient et je parus moi-même
> Qu'ont formé tous les corps et les choses
> > humaines

(All those arriving who weren't myself / Brought one by one the pieces
of myself / They built me piece by piece like a tower / The people piled
up and I myself appeared / Formed by all bodies and all things human)

And in "Vendémiaire" he hymned his new Jerusalem, Paris, as the
center of the universe.

Simultanéisme became the order of the day to him as it did to
unanimists and to the poets of dozens of little artistic movements
with names ending in -*isme* that were flourishing all over France
(André Salmon counted as many as fifty in Paris alone). Many of

them felt the need to impose art—especially French art—upon a
rapidly moving twentieth century by a universal synthesis of all the
arts and all the genres, with historical and legendary perspectives,
and geographical and scientific cosmopolitanism. Science fiction,
the literature of travel through space and time, fantasies on the
machine, travels in the Orient and in America, poems by Valéry
Larbaud and Marinetti, and the novels of Gide, Claude Farrère,
John-Antoine Nau, and Paul Adam provided readers in the new
century with a new world outlook. Apollinaire found himself somewhat ahead of the game. His first published prose had been a science
fiction account of a brain surgeon who played God *(Que faire?)* and
the travel stories of *L'Hérésiarque et cie. L'Enchanteur pourrissant* was
a simultaneous play-novel-poem uniting druids, prophets, heroes,
and princesses in an anachronistic vision of one night; and "Salomé"
(Alcools), like a Flemish painting, leaped frontiers and centuries to
bring Saint John's decollation up to seventeenth-century Europe—
and on into the twentieth-century world of Freud. Lesser travel
poems like "Hôtels," "La Porte" ("The Door"), and "1904" were
written alongside major cosmopolitan works like "La Chanson du
mal-aimé" and "L'Emigrant de Landor Road." After 1908, he became even more of a world citizen.

L'Hérésiarque et cie had terminated with a series of five short stories
that included a linguistic misapprehension in Tuscany and cannibalism in Canada together with the rise and fall of the Antichrist
Dormesan. New short stories, later collected in *Le Poète assassiné*
(1916), treated of a Dutch millionaire who gained his wealth in
South America ("La Rencontre au cercle mixte" ["The Meeting at
the Mixed Club"]), a lonely ventriloquist in a London rooming
house ("Les Souvenirs bavards" ["The Talking Memories"]), and a
phantom fiancée in Cannes ("La Fiancée posthume" ["The Posthumous Fiancée"]). And in the title story of the collection, "Le
Poète assassiné," the semiautobiographical protagonist, Croniamantal, travels from Belgium to Paris, Rome, Munich, Monaco, and
Aix-en-Provence before he embarks at Paris upon a literary career.

The young critic André Billy, in the summer of 1910, directed
a symposium to which some leading new novelists, including Aurel,
Montfort, C.–F. Ramuz, and Lucien Rolmer, contributed their
views on contemporary trends in the novel. Summarizing their opinions, Billy wrote, perhaps referring to Apollinaire's three-year crusade for novels of fantasy in his critical reviews for *La Phalange,* "A

resurgence of the novel of imagination or adventure has been predicted. None of my correspondents refers to it. . . . The novel
will thus continue to be realistic."³ Apollinaire was writing at this
time his novella "Le Poète assassiné," one of the most Rabelaisian
and least naturalistic works of fiction written since the death of
Alfred Jarry.

In chapter 14 of this work, the triviality of realistic novels is
humorously alluded to, and in the work as a whole the alienation
from poetry of the humble people of the crowd—those eternal
subjects of naturalistic novels—is proposed as the major theme.
New imagined worlds are united with a symbolic plot and auto-
biography, until the whole becomes an exotic world in which the
fantasy has an edge of satire. The following is a piece of pure poetry,
"free of all chains":

MAHEVIDANOMI
RENANOCALIPNODITOC
EXTARTINAP + v.s.
A. Z.
Tél: 33–122   Pan:Pan
OeaoiiiioKTin
iiiiiiiiiiii

The last line is plagiarized from Francis Jammes's "Le Poète et les
oiseaux" (The poet and the birds).

In a few passages, the self-sufficient worlds of poetic imagination
of the 1908 period are represented. The hero Croniamantal, a solar-
Christ figure like his author, having become a poet at Paris, has
only to close and to open his eyelids like jaws to swallow and renew
the universe, and to imagine the least details of enormous worlds.
When he finds refuge from external reality in his memory, truth,
outside of time, appears to him. In a book that satirically describes
the people of the world following Lycurgus's and Plato's lead and
banishing poets from the Republic, he turns Plato's cave inside out
and reveals that the poet's imitations of reality have the highest
reality ("opposite Art there is its appearance into which men put
their trust and which lowers them when Art has elevated them").
At another point, he sings to a spring of his own creation, the
immortal source of poetry (the poet, like Moses or Merlin, is a
sourcier, a dowser):

Croniamantal

O spring! You who gush forth like endless blood. You who are cold as marble, but living, transparent, and fluid. You, always new, always the same. I adore you, you who animate your verdant banks. You are my peerless divinity. You will quench my thirst. You will purify me. You will murmur your eternal song to me and lull me to sleep in the evening.

(chapter 12)

This mood is a passing one in "Le Poète assassiné," however; Croniamantal soon turns back to the literary world of Paris with its realistic fiction ("A woman stepped on his toes. She was an author and declared that the meeting or collision would provide her with the subject of a delicate story") and to his pursuit of love in the person of Tristouse (Marie) Ballerinette across Germany, Czechoslovakia, and France.

In poetry as well as fiction the traveler continued to move, sometimes, as in "L'Emigrant de Landor Road," into places he had never been in actuality, and sometimes, as in the Amsterdam of "Rosemonde" *(Alcools),* into familiar foreign lands. In this last poem, a variation on the theme of Baudelaire's "A une passante" ("To a Passerby"), he glimpses *en passant* a Dutch rose in his eternal quest for the *rosa mundi* *(rooze Mond* means "rosy mouth" in Dutch):

> Je la surnommai Rosemonde
> Voulant pouvoir me rappeler
> Sa bouche fleurie en Hollande
> Puis lentement je m'en allai
> Pour quêter la Rose du Monde

(I nicknamed her Rosemonde / Desiring to recall / Her flowered mouth in Holland / Then slowly I passed on / To quest the Rose of the World)

In "Annie" *(Alcools),* the roses are in America, with the oriental rose-palace of "Palais" becoming an occidental villa surrounded by another garden full of roses (and equally sterile)[4] "between Mobile and Galveston" (!). In "Ispahan," he visits in his imagination the Persian city of roses, yet the voyage to the Orient this time is more realistic and more self-fulfilling than in "Palais." He poetically transposes a chapter of a 1908 travel book written by the Princess Bibesco into beautiful symbols of Pan, of the poet's new Madonna, Marie, and of the phoenix sun:

Pour tes roses
J'aurais fait
Un voyage plus long encore

Ton soleil n'est pas celui
Qui luit
Partout ailleurs
Et tes musiques qui s'accordent
    avec l'aube
Sont désormais pour moi
La mesure de l'art
D'après leur souvenir
Je jugerai
Mes vers les arts
Plastiques et toi-même
Visage adoré . . .

J'ai parfumé mon âme
A la rose
Pour ma vie entière
                    ("Ispahan")

(For your roses / I would have taken / An even longer trip // Your sun is
not the one / Shining / Everywhere else / And your music attuned with
dawn / Is for me henceforth / The measure of art / After its recollection /
I shall judge / My poems the plastic / Arts and yourself / Beloved face
. . . // I have perfumed my soul / In rose / For my entire life . . .)[5]

The voyages into his own past of "La Chanson du mal-aimé" and
"Les Fiançailles" continued also, with, however, an unexpected and
frightening new dimension. In his symbolic use of the legends of
Orpheus and Ixion in 1908 he had pridefully assimilated into his
optimistic philosophy of poetic death and resurrection the tragic
fate of those heroes, the pinning of Ixion to a wheel in the sky
(turned into a stellar theater seat in "Le Brasier") and the decapitation
of Orpheus by homophobic women (the martyred poet-god had
become the decapitated and resurrected sun in the fifth and ninth
section of "Les Fiançailles"). Now his own hubris was struck with
such violence that he assumed that the thunderbolt came from the
God he had forsaken (". . . O God who knows my sorrow / You
who gave it to me"[6]). Lilith again took revenge on him, this time
through the person of the *Mona Lisa:* he was imprisoned on 7

September 1911—although innocent—for the theft from the Louvre of Leonardo's fatal lady. The shock was so great that he momentarily regained his lost faith. Moreover, the slow or rapid passing
of time, the major concern of the prisoner, entered his poetry and
became one of his major themes. A latent melancholy was again
released ("I've lived like a madman and wasted my time," he wrote
the following year) which made his search for himself through the
events of his past in such new poems as "Le Voyageur" ("The
Traveler") and "Zone" intensely poignant. Yet even as a chained
and repentant Prometheus in the Santé prison in Paris, he never
completely lost his poetic omniscience:

> Je viens de retrouver la foi
> Comme aux beaux jours de mon enfance
> Seigneur agréez mes hommages
> Je crois en vous je crois je crois
>
> Monde souffrant de mon orgueil
> Vous n'avez une vie qu'en moi
>   (ms. of "A la Santé")

(I have just recovered my faith / As in the lovely days of my childhood /
Lord accept my praise / I believe in Thee I believe I believe / / World
suffering by my pride / You have a life only in me)

The bittersweet myth of the Wanderer is never better expressed
than in "Le Voyageur" *(Alcools)*. Beginning his poem with an ancient
Greek genre, the *paraklausithyra* (song-of-the-lover-weeping-outside-
his-beloved's-locked-door),[7] and extending it into a search for meaning behind the mysteries of life and dream, Apollinaire touches on
the more Germanic side of the symbolist muse—a side that often
surfaces in modern French poetry—wherein "door" becomes Ho-
mer's (and Gérard de Nerval's) "gate of ivory and horn," the door
of "the key of closed eyes" (see the early poem, "La Clef" [The key])
into the marvelous land of shadow and night (see *porte* in the Glossary
of References).

As in "Les Fiançailles," the poem of the search in "Le Voyageur"
is the only discovery, but here the search is not so much for the
self's creative transcendency as it is for a meaning of self *outside* the
artistic experience. Poetic technique is accordingly reversed: instead

of following a fairly exact chronological and dialectical progression that turns images from experience into trinitarian symbols of the creative process—the Purgative, the Illuminative, and the Unitive ways of Saint John of the Cross—here the poet takes memories out of his past and *disorders* them, or, better, brings them to the poem in their natural disorder, thumbing through old travel photographs out of sequence in order to discover their secret significance—the whole beyond the sum of the parts. "Whom do you recognize in these old photographs?" he asks; the question is reminiscent of André Breton's surrealist query, "You say that this photograph doesn't look like me; then *who is it?*"[8]

Taken separately, most of the images came out of the real life of the poet, his childhood in Monaco, his travels in Belgium and Germany, his loss of sacred and profane love, his admiration for brotherly friendship.[9] Pieced together with one imagined image, a shadowy Homeric or Wagnerian scene (stanzas 12–15), they become a view of life with reverberations far beyond him—just as two stones, washed together and shaped into a symmetrical whole by a river, may include the vast, silent perspectives of two different geological ages. And the poet, the enigmatic image-shaper, can only marvel at what has been created *through* him. All that he really knows is that he is moved by the natural forces of change: "Life is as variable as the Euripus."[10]

The Poet of the Twentieth Century

"A la fin tu es las de ce monde ancien" ("Finally you are weary of this ancient world") "Zone" *(Alcools)* begins, with a line that became a rallying cry for twentieth-century poets: founders of surrealism Philippe Soupault, Louis Aragon, and André Breton, for example, repeated the line like a slogan in 1917. One must be modern; and what is most modern? Aviation, of course, flight! Christ who holds the world's altitude record, Christianity, Icarus, Simon Magus, and the immortal phoenix, the latter accompanied as in the Latin writings of Tacitus, Lactantius, and Claudian by all the birds of the world. Not to forget those other immortals, Elijah, Enoch, and Apollonius of Tyana. Even you, Pope Pius X, you the professed foe of modernism, you who nevertheless blessed our French aviator Beaumont last year in Rome,[11] you are the most modern European! But the supreme flyer of all, the most wondrous, the New Messiah, "the first airplane," is the twentieth century itself:

> . . . changé en oiseau ce siècle comme Jésus
>   monte dans l'air
> Les diables dans les abîmes lèvent la tête
>   pour le regarder
> Ils disent qu'il imite Simon Mage en Judée
> Ils crient s'il sait voler qu'on l'appelle
>   voleur
> Les anges voltigent autour du joli voltigeur
> Icare Enoch Elie Apollonius de Thyane
> Flottent autour du premier aéroplane

(. . . changed into a bird this century rises in the air like Jesus / The devils in the abyss lift their heads to watch it / They say it's imitating Simon Magus of Judea / They cry if it knows how to fly *(voler)* let it be called thief *(voleur)* / Angels hover over the pretty acrobat / Icarus Enoch Elijah Apollonius of Tyana / Float about the very first airplane . . .)[12]

It is a tragic irony that down below Night has turned into the old enemy again and has cut off the poet's flight:

> Tu te moques de toi et comme le feu de l'Enfer
>   ton rire pétille
> Les étincelles de ton rire dorent le fond de
>   ta vie
> C'est un tableau pendu dans un sombre musée
> Et quelquefois tu vas le regarder de près . . .
>
> Adieu Adieu
>
> Soleil cou coupé

(You mock yourself and your laughter crackles like hell-fire / The sparks of your laughter gild the depths of your life / It's a painting hung in a dark museum / And sometimes you go look at it close up . . . // Farewell Farewell // Sun throat cut)

Alcools

Once again, in "Zone," the poet-Christ is crucified: Marie Laurencin, who is present as the Virgin, a possessive image, and a beautiful mulatto equivalent to Night,[13] has finally left him for good. But if *Alcools* begins with a love-death, the work is so arranged that it embodies as a whole a new birth: it rises finally like the twentieth century and takes our poet along with it.

In *Alcools* Apollinaire assembles the principal poetic achievements of his life, introduces them with "Zone" and summarizes them with the triumphant "Vendémiaire" in the frame of the present. He breaks away from chronology to establish a simultaneous unity of poetic personality and theme as consistent as that of "La Chanson du mal-aimé," "Les Fiançailles," or "Le Voyageur." Except for a section of Rhenish poems and one of prison poems, he has placed after each poem one of a different period (usually) and of a different type (always). Throughout he has spaced the long poems, outnumbered by the short ones, in such a way that two never come together, which he has also done for the majority of the poems written in or about Germany, a group that constitutes a little less than half of the collection. The variety of subject matters, themes, and styles is thereby so well balanced that never does one section have ascendancy over another, and the work gives the appearance of containing much more variety than it actually does; how much more limiting a chronological arrangement would have been can be seen by the list included in the chronology of this book.

It is evident what he is about. With the assiduity of a town planner rather than the overliterary "junk dealer" he was accused of being by unfriendly (and even friendly) critics at the time of publication of the work in 1913, he desires to lend his constructions the greatest horizontal and vertical relief possible within the unity of his enthusiastic—yet ordered—vision of himself, life, and art. Marcel Raymond was seeing the trees but missing the forest when he remarked that each poem seemed to be written by a different poet and that some of the poems were unfinished *(De Baudelaire au surréalisme);* he should have seen that the sum of the poems was the organic myth of a poet.

An examination of the main themes and symbols takes us closer to the heart of that myth. The negative sun-night theme of the crepuscular poems written before 1908 is now completed and brought full cycle by the positive phoenix theme of "Les Fiançailles," the epigraph of "La Chanson du mal-aimé," the last stanza of "Cré-puscule" ("Twilight"), and the dawn at the end of "Vendémiaire." In a countercyle, the beloved's ascension at sunset in "Un soir" is transcended in "Les Fiançailles" and "Le Brasier" and ended in "Zone." The theme of the death of love in autumn remains a strong one, with, however, a new emphasis: in the new poems "Cors de chasse" ("Hunting Horns"), "Le Pont Mirabeau" ("Mirabeau Bridge"), and "Marie," images of reluctant acceptance, of the melancholy enjoyment of dying sounds and passing waves replace those of sterility and suicide. "Zone" is an exception, of course; but it in turn is balanced by the autumnal victory of "Vendémiaire." Particularly does the eternal, cyclical river become an important symbol of the passing of time and love, replacing in "Le Voyageur," "Clotilde," "Le Pont Mirabeau," "Marie," and "Zone" the murderous sea of the early poems. The poet has become more a pathetic, fated hero—in spite of what he says in "Cors de chasse"—than a tragic victim. Only in "Zone" does he tragically set when a bloody sun rises; but this poem with its parallel admiration for Jesus and for its wounded, messianic hero-poet, and with its description of the countermovement upwards of the century serves as an excellent introduction to all the rising and falling themes in *Alcools,* day and night, light and shadow, the joys and griefs of a poet-errant. "La joie venait toujours après la peine" ("Joy always came after sorrow") ("Le Pont Mirabeau").

Light and shadow form one of the five principal categories of symbols in *Alcools;* the others are liquids, plants and animals, the human body, and the mythic poet-creator himself. The latter is subdivided into all the men and women, heroes, heroines, kings, queens, saints, gods, and goddesses who combine to form his vision—a process described in microcosm in "Cortège." All the symbols in all the categories are at the same time both independent of and dependent upon the poet's psyche: he writes about shadows, "The sun which makes them somber / With them will disappear" ("Clotilde"), what he writes about himself: "I have given all to the sun / All except my shadow" ("Les Fiançailles"). About everything else, *fire* is primary: Apollinaire, a poet of growth and movement like Shelley, makes the flame the source of all things. In this, he reflects the pre-Socratic philosophy of Heraclitus, "who saw in fire the symbol of general life, the emblem of the organizing and dissolving force."[14]

After light and fire, liquids are most frequently alluded to in *Alcools.* The poems are enclosed between two generalizations—"Et tu bois cet alcool brûlant comme ta vie" ("And you drink this alcohol burning like your life") ("Zone") and "Je suis ivre d'avoir bu tout l'univers" ("I am drunk from having drunk the whole universe")

("Vendémiaire")—just as they begin and end on the edge of the Seine. The poet's *soifs* (thirsts) for the bittersweet, poisonous-renewing *alcools* of life are present throughout, from the bitter Cyprus wine of "Palais" and the fairy-tale wines of the Rhineland to the *apéritifs* of the smoke-filled Parisian cafés ("La Chanson du mal-aimé") that Apollinaire knew so well. In 1901 it was the Rhine that was drunk ("Nuit rhénane"), in 1909 it was Paris ("Vendémiaire"); even his broken wine glasses give rise to laughter in "Nuit rhénane" and "Poème lu au mariage d'André Salmon"; and they all form a part of the poet's Eucharist, which rises to a messianic climax by the end of the book.

Yet for an intoxicated urban poet who hymns his beloved Paris as the throat of the universe, Apollinaire is revealed in *Alcools* to be a remarkable nature poet as well: the rural countryside is everywhere, all seasons and all weather are represented, and he cites about forty kinds of plants and trees, taken mainly from his own personal observation, knowledge, and love (he was an excellent botanist). The more than fifty animals, on the other hand, derive primarily from literary sources: even the ferret and the hedgehog of "Le Voyageur" are probably erotic symbols—like the ferrets, moles, panthers, tigresses, etc., elsewhere in his writings. But there is scarcely a natural phenomenon or object, plant, stone, or animal, that is not personified to some extent, just as in the pantheistic side of his philosophy nature is largely made up of slumbering gods and demons to be aroused by the poet. The stars, the sun, the sea, and currant bushes bleed; petals are fingernails or eyelids; leaves are hands, prayers, or tears. Hair is flowing water or foaming sea; eyes are oceans, stars, fire, crocuses, or gems; hands are sunsets, rivers, leaves, doves, or white birds. Inevitably most of these nature symbols relate to women; they constitute a veritable *carte du Tendre* (map of the country of Tender Love) of an anthropomorphic external universe to be penetrated, explored, and fertilized by the poet's body and mind. Reciprocally, as the poet is seeking the Divine (or lubricious) Mother in most of the poems, the roses—both pure and impure—of her natural world become his creative power: "Flowers in my eyes turn back to flames / I meditate divinely" ("Les Fiançailles").

Thus the first four categories of symbols unite to become part of the fifth major category, the myth of the erotic sun-poet. The supreme statements of the poet's divine creativity are undoubtedly "Le Brasier" and "Les Fiançailles," but almost every poem reflects his omniscience in some way—even the poems that lament love's loss. For example, in "La Tzigane" ("The Gipsy"), another poem of unrequited love for Annie, the poet is still a picturesque ring-master of his own sad fate. In the triumphant "Crépuscule" ("Twi-light") on the other hand, the poet's alter ego is a Picasso-like Harlequin who incorporates the Christian triad in his act as he rises trismagistically to juggle a star between a dwarf and a hanged man (probably the Judas-Anteros figure again) just as Jesus rose tran-scendent from his Crucifixion between the two thieves—and as the phallus rises between its two *témoins*. Finally, in the remarkable little one-line poem-synthesis "Chantre" (choir director, cantor): "Et l'unique cordeau des trompettes marines" ("And the single cord [pun: body of water, water horn] of the trumpets marine"), he is the one-man conductor-musician who plays at the same time a phallic single string instrument and vulvic sea trumpets; he is both the cord, chord, and *con*cord for the feminine, oceanic forces of the *trompette marine*—which is both a stringed and a wind instrument, a large bass fiddle with one string and a Mediterranean conch shell. The "breath" of the poet becomes thereby a new Yaveh's wind moving upon the water in the first chapter of his own Genesis.

Even "Le Pont Mirabeau," one of the best-known poems in French literature, has a mythic subtext unsuspected by most of its admirers. Mirabeau was one of Apollinaire's favorite erotic writers, and his bridge, besides being the one in Paris at which the Seine seems so suddenly to take off to the sea, is a symbol to the poet of his own *bridge of flesh*, "the link," as he will write in 1913, "joining all lovers" ("Liens" ["Chains"], *Calligrammes*). As for the river itself, it should come as no surprise to learn that it is an essential part of the anthropomorphic feminine mystique, the central river of Anima (and Tendre) that flows through all our psyches, male as well as female. As well as through Paris, the heart and soul of the universe (see "Vendémiaire").

In summary, all the symbolism of *Alcools* forms itself inevitably into the pantheistic triad, the creation myth, of Apollinaire's aes-thetics: marvelous external reality unites with inner vision to form a new universe of art. External reality is a world of multiple rela-tionships, or, to use Baudelaire's term, *correspondances*, between the symbols of other worlds in this one (the sea, shadow, masks, destiny, dreams, the occult, mirrors, legendary plants and animals, legendary and historical characters) and symbols of contemporary reality (rivers, light, houses, streets, cities, countries, clothes, games, the body, the dance, seasons, animate and inanimate nature, contemporary personages). The inner vision is that of the poet as Eros and Christ and Anteros and Antichrist, a wandering god and fallen king betrothed to Psyche and the Virgin, undergoing the death-birth cycle of love and life in melancholy and joy. Both visions, the inner and the outer, combine like Ixion mating with his cloud-vision of Hera, the Mother Goddess, and the result is *Alcools,* a balanced, clear-obscure, mysterious-realistic, bittersweet, Dyonisian-Apollonian dance of life, represented by the three major symbols of the poet's *moi,* fire, shadow, and *alcools.* All the imagery ultimately runs together into one superior view:

> Actions belles journées sommeils terribles
> Végétation Accouplements musiques éternelles
> Mouvements Adorations douleur divine
> Mondes qui vous ressemblez et qui nous
>   ressemblez
> Je vous ai bus et ne fus pas désaltéré
>
> Mais je connus dès lors quelle saveur a
>   l'univers
>   ("Vendémiaire")

(Actions beautiful days terrible sleeps / Vegetations Couplings eternal music / Movements Adorations divine sorrow / Worlds which resemble each other and resemble us / I drank you and was not satisfied // But I knew thereafter the savor of the universe).

Vintage

The concluding poem of *Alcools,* "Vendémiaire," thus serves as both climax and epilogue for the collection. A hymn to Paris as the central star in the galaxy of Europe, it raises the Parisian poet to heights from which he can command the panorama of his entire poetic experience. This experience is first embodied in the cities and regions of Europe he has known, and then assembled into his absorption of the cosmos. "Vendémiaire" is a simultaneous synopsis of his past like "Le Voyageur" and "Zone," but unlike those meditative, questing poems, it is a poem of triumph, in which, in one lyrical, intoxicated vision, Apollinaire makes his bid for immortality in semimystical fervor and joy.

Again as in "Le Voyageur" and "Zone," he disorders his geographical past to bring it up to the plane of the present. From the ancient cities of Brittany, symbolizing one of his earliest enthusiasms, the mysterious medieval romances, he leaps to the modern industrial cities with their proletarian vigor, also celebrated in his first poetry. Lyons, which he visited in his youth, now enters with its violent history of religious wars, revolutions, and the recent bloody suppression of the anarchists; it then cedes the spotlight to the cities of Provence with their symbols of sacred and profane love. A lament for his beloved Sicily, which suffered severely from the earthquake of 28 December 1908, follows next, with a beautiful description of the subsequent flight of the Sirens from the Strait of Messina into the unknown. Rome represents other events that profoundly influenced him, the definitive end of Gallicanism in 1870 and the 1905 separation of church and state; and the songs of the cities end with Coblenz speaking for the Rhineland.

It is significant that these regions of Europe describe themselves partly or wholly in religious terms. The church steeples in Brittany and the meeting of the Rhine and the Moselle are pictured as praying hands; the Rhone and the Saône are Lyons's lips uttering divine words; the cities of the Mediterranean are broken Eucharistic Hosts; even the northern manufacturing towns speak of the metallic saints of their sainted factories. Prayers alternate with songs on the September night.

At the end of "Vendémiaire," in a joy reminiscent of that of Whitman or Nietzsche, Apollinaire sums up his main themes, symbols, and ideas. Turning his back on Rome and still a spokesman for the anarchist's heroic world of the future, he becomes the prophet of the New City—Paris—in which "God can become" (the phrase is Nietzsche's). This god will be the marvelous god created by man— by the poet. Yet humble religious experiences of other men ("men on their knees on the shore of the sky") form part of his song on the calm autumn night. The theme of "Vendémiaire"—the theme of *Alcools*—is the poet's superhuman acceptance of and transcendency over everything in the universe, from "good immortal worms" (pun: *vers*, "worms," also "verses") to fire "which you must love as you love yourself." He sings of many of his main symbols: seas, animals, plants, cities, destinies, stars, and fire, and he employs all his main themes: the past living within him ("All the proud dead united in my head"); the poet's swim to the stars ("He smiled young swimmer

. . ."); and lyrical beauty ("Flowers out of mouths"). He sings even of the lands on the limits of life ("terrible sleeps") and those beyond his ken ("All I shall never know"). On the top of existence, containing all mankind in him, he is a cosmos drunk on all the wines; he cries,

> Ecoutez-moi je suis le gosier de Paris
> Et je boirai encore s'il me plaît l'univers
>
> Ecoutez mes chants d'universelle ivrognerie

(Listen to me I am the throat of Paris / And I'll drink the universe again if I like // Listen to my songs of universal drunkenness)

Another world has been added to the universe of art as he finally turns away:

> Et la nuit de septembre s'achevait lentement
> Les feux rouges des ponts s'éteignaient dans
>   la Seine
> Les étoiles mouraient le jour naissait à peine

(And the September night gradually ended / The red fires on the bridges put themselves out in the Seine / The stars were dying the day was barely breaking)

Chapter Five

The New City

Je suis dans le ciel de la cité

—*"La Victoire"*

Back to the Crowd, 1913–14

Apollinaire's word was absolutely committed when he was a young poet in the service of the Revolution; it became equally committed when he devoted the last years of his life to serving a revolution in twentieth-century art. *Alcools* began with the ascension; *Calligrammes (Calligrams),* its successor, which he published in the last year of his life and in which he included poems written from 1913 to 1918, begins and ends with authoritative plans for the building of the New City viewed from his own exalted position as artist and seer.

He had striven toward this City all his life; only, he had changed in the years between 1904 and 1910 from a political revolutionary to an aesthetic one. In this sense, "Vendémiaire," which was first conceived in 1909 as part of a revolutionary calendar,[1] can be viewed as one of his most apocalyptic works. In that year he became a regular contributor to the strongly anti-royalist and anticlerical paper *La Démocratie Social* and was made even more aware that he had arrived at the historical, eschatological moment of "the death of kings" (announced by the Book of Revelation). In the stanza of "Vendémiaire" in which he calls for the death of Rome's traditional emblems, the she-wolf, eagle, lamb, and dove, he prophesies the arrival of a new crowd of "enemy and cruel kings"—perhaps socialist demagogues—to take their place at the eucharistic table and drink Paris's "twice-millenary wine."[2]

Nevertheless, he retained his mistrust of the mass demagoguery that he had seen so dramatically demonstrated by the rampaging anti-Semitic mobs at the time of the Dreyfus affair. As an anarchist he had joyfully anticipated the people's coming; but he had not, for all that, made sympathetic the worldwide lynching of Catholics at the end of *La Gloire de l'olive,* and he had even had the massacre denounced by Enoch the bellboy. In 1911 he wrote Gide that the latter's Nietzschean parable in *Prétextes,* that inferior flowers in flower gardens crowd out the superior ones, was "unfortunately true,"[3] and he wrote a story, "L'Ancien Tailleur" (The former tailor), in which a tailor attacked the public for its idolatry of science and its destructive hatred of beauty.[4] "L'Ancien Tailleur" is reminiscent of Baudelaire's parables in which dogs are shown to like excrement and shun fine perfume just like the vulgar crowd; similarly, the end of "Le Poète assassiné," where Enoch has turned into the divine poet Croniamantal excoriating the crowd for its lynching of *poets,* reminds one of Baudelaire's dire prediction of a bourgeois end of the world in *Fusées.*

Apollinaire had reasons for his elitism. After 1908 he had campaigned widely for Orphic poetry, the novel of fantasy, the philosophy of the Marquis de Sade and other erotic writers, and the art of his friends the fauvists and the cubists. In return, he was attacked for the poetry by the naturalists; the novel would remain realistic, wrote André Billy; the apologies for de Sade and others put him in jeopardy with certain authorities; and the new paintings were the laughingstock of the town. Remarkably, he was only the more convinced of the soundness of his ideas before a growing number of enemies and the public scorn; but one can assume that the anarchistic violence of his futurist manifesto of 1913, singing *merde* to

> . . . Academisms
> The Siamese twins D'Annunzio and Rostand
> Dante Shakespeare Tolstoy Goethe
> *Merdoyant* dilletantism
> Aeschylus and the theater of Orange
> India Egypt Fiesole and theosophy
> Scientism
> Montaigne Wagner Beethoven Edgar Poe Walt
>   Whitman and Baudelaire

and *rose* to

> Marinetti Picasso Boccioni Apollinaire Paul Fort Mercereau Max Jacob
> Carrà Delaunay Henri-Matisse Braque etc.
>
> *(L'Antitradition Futuriste)*

was hardly the joke some of his friends took it to be. In "Le Poète assassiné" there is a passage where all the she-wolves of distress are described as waiting outside Picasso's door ready to devour the two friends "in order to prepare in the same place the foundation of the New City" (chapter 10). It was not his nature to take devouring lying down; he intended to do as much of the tearing down of the old world and the building up of the new as he could himself:

> En somme ô rieurs vous n'avez pas tiré grand-
>   chose des hommes
> Et à peine avez-vous extrait un peu de graisse
>   de leur misère
> Mais nous qui mourons de vivre loin l'un de
>   l'autre
> Tendons nos bras et sur ces rails roule un
>   long train de marchandises
>   ("Le Musicien de Saint-Merry")

(In short O scoffers you haven't gotten much out of mankind / And barely have you extracted a bit of fat from its misery / But we who die from living far from one another / Let us stretch out our arms and on these rails rolls a long train of merchandise)

In 1913 he found some new tools for the new construction. He turned his review, the *Soirées de Paris* (Evenings/Parties of Paris), into a crusading journal in favor of "that motor with every tendency impressionism fauvism pathetism dramatism orphism paroxysme DYNAMISM PLASTICITY WORDS IN LIBERTY INVENTION OF WORDS" which he celebrated in his futurist manifesto. In it he published the political writings of his anarchist friends René Dalize and Charles Perrès along with articles on science fiction, the American imagists, Henri Rousseau, Marinetti, Claudel, drama-tism, futurism, and calligraphic (concrete) poetry in a valiant at-tempt to rally the dozens of feuding groups of avant-garde artists throughout Europe around a united front. He began joining organi-zations for the defense of arts and for aid to indigent writers; he gave lectures; he supported a writers' union; he wrote prefaces to catalogues; he brought his articles on modern art up to date in *Les Peintres cubistes (The Cubist Painters);* and he continued defending the new painting in the press. As could be expected, his poetry became one of his main weapons, as he accelerated his lifetime trend toward *simultanéisme* and the unification of the arts, by breaking up his form and prosody to fit a more dynamic, more popular muse.

His new prosody contrasted markedly with that of *Alcools*. The latter had been primarily traditional, with approximately three-fourths of the lines in regular meter, mostly twelve-syllable Alexandrines (with a certain amount of play in the mute *e*'s however) and octosyllabic lines (he boasted that he had revived the importance of the octosyllable). Masculine and feminine rhymes alternated regularly for the most part as in the most classical verse of Malherbe, while traditional four- or five-line stanzas with alternate or enclosing rhymes predominated. Rhyming was usually conservative except in some of the regular narrative poems in which striking rhymes were used for comic and exotic effects; in "Palais," for example, "Lul de Faltenin," "L'Ermite," "Le Larron," "Rosemonde," and the beginning of "La Chanson du mal-aimé." Chronologically speaking, the freest prosody was in the omniscient and occasional lines of 1908–9 ("Le Brasier," "Les Fiançailles," "Poème lu au mariage d'André Salmon," and "1909") written at a time when Apollinaire was celebrating the symbolist discovery of free verse in his critical work *La Poésie symboliste;* whereas the musical love lyrics of 1910–12 ("Le Pont Mirabeau," "Marie," "Cors de chasse," and probably "Clotilde") and the prison poems of 1911 returned to the more regular prosody of the Rhenish lyrics. This last period, however, did see the beginnings of a new style in which the relaxed prosaic qualities of 1908–9 were magnified horizontally to include the long, undisciplined couplets, the free verse, and the emphasis on content over form of "Cortège," "Vendémiaire," "Le Voyageur," and "Zone."

Alcools's changes in prosody, then, came out of traditional nineteenth-century forms and were rather evolutionary than revolutionary, with one major exception: the futuristic deletion of punctuation—for the whole work!—on the eve of publication in 1913. Legend would have it that Apollinaire was so upset over the many typographical errors in punctuation in the proofs that he gave the sweeping order to delete all punctuation; but sober critics have shown that this radical innovation that has influenced a major part of French poetry up to the present time actually continued nineteenth-century symbolist syntheticism, bringing the lines closer to the musical, the marvelous, and the metaphysical (Mallarmé's famous blank spaces) which lay between them. Apollinaire and fellow poet Pierre Reverdy agreed that punctuation interrupted the free flow of their poetry, as they put it, "from the source."[5] With the exception of minor occasional verse like "Hôtels" and parts of "A la Santé," the major part of Apollinaire's poetry, rising as it does from pantheistic ambiguity into ultimate erotic unity, profited from the change. Subsequent dadaist and surrealist visions of the modern marvelous profited likewise.

The prosody of the new poems, collected in the first section of *Calligrammes* and called "Ondes" (Air waves), is strikingly freer than that of *Alcools,* the freest in Apollinaire's poetry since his first adolescent experiments. Perceiving the need of bringing even more of the twentieth century into his simultaneous vision of it in order better to influence it in return, he adopted a synthetic style, incorporating various techniques of European art and poetry around him: futurism's telegraphic leaps and shocks, its concrete structures, and its "SUPPRESSION of the elegy syntax adjectives punctuation classical prosody plot music typographical harmony . . ." (*L'Antitradition Futuriste);* the advertising handbills, billboards, and signs which he and Fernand Léger so admired with their diversity of typography and style and their directness of appeal (see the beginning of "Zone"); dramatism's antidescriptive, simultaneous choral poetry; cubism's collages and its reconstruction of shattered reality; orphism's use of complementary colors and colorful instinctive rhythms to create association by contrast; Mallarmé's experiments with visual mimesis in *Un coup de dés* (A roll of the dice), republished in 1912;[6] and of course his own old stream-of-consciousness techniques bringing "Ideas, old gossip, oddments of all things / Strange spars of knowledge and dimmed wares of price" (Ezra Pound, "Portrait d'une femme") to a modern idiom. Classical meter and rhyme, for the most part, fell by the wayside.

The subject matter of the modern world became correspondingly more important; the early trolleys, gas lamps, and "roses of electricity" now joined with buses, airplanes, telephones, trains, telegraph poles, and the Eiffel Tower with its complementary ferris wheel, and alternated with distant places, legends, historical events, and myths. With his friend Blaise Cendrars, whose famous poem "Pâques à New-York" ("Easter in New York") had been a major influence on "Zone,"[7] he shattered the romantic, anecdotic "I"— already objectified by the "you" (referring to himself) of "Le Voyageur" and "Zone"—as he made great leaps between his memories, his immediate experiences, and his imagined experiences of others.

Like the sensuous futurists—the opposite of the conceptual cubists—he made concrete poems in the shape of external subject matter, beautiful and profound little *calligrammes* (he called them *idéogrammes lyriques* at that time) of watches, mirrors, neckties, etc., which not only have opened up rich new possibilities for the graphically oriented poets of the twentieth century but have given a new impetus to the growing collaboration of all the arts—especially literature, art, and music (Apollinaire hoped that his poem-paintings would be read as a musical score)—which has been taking place since the beginnings of romanticism.

The most complex, profound, and influential of these concrete poems was one of the first he ever wrote, "Lettre-Océan" ("Ocean-Letter") *(Calligrammes)*. Basically a double circle, it should be read, seen, and heard simultaneously for a new audio-visual reality to be created. Indeed, it might be considered as something of a four-dimensional *mappemonde* (the fourth dimension here being sound) that celebrates 1) the audiovisual experiences and fraternity of two brothers in two hemispheres; 2) the complementarity of the male-female forces of the universe depicted by the male (vertical) tower-sun and the female (horizontal) wheel-sea-moon; and 3) the technological revolution and new synthesis brought about by telegraphy, radio, cars, ships, and trains. All in the prosaic framework of a simple ship-to-ship or ship-to-shore telegram-letter (a *lettre-océan*) that Wilhelm in Paris actually received from his brother Albert in Mexico; and all crammed with the trivial fragments of a great city's sounds, the slang, slogans, songs, insults, jokes, radio broadcasts, and inarticulate noises of street and café (see the Glossary of References for an explanation of some of these). The work's universality, as Roger Shattuck writes in his penetrating analysis of what he calls the first great *poème-événement ("poem-happening")*, makes it the literary equivalent of those other two pre-World War I seminal works, Stravinsky's *Sacre du printemps* and Picasso's *Demoiselles d'Avignon*. It is "the mind raised to the level of omniscience, ubiquity, self-transcendence in the complete instant: a form of self-divinization."[8]

To use a favorite critical term of Apollinaire himself, his calligrams artistically *ennoble* the sights and sounds of everyday reality. "Anch'io son pittore!" ("I, too, am a painter!"), he cried, suddenly discovering a whole new noble dimension for himself. Like the cubists and orphic painters, he found himself in the enviable position of being able to give a new, orphic dimension to the most com-

monplace reality that was all about him in his eternal wanderings
through Paris. And all through the power of his own godlike observation! His new aesthetic was both a new, simultaneous *impressionism* (letter to Madeleine, 1 July 1915) and a new *realism* for the
future to build upon:

> And to renew inspiration, to make it fresher and more orphic, I think
> that the poet will have to refer back to nature, to life. If he should even
> limit himself to noting undidactically the mystery he sees and hears, he
> would become habituated to life itself like nineteenth-century realists who
> thus raised their art very high, and the decadence of the novel came at
> the very moment when the writers ceased observing external reality which
> is the very orphism of art.
>
>   (*Soirées de Paris*, 1914)

His favorite illustration of his new aesthetic was "Les Fenêtres"
("The Windows") (*Calligrammes*). In this conversation-catalog poem,
apparently unrelated elements of *reality* are brought together *impres-
sionistically* like *papiers collés* and deftly shaped into a new reality, a
new unity.

> Du rouge au vert tout le jaune se meurt
> . . . .
> Tu soulèveras le rideau
> Et maintenant voilà que s'ouvre la fenêtre
> Araignées quand les mains tissaient la lumière
> Beauté pâleur insondables violets
> . . . .
> La fenêtre s'ouvre comme une orange
> Le beau fruit de la lumière

(From red to green all yellow dies / . . . / You will lift up the curtain /
And now the window is opening / Spiders when hands were weaving light /
Beauty pallor unfathomable violets / . . . / The window opens like an
orange / The beautiful fruit of light)

This basic structure of lyrical evocation of his friend Robert Delaunay's orphic paintings "Fenêtres"—written for a catalog to Delaunay's exhibition in Berlin while looking out upon his famous
Eiffel Towers ("Tours / Towers are streets") and the rest of the world
("sparkling   diamond /   Vancouver")—serves   as   a   framework   for

snatches of real or imagined conversation in a café, a sunset over the Mediterranean, an enumeration of objects in a room, and some arbitrary associations culled among friends. As in Delaunay's pointillist-inspired spectrum-smashing, the poet proceeds by a technique of association by opposites to encompass as much as possible in his airy view. His old fatal rhythm of art moving between the individual and the world, adventure and order, surprise and inevitability, the human and the inhuman, and creation and death, becomes extremely overt as he takes leaps in time and space from the jungle to the telephone and from the Antilles to Vancouver in a cosmopolitan, very simplified stream of consciousness. Red and green, night and day, ancient and modern, tower, street, and well, "Paris, Vancouver Hyères Maintenon and the Antilles" (note the space-time puns on *hier* [yesterday] and *maintenant* [now]) find their unity in their variety when shaped by instinct and art.

What has happened to Apollinaire's myth of himself? This poetry's extreme externalization, tending away from chronological and narrative progression, inevitably weakens the role of the poet-creator, while it makes the poet-wanderer all the more omnipresent.[9] Yet even though Apollinaire became for the moment more of an observer and a builder than a flaming demiurge, he still had potent phallic power ("Le Musicien de Saint-Merry"); and he could still find a prototype for Christ and Ixion in a dancing harlequin boy on a sidewalk of Paris ("Un fantôme de nuées" ["Phantom of Clouds"]). He was, in short, still the superior artist:

> Rails qui ligotez les nations
> Nous ne sommes que deux ou trois hommes
> Libres de tous liens
> Donnons-nous la main
> ("Liens" ["Ties"])

(Rails lashing nations together / We are only two or three men / Free of all ties / Let us hold hands)

He could still ascend: "We are going higher now and no longer are touching the ground" ("Le Musicien de Saint-Merry"). But he now suggested that the new aesthetic revolution could be adopted by the people. Walking through Paris on 13 July 1913, on the eve of the anniversary of the old failed, political revolution (ironically, by the statue of Danton in the Latin Quarter[10]), the poet observed this revolution taking shape: the artist, a little harlequin acrobat, in a Christ-like transfiguration, was actually succeeding in transmitting his Ixion-like creativity—a *musical* creativity of form—to the crowd:

> Le petit saltimbanque fit la roue
> Avec tant d'harmonie
> Que l'orgue cessa de jouer
> Et que l'organiste se cacha le visage dans les
>   mains
> . . . .
> Mais chaque spectateur cherchait en soi l'enfant
>   miraculeux
> Siècle ô siècle des nuages
>   ("Un Fantôme de nuées")[11]

(The little saltimbanque did a cartwheel / With so much harmony / That the barrel organ stopped playing / And the organ grinder hid his face in his hands / . . . / But every spectator was seeking in himself the miraculous child / Century O century of clouds)

A Revolution in Art, 1908–18; Picasso, Duchamp, Chirico, Archipenko

In chapter 3 I have discussed how Apollinaire's general theories of painting represented an evolution out of symbolist ideas about art and were the same ones that he held for poetry; yet his close association with the actual creations of the young painters resulted in a large body of impressionistic criticism concerning more individual efforts. Largely reportorial and sometimes distorted by overconceptual considerations, this criticism was nevertheless extremely perceptive, revealing an acute sensitivity to anything aesthetic, an amazing range of taste, and an intuitive ability to pick the best talents from literally thousands of artists. He was one of the principal critics to establish the importance of the term "plastic" in modern art history ("the plastic arts," "plastic constructions"). Yet, not surprisingly, he also gave importance to the contrasting literary term "poetic" to describe aspects of painting not covered by the cubist experiments: Matisse's colors, for example, or Metzinger's subject matter, Willette's animated caricatures, Roussel's myths, the minutiae of the primitives, and the painting of José-Maria Sert, the painter who "did not keep himself from having a poetic imagination" (he added, almost wistfully, "that's rare in our time").[12] Throughout his life his own drawings and doodles owed much to symbolist paintings by artists such as Paul Ranson, Maurice Denis, and Gustave Moreau, and his taste for literary art combined with his interest in everything from nudes and artificial flowers to Chinese watercolors and religious subjects. This breadth of taste resulted in a large, eclectic, sometimes irresponsible, and often satirical body of journalistic criticism that occasionally sounds like Baudelaire's professional writings on art:

. . . At the Library circle, "The Salon of Mountain Painters" has opened. This exhibition shows that mountain climbing is a sport and not an art.
(Chroniques, 14 March 1910)

. . . M.Cachoud loves night and proves it by exhibiting a great number of nocturnal paintings at the Georges Petit gallery. "They make you dream," says the catalog. Pleasant locution for "they put you to sleep."
(Chroniques, 7 May 1910)

. . . The lunar nights of M. Cachoud take on importance as soon as one discovers that the painter is, like Henri Matisse, a student of Gustave Moreau.
(Chroniques, 29 April 1913)

Indeed, one of the main tenets of his criticism was the artist's freedom from systems, a fact which above all else explains his ambivalent attitude toward cubist paintings; in the catalog of the first all-cubist exhibition at Brussels in June 1911, in which he accepted the designation *cubisme* on behalf of his friends, he summed up, "I think I have given in a few words the true sense of Cubism: a new and very elevated manifestation of art but not at all a system constraining talents" *(Chroniques).*

The following review of Apollinaire's opinions on four representative artists, therefore, requires a certain relativity of judgment on the part of the reader. One must bear in mind that, at the time of the criticism, Apollinaire was attempting to preserve his aesthetic

integrity while at the same time trying to further the (French) cause
of the new art, inculcate more poetry and higher standards upon
it, keep his Philistine readers informed and unsuspicious (he was
often writing for the Enemy, particularly in the conservative *Intransigeant,* where grudging praise was a better weapon than unqualified enthusiasm), and walk the tightrope of support for certain
superior talents over the savage jungle of avant-garde egotism and
partisanship. That he managed to further the careers of many of
the most important artists of our time under such adverse conditions—a list of his favorites reads like a syllabus for a course on
modern art: Picasso, Matisse, Braque, Rousseau, Laurencin, Derain,
Dufy, Vlaminck, Gris, Delaunay, Chagall, Chirico, Duchamp, Picabia, Archipenko, Kandinski—is a tribute to his taste, his per-
serverence, and his loyalty to his friends—which was not always
paid back in kind.

    Pablo Picasso.   It is significant that after the lyrical article of
May 1905 about the blue and rose periods (see above, chapter 3)
Apollinaire only rarely referred to specific later works of Picasso;
and he never mentioned the *Demoiselles d'Avignon* (1907) even though
in 1912 he continued the 1905 article in the first chapter of *Les
Peintres cubistes.* In this continuation as in later articles, there is a
noticeable diminution of enthusiasm. The tone is always one of full
confidence in Picasso's genius, in his absorption with reason, art,
symmetry, and proportion, and in his potential to produce divine
masterpieces in the future; but Apollinaire finds no single works to
wax enthusiastic over other than the sculpture *Head of a Woman* and
the décor for the surrealistic spectacle *Parade* in 1917. The curtain
of *Parade* is mentioned in the calligram "Pablo Picasso" *(Il y a);*
but almost the entirety of that mystical word-painting on Picasso's
work is based on the paintings of the blue and rose periods. In the
short critical study "De Michel-Ange à Picasso" *(Chroniques,* 1912)
and in the novels "Le Poète assassiné" (1916) and *La Femme assise*
(1918), Picasso is always evoked as the author of the precubist
canvases, "the painter with the celestial blue hands." Significantly,
in a watercolor that he sent to the painter in 1906, he drew a
harlequin figure juggling the words "Les oiseaux chantent avec les
doigts" ("Birds sing with their fingers"), a phrase made famous and
given a surrealistic extension by Cocteau in his play and film on
Orpheus;[13] but in its first context it was obviously meant to mean

that Picasso was a divine harlequin like the "fantôme de nuées" who made music with his hands.

Thus the great influence he exerted on Apollinaire after 1906 and up until 1917—when his temporary return to a classical conception of the human figure coincided with the partial classicism of Apollinaire's "Esprit nouveau" ("New Spirit")[14]—must be measured in terms of his personality, his methods, and his goals rather than in terms of concrete realizations of those things. As Apollinaire's world was at once materialistic, religious, and anarchistic, both ordered and adventurous, he felt a close spiritual kinship with an art he believed to have derived from the Hellenic purity and truth, the Spanish realism, and the mysterious angelic violence characteristic of the art of El Greco, the Greek painter of Toledo *(La Femme assise)*. He also believed that Picasso was attuned to the erotic mysticism of Saint Teresa de Avila *(Chroniques,* April 1905). From "Les Fiançailles" to "Les Collines" ("The Hills") the impact of an elementary, omniscient, constantly renewed and renewing art can be felt in Apollinaire's works; but the greatest manifestations of that art were always those lonely phantom figures on the confines of humanity of the early paintings.

Perhaps the most revolutionary contribution made to twentieth-century art by both poet and painter, however, was their common discovery and propagation of the religious implications of African sculpture—and this thirty years before André Malraux's art criticism! In an interview made sometime between 1909 and 1912 and first published by Pierre Caizergues in 1979, Apollinaire quoted his taciturn friend on these implications:

I felt the greatest emotion of my life [said Picasso, according to Apollinaire] on the sudden appearance of the sublime beauty of the sculpture created by the anonymous African artists. These passionate and rigorously logical works of religious art are the most powerful and beautiful works ever produced by the human imagination.[15]

Little wonder then that after such an aesthetic and religious shock (and undoubtedly after being oriented toward it by the writings of Gauguin, Rimbaud, Nietzsche—and Apollinaire), Picasso passed in so short a time from the Eves, Magdalens, and Madonnas of the blue and rose periods to the realization of his great erotic icon, the

114 GUILLAUME APOLLINAIRE

Demoiselles d'Avignon, with its five primitivistic exorcisms of the *Mater Magna.* Or that Apollinaire's Pans and Orpheuses should now be accompanied by the "passions" (one of his favorite words when discussing this art, as Jean-Claude Blachère has indicated[16]) of African fetishes, those "inferior Christs of obscure hopes" ("Zone") he now surrounded himself with in his apartment in the Latin Quarter. For among all the cubist and orphic negrophiles, Apollinaire and Picasso were almost the only ones to understand that these sculptures were more than new kinds of plastic constructions to be integrated into Western art; they realized that the works released new kinds of gods and goddesses—new forms of the divine artist—both similar to and radically different from the ones they, too, had been releasing into Western society in their own works. This into a society which had been dominated iconographically for three thousand years by the figures of Apollo, Aphrodite, Christ, and Mary. To Apollinaire, African art was, therefore, literally *a new creation* in the biblical sense of the word; in another important text, prudently not published during his lifetime and just come to light in 1984, he made this point clear, sacrilegiously suggesting that both his new art and African art were based on the same basic, Luciferian laws:

The elementary laws that govern the existence of the world allow themselves to burst forth whenever an artist dangerously creates according to the serpentine formula, *you will be as God* [my emphasis]. For a long time artists had lost both the consciousness of and the interest in their own divinity. Finally today, man's pride is manifest. The painters (and the poets), after having consciously established their ignorance have taken the logical step of *creating* [Apollinaire's emphasis]. It is amazing to think that this profound moral lesson has been given to Europe by Africa and Oceania.[17]

On the journalistic level, Apollinaire campaigned almost single-handedly over the last six years of his life for government recognition of the importance of African art, priceless examples of which had been relegated to a dusty corner of the Musée de l'Homme in Paris (where Picasso had his revelation in 1906). In 1917, he gave public lectures on it and wrote an important preface to the first album of photographs of African and Oceanian sculpture.[18] Furthermore, during 1917–18 he originated the thesis, overlooked at the time but taken seriously by art historians and anthropologists today, that black African art was the source of Egyptian art.[19] As for Picasso, he spent the rest of his long and productive life confirming the supremacy of the primitive gods in his psyche, especially the gods of fertility and war, mother goddesses, and animal gods like Mithra and the Minotaur.[20]

Unfortunately, on the negative side of the picture, Picasso's immolations—like the ones in Apollinaire's final prose works of 1916–18—were to a great extent misogynic. When in 1912 the poet said of an anonymous pornographic work, the *Zoppino,* "These almost macabre details, these nauseating descriptions, . . . these bizarre, appalling, even apocalyptic metaphors, indicate, in my opinion, a Spanish author" ("Délicado," *Les Diables amoureux*), he not only indirectly described certain passages of his own *Onze Mille Verges,* but suggested some of the psychology that lay behind Picasso's visions. Picasso was portrayed in *La Femme assise* as a lecherous faun "who with women only knew violence and who despised them" (chapter 8); and according to several of his friends, he considered *Les Onze Mille Verges*—probably written about the same time as *Les Demoiselles d'Avignon* was painted—Apollinaire's greatest work. The evolution of his life and work since the poet's death partly bears out this portrait. His two published plays are remarkable for their Lautréamont-like (and Jarry-like) misogyny and scatology; and perhaps no major artist since Bosch and the medieval painters of the seven deadly sins has been so obsessed with virility symbols, cruelty, and the masochistic violation of the female form. If Apollinaire had lived, he might have been disappointed by Picasso's failure to become the new Michelangelo he prophesied; and he would probably still have regarded the symbolist works that he held up for thirteen years as masterpieces of world painting as his best works.

Marcel Duchamp. In an astonishing preview of the goals of dada and surrealism, Apollinaire suggested in his discussion of the art of his chess-playing friend that an artist might reproduce irrational elements in nature that do not require aesthetic arrangement for their moving qualities; these elements would pass beyond beauty into regions of pure force, power, and energy. An art containing them could depart from the aesthetic, higher domain of the artist for the domain of society, thus reconciling art and the people; and Apollinaire already described the "ready-made": "Just as a work of Cimabue was paraded about, our century has seen Blériot's airplane, laden with humanity, millenary efforts, and necessary art, escorted in triumph to the Arts and Crafts Museum" *(Les Peintres cubistes).*

These conjectures only found a place in Apollinaire's aesthetic through his discussion of Duchamp's painting, however; it was not until 1917 that he suggested the possibility of important surrealist worlds through and beyond art for himself.

It was in 1917, moreover, that Apollinaire may have been influenced by Duchamp's most famous *ready-made* in his play *Les Mamelles de Tirésias (The Breasts of Tiresias)*. Duchamp's upside-down urinal entitled "Fountain" and referred to by its discoverer as "the Buddha of the Bathroom" (since it resembles a seated Buddha) was rejected by the Society of Independent Artists of New York in the spring of 1917 and was the subject of an Apollinaire article in 1918 in which he criticized the Society for depriving the artist of the right to elevate a hygienic object into the realm of art. Thus it was likely that Apollinaire's own hygienic object, a chamber pot which is elevated into a "piano" in act 1 of *Les Mamelles,* was serving the same aesthetic end. The poet and the painter were often on the same wave length: Robert Lebel has shown that Apollinaire was undoubtedly a major catalyst for Duchamp's dadaism as early as 1912 by introducing him to Raymond Roussel's play *Impressions d'Afrique.* Katiä Samaltanos discusses at length the two friends' explorations with Picabia of such new sources for art—and antiart—as psychiatry and the occult; the paintings, writings, and calligrams of the insane; dictionary quotations (verbal ready-mades); jokes and puns; brute sounds; and children's drawings.[21] Reverberations from these mutual influences turn up in Apollinaire's works everywhere from the dada-like explosion of *L'Antitradition Futuriste* in 1913 to the *Quelconqueries,* the more iconoclastic calligrams, and the childish new realms for poetry mentioned in "La Victoire" ("Victory," 1917).

Giorgio de Chirico. Apollinaire wrote little on the Italian precursor of the surrealists who frequented his apartment with his brother Savinio in 1912 and who painted the prophetic "target-portrait" in 1914 that marked the place where Apollinaire would be wounded in 1916.[22] Nevertheless, he consistently praised the metaphysical poetry of his strange plastic enigmas and at one point called him "the most astonishing painter of the younger generation." He was influenced by his 1913 paintings himself, as Willard Bohn has shown convincingly, especially in his use of Ariadne in "Arbre" and in "Le Musicien de Saint-Merry" as a symbol for the female archetype, wedded to Dionysus. In turn, Chirico was probably inspired by the poet's phallic *Musicien* in his mannequin figures of

1914, which were to play such an important role in the subsequent history of dadaism, expressionism, and surrealist art.[23]

Alexander Archipenko. Apollinaire's enthusiastic preface to Archipenko's Berlin exposition in March 1914 climaxed several years of admiration for the pioneer sculptor and constituted his major critical text on the parallel role that sculpture was to play in tandem with the works of the new painters in creating the transcendent ("divine") new reality of modern art. In the works of his new friend as in the works of Picasso and Matisse he found the influence of the great mystical art of the past—in this case of Catholic, Greek, Egyptian, Chinese, African, Indian, and Polynesian works—subordinated to the "chaste and marvelously childlike soul" of the creator. His sculptures, therefore, were both plastic and religious syntheses in the service of the higher divinity of his own personal enlightenment. They were the first chords of a *harmony,* he said, in an art that had provided heretofore, with a few exceptions, only a *melody* (from Apollinaire's general references to sculpture, I suspect that these exceptions were Michelangelo, Rude, and Rodin). I add as an historical note that Apollinaire's unqualified enthusiasm for the sculptor brought about the end of his employment as art critic for the *Intransigeant:* when he defended Archipenko's contributions to the Salon des Indépendants in February 1914 against an attack by a fellow writer on the same newspaper, the editors published a picture of one of these works, "Médrano," with the caption "We reproduce here a photograph of the work of art (?) praised elsewhere in this issue by our collaborator Guillaume Apollinaire, who assumes sole responsibility for his opinion." Apollinaire resigned shortly thereafter *(Chroniques,* 356, 503).

The New Woman, 1898–1918

And there appeared a great wonder in heaven; a woman clothed with the sun, and the moon under her feet, and upon her head a crown of twelve stars . . .

And she brought forth a man child, who was to rule all nations with a rod of iron . . .

And to the woman were given two wings of a great eagle, that she might fly into the wilderness . . .

(Revelation 12:1,5,14).

. . . The Marquis de Sade, the freest spirit that has lived until now, had special ideas on woman, wanting her to be as free as man. These ideas which will be brought out one day produced a double novel: *Justine* and *Juliette*. It was not by chance that the marquis chose heroines instead of heroes. Justine represents woman of the past, subservient, miserable, and less than human; Juliette, on the contrary, represents his perception of the new woman, a being of whom we have as yet no idea, who is detaching herself from humanity, who will have wings, and who will renew the universe.

(Les Diables amoureux [The amorous devils])

Who or what was Apollinaire's New Woman? And what role would she play in the creation of the millennium of art? The answers to these questions lead to the core of the poet's thought, his hopes for an externalization of Psyche and Hera, Cybele and Isis, Aphrodite and the Madonna, Lilith, Eve, Helen, Salome, and Rosemonde, in a female spirit of the universe, the Panther to his Pan ("Deuxième poème secret" [Second secret poem]), the essential second member of his erotic trinity. As Jean-Claude Chevalier sums it up in his structural analysis of *Alcools*, "What [Apollinaire] ultimately seizes in the farthest nest of the oblong stars is Woman."[24]

In "Arbre" (1913) there is the mention of "the Mole-Ariadne" *(la Taupe-Ariane),* a curious expression that, as we have seen, derives from Nietzsche and from Chirico's paintings. It probably has at least two other sources as well: the common slang use of *taupe* for "prostitute," and Remy de Gourmont's well-known description of the female mole's annual labyrinthine flight through a subterranean palace to elude the amorous male.[25] In 1913, however, Ariadne was not Juliette; Apollinaire, suffering from the flight of love (Marie Laurencin, tired of his many infidelities, had finally left him) pictured her in another 1913 poem "Le Musicien de Saint-Merry" as a member of a new flock of sphinxes following a Pan-like flutist into the stars. But at this point, the symbols seem to become jumbled. *Dionysus* was the god who led Ariadne astray according to legend; and, although he traditionally could be said to have a following of Bacchantes and flute-playing satyrs, he was not celebrated for his own musicianship as were Pan and Apollo. Apollinaire followed Pan's flute himself in "Le Brasier" and wrote the music in "Le Musicien." In the latter poem, moreover, the flutist was also a sort of Eros-Thanatos figure, a "passer of the dead," amid millions of flies and death-dealing prostitutes; the image reminds us of the line "I am awaiting the passage of Thanatos and his flock" from an early poem about the death of love, "Le Mendiant" (The beggar).

To unravel this tangled skein of symbols, let us embark on our own
labyrinthine pursuit, following Eros and his twin brother in turn
through the sunlit or twilight streets of a few representative prose
works and plays, in a search for Her, the "Unknown" ("L'Ermite"),
the goddess he pursued all his life.

These works are *L'Enchanteur pourrissant* (1903–9), *Les Mamelles
de Tirésias* (1903–17), *Onirocritique* (1907?), prefaces to erotic classics
(1909–13), *La Femme assise* (1917–18), and *Couleur du temps* (1918).
Three main points may be affirmed at the outset: 1) Apollinaire's
early adolescent cult of the Virgin Mary set the stage for his lifetime
pursuit of a secular female divinity; 2) his love-hate relationship
with his mother, she who was a combined Eve, Mary, and Lilith
figure to him, profoundly reinforced his need for this ideal; and 3)
the ideal varied with the varying stages of the birth-death cycles of
his loves for Annie (1901–4), Marie (1907–13), Lou (1914–15),
Madeleine (1915–16), and Jacqueline (1917–18).

Before Anna Maria Playden, "Annie," departed to America and
Apollinaire was first entombed as Merlin in 1904, he had recorded
his earliest ideas on eroticism in a number of poems of seduction
and frustration. Obviously counting on profiting from his materialistic anarchism and ideas of free love, he had oscillated between
the classical "Don't you know we are dying?" and "I'll make you
immortal by my poetry" themes, both tempered by a poetic, fin-
de-siècle pleasure in watching his rosebuds wither and his princesses
sail away. In a good adolescent tradition, onanism, scatology, and
masochism were everywhere, with, however, suprisingly little guilt,
his revolutionary beliefs in feminism, sexual freedom, the sainted
working girl, anti-Malthusianism, and Helen the fecund muse of
liberty, having been enough to justify his erotic desires:

> Au siècle qui s'en vient hommes et femmes
> fortes
> Nous lutterons sans maîtres au loin des cités
> mortes
>
> ("Les Poètes")

(In the century to come strong men and women / We shall fight without
masters far from the dead cities)

> Quand te nomme un héros tous les hommes se
> lèvent

Hélène ô liberté ô révolutions
                                        ("Hélène")

(When a hero calls you by name all men stand up / Helen O liberty O
revolutions)

   Alas, by 1904 the revolution was stale, love was dead, and the
sexes, said Remy de Gourmont in a book that was Apollinaire's
bible, had never been farther apart—an inevitable condition, he
added, of a superior civilization ("Let us dream, if it is permitted
to dream, of multiplicity rather than unity"—*Epilogues*). Gourmont
had elaborated on this idea in his *Physique de l'amour (Physiology of
Love)* of the year before, another book much admired by Apollinaire,
which was one of the first comparative studies of animal sexuality.
Primarily influenced by J.-H. Fabre's entomological volumes, its
main thesis is "We are animals . . . and when we make love, it
is definitely what the theologians call *more bestiarum.*" All sexual
tastes, all so-called perversions and cruelties, said Gourmont, are
in nature: "In love, all is true, all is just, all is noble the moment
it is a matter of play inspired by the procreative urge." Dimorphism,
based on sexual differences, is the rule of life; the reproducing female
is the important member of the couple, and the female of the human
species is no exception—although physically and mentally she is
inferior to her partner. For civilization to persist, dimorphism is
essential: "The sole aim of the couple is to free woman of all care
that is not purely sexual to permit her a more perfect accomplishment
of her most important function." In society, her most important
function is to attract the male. Thus she is beautiful; her arms are
sexual attributes, whereas man's arms are only tools.
   I deduce from several passages in *L'Enchanteur pourrissant*, especially those concerning flies, bats, and dragonflies, that Apollinaire
knew *Physique de l'amour* well when he wrote his novel. He gives
us a key to the manner in which his book—and many of his short
stories—should be analysed in the following revealing passage from
a letter to Madeleine:

I read today the news of the death of the entomologist Fabre whose books
I used to enjoy tremendously for his studies on insects taught me to know
men and if I had the leisure for it I should like them to be studied in my
romanesque work as minutely as precisely and as amorally. . . . But I

occasionally used to amuse myself by changing in Fabre's pages the names of insects into names of men and women, which gives those pages a terrifying aspect of overly real humanity à la Marquis de Sade. . . .

(14 October 1915)

This behaviorist view of human nature is combined by both Apollinaire and Gourmont with the Nietzschean dichotomy of Ariadne and Dionysus, the passive and active, the female and male poles of the universe.

In the last section of *L'Enchanteur pourrissant,* man is characterized as an active idealist, bestial and aspiring; he is a drift of pigs with its swineherd who is either earthbound reaching for the sun, or walking on the sky longing for the earth—and turning his back on it; he is consciously creative, "a field with its harvester." Woman is the opposite, an unconscious, passive realist who expresses herself either as aimless natural beauty ("useless spring") or nature's turmoil, "the restless ocean, bloodshed." Her best prediction is childbirth. Viviane, the Lady of the Lake and Merlin's beautiful nemesis, reveals herself to be neither the phantom of Remy de Gourmont's earlier Decadent works nor the enchantress of legend, neither Psyche nor Medea, but an ordinary woman. She is merely *organically* different from the male and thus inaccessible to her lover. "We are at a distance," she maintains, "but at a distance before and behind so that man is in the center of our remoteness, he prefers to try to grasp us in order to make love." Solomon and Socrates, summoned to confer the aggregate of man's wisdom in matters of love, can speak only in terms of carnal satisfaction, heterosexual and homosexual. Viviane at heart detests men and admires the female consort of Lilith, the lesbian dragonfly (see *demoiselle* in the Glossary). Ideal love is dead: "Circe came . . . into the forest the evening of the death of the enchanter" (version of 1904). In spite of their protestations, Merlin and the Lady of the Lake are surrounded by copulating animals. The opening question of the book, "What will become of my heart among those who love one another?" becomes a cosmic absurdity.

Then how and why, Merlin asks, did a woman enchant and bury him? Viviane remains silent (she speaks but is censored by the author in the 1904 version). Her dancing, her fertility, and the creative blossoming of spring come to an end at the end of the book amid scenes of lesbianism and menstruation.

If the impotence and hopelessness of romantic love is the subject
of *L'Enchanteur pourrissant,* conjugal fecundity and the repopulation
of France are advocated in *Les Mamelles de Tirésias (The Breasts of
Tiresias).* This dramatic farce, a landmark in the history of surrealist
drama (Apollinaire invented the word *surréaliste* to describe it), was
first sketched out in 1903 at a time when France's underpopulation
was much discussed by intellectuals. It was natural that the illegitimate Apollinaire should have been interested in marriage and
children—he did ask each of his major mistresses to marry him,
with the possible exception of Lou. What were less obvious were
the reasons for his obsession with repopulation. Some critics and
friends have considered the propaganda of *Les Mamelles* to be a
Jarryesque joke not to be taken seriously. Let us look at the record.

The anarchist poems had forecast postrevolution fecundity. In
1901, the year Apollinaire asked Molina da Silva for his daughter
Linda's hand, his hero of *Que faire?* criticized duels for "depopulating
instead of repopulating." The next year he heard Isaac Laquedem
maintain that the sole beauty of women was a pregnant appearance
("Le Passant de Prague"), and he himself praised the fecund beauty
of German girls (1902 version of "La Rose de Hildesheim"). In "Le
Larron," the pagans admitted being moved by pregnancies and used
them to attack the Christian doctrine of aseity. In *L'Hérésiarque et
cie,* Gaétan Gorène overcame the sterility of his wife by the grace
of science and the sex of his priest ("Un monstre de Lyon ou l'envie"
[A monster of Lyons or Desire]); the ubiquitous Baron Dormesan
conceived three children of his mistress while she was in Paris and
he in Chicago, Jerusalem, and Melbourne; and Pertinex Restif, the
incestuous ragpicker of "Histoire d'une famille vertueuse, d'une
hotte et d'un calcul" (Story of a virtuous family, a sack, and a
gallstone) got his sister pregnant with "a beautiful pearl" for a belly.
In 1906 the young Don Juan impregnated his sister, his aunt, and
a peasant girl, accomplishing thereby his "patriotic duty, that of
increasing the population of my country." In "Le Poète assassiné,"
Croniamantal's mother preached that the duty of women was to
have children and listened to a Vatican priest tell her that France
was being depopulated by anticlericalism ("yes, *baronnesse,* it is
proved"). She also went to a naturalistic play in Paris whose plot
concerned a woman without ovaries who became pregnant thanks
to love and surgery. Further on in the same book there was a recipe
for an antihygienic powder for having many children, to be spread

on bedsheets. In 1915, during the war, Apollinaire was proud of his cat giving a good example of repopulation, praised his fiancée's large family, and planned to have many children by her ("nothing is more prolific than Polish blood"). In the pages of the *Mercure de France* he seriously recommended a national policy of giving the military salute to pregnant women. He had a book on determining the sex of children in his library.[26] And finally, he wrote throughout the latter part of his life a novel about a decadent European lesbian and about her grandmother who emigrated to Salt Lake City as a Mormon convert, a woman whose sterility and dilettantism he contrasted to the spectacular fecundity of the Mormon women:

. . . Like swelling rivers, the women were flowing in from every street, and now everywhere they looked the emigrants saw nothing but women, and almost all of them were pregnant . . . And, little by little, there were so many pregnant women that there appeared to be nothing in Union Square but their enormous bellies moving like the little waves of a lake on which little heads made ugly with childbearing were floating like corks.
(La Femme assise)

"I claim that the farcical (and Surrealistic) drama of Monsieur Apollinaire is whether he will it or no, a polemical play *(une pièce à thèse),*" wrote a reviewer of *Les Mamelles de Tirésias* in 1917, in an article that the playwright called "interesting and judicious." In truth, he was using farce à la Aristophanes to stuff his ideas with; and those ideas were essentially the same ones of the philosophers who influenced him in 1903, when he first conceived the play. Nietzsche, for example, had written that the solution of women was maternity (he had also advocated the whip) and hymned the sacred fire of pregnancy *(Dawn)*. Remy de Gourmont, who had, on the other hand, attacked "the folly of repopulation"—usually relegated, he wrote, to poor families by impotent administrators—nevertheless opposed Malthusianism, free love, and the opposite of free love, puritanical Anglo-Saxon feminism *(Epilogues)*. Feminism, he said, if successful, would move civilization toward human parthenogenesis and a beelike society with a Queen Mother, female workers, and male drones; while complete sexual promiscuity would only turn the world into chaos, destroy the couple, and lead to even greater subjection of the weaker female than in the past. The basis of society and of all higher animate nature is *the couple:* woman is liberated when she is free to cultivate at leisure her reproductive attributes; while her male counterpart with his animalistic promiscuous instincts must sustain her in this freedom while indulging at times in a freedom of his own, in the joys of "temporary polygamy," the safeguard of marriage (La Physique de l'amour).

In Les Mamelles de Tirésias, Apollinaire satirizes feminism in the person of his female protagonist Thérèse, who exchanges her pneumatic symbols of maternity for a beard, names herself Tirésias, and leaves her husband to become a "deputy lawyer senator . . . mathematician philosopher chemist." But her creator, in a supreme Oedipal statement, goes Remy de Gourmont one better: his male hero, the abandoned husband, becomes the Father, the phoenix, the phallus, and France—and the conqueror of death—in one mighty act of will by giving birth to "40,049 children in a single day." Has Apollinaire abandoned the couple? Not in the least: a repentant Thérèse returns to her husband at the end of the play, ready, as the dramatist wrote in his own review, to do the double!—now that she has shed her beard, donned her breasts, and is back home again where she belongs. Eve unchained would then transcend herself by following her husband's Promethean example—and the example of the codfish—by having multiple progeny. Leaving the husband free, of course, to cultivate his male prerogative of "temporary polygamy"—"scratching himself where he itched" (act 2). Never would King Ixion ride higher.

We find, therefore, that Apollinaire carried along with him a pregnant Eve symbol on his quest for the Superwoman and in his flight from (and to) the sanguinary womb; and he finally bequeathed her and her children to France for the cause of French culture and his own immortality. As well as his own immorality: there is no doubt that his patriotic zeal owed much to his own promiscuous tendencies.[27] Over the passion flowers and the venomous plants hung the ripe fruits that he loved, part of the beauty—and irony—of autumn. They were like the breasts and the body of woman in full maturity. His most admiring description of Eve was of her portrait in the magnificent painting on the ceiling of the Sistine Chapel: "When Michelangelo painted the resplendent Eve of the Sistine, he gave her the splendor of creative forces, breasts of abundance, copious, saturated breasts that were to nourish a Race, a whole Race. . . ."[28]

For three years after Annie's departure, however, he was far from both male parthenogenesis and female fertility. He believed that he could no longer love. His onanistic tendencies and black humor broke into clandestine print in the incestuous fantasies of *Les Exploits d'un jeune Don Juan (The Memoirs of a Young Rakehell)*, and especially in that apocalypse of copulating beasts, *Les Onze Mille Verges*, with its multiple episodes of sadism, masochism, fetishism, saphism, transvestism, urolagnia, coprolagnia, coprolalia, necrophilia, poedophilia, gerontophilia, and zoophilia erotica, and with its close understanding, as Robert Desnos has pointed out, of the essentially modern role played by masochism and the whip *(De l'érotisme)*. Typically, Apollinaire was extending his death of love to the rest of society; in one of the few thoughtful passages of the book, he carried Gourmont's civilized dimorphism as far as Sodom and Gomorrah. One of his characters comments:

. . . Masturbation is a very laudable action, since it permits men and women to get used to their approaching definitive separation. The customs, the spirits, the clothes, and the tastes of the two sexes are becoming more and more distinct. It is about time we recognized this fact, and if one wants to dominate on earth, it would appear to me to be necessary to take into account this natural law which will soon impose itself.

(chapter 7)

Apollinaire wanted to dominate, to be king. He later wrote to Lou after he had taken a vow of chastity at the front, that it was a joy to dominate his carnal desires "in order to dominate others some day" (letter of 14 April 1915). In the next few years, he became the loveless poet-god of "Le Brasier," the chaste Templar of "Les Fiançailles," and the solitary enchanter of *Onirocritique* (Dream-criticism). This last work was published in 1909 as the last section of *L'Enchanteur pourrissant;* its leitmotifs are, "But I was conscious of the different eternities of men and women," and "Two dissimilar animals were coupling." In surrealistic prose the lone poet wanders through a dreamlike chaos left by the splitting apart of the universe into two eternities, until, as the two animals melt away to shades, he becomes *the last man* in harmony with the empty cities, the rivers, and the undefiled mountain snows.

In his prefaces to such erotic classics as *The Memoirs of Fanny Hill* (1910), Aretino's *I Ragionamenti* (Dialogues) (1909–12), and the works of the Marquis de Sade (1909), Apollinaire, now in love with

Marie Laurencin, became a polemicist for free erotic experience, that
is to say, the greatest range of erotic possibilities within and between
the two separate eternities of male and female. *Les Onze Mille Verges*
had been a de Sade-like compendium of erotic experience, revealing
great knowledge of the subject on the part of its young author both
through his personal life and through literature, and it had contained
a number of insatiable Juliettes in the midst of its violently anti-
Russian mayhem.[29] Now he advocated the sixteenth- and eighteenth-century cult of the flesh, of "sublime obscenity," as against
the limited range of sexual freedom advocated by puritanical apologists for free love in the twentieth century. Their Eros had become
"a statue of a little naked, sick god, his bow unstrung, a shameful
object of curiosity, a subject of medical and retrospective observa-
tions" ("Andréa de Nerciat," *Les Diables amoureux).* De Sade, on the
other hand, the creator of the new-Juliette-with-wings-to-renew-
the-universe, was the great libertarian of sex, as well as an important
precursor of Lamarck, Spencer, Nietzsche, and Krafft-Ebing. His
ideas were best expressed in "that opus sadicum par excellence," *Le
Philosophe dans le boudoir (The Philosopher in the Boudoir).*

In this chaotic but fascinating treatise, the ideal woman is sketched
out by de Sade in terms reminiscent of those used by Fabre to
describe certain female insects. Her only desire would be to be made
carnal love to from morning to night. She would be unmarried, she
would live in a state house of prostitution—there would be male
houses for *her,* too—and she would be completely *free,* "with no
restraints but her penchants, no laws but her desires, no morality
but that of nature." Her children, if any, would be brought up by
the state. Virtue and vice being nothing but relative social terms
for natural phenomena and love being nothing but desire, incest,
sodomy, and crime, including murder, as well as egoistic altruism,
humanity, fraternity, and charity would all be permitted. Inequality
is the rule of nature; one should profit by any superiority one is
lucky enough to have. The anarchistic rule of the strongest will
finally dawn; men and women will grow in strength, primitive
beauty, and godliness; "charming sex, you will be free."

Apollinaire's New Woman did not entirely fit this portrait, but
she was partly formed by it. He mainly compromised de Sade's ideas
with those of Remy de Gourmont—and Proudhon's belief in the
family—in his advocacy of as much erotic freedom as possible within
the limits of monogamy, "the licentiousness which is the health

and safeguard of marriage." He lauded Aretino's sonnet sequence on love's positions: "Variety is the only arm we possess against satiety. And the man [Aretino] who, directly or indirectly, furnished love with a pretext never to become stale should be honored by all married people." Evidently Apollinaire saw Juliette as the mistress of both Eve and Mary; he would later instruct his virgin fiancée Madeleine in the same ideas.

Not long after Marie Laurencin left him for a German artist, he was attempting to enlist in the French forces at the beginning of World War I, driven by a need to fight with the angels on the right side of what he considered to be a kind of Armageddon of Aesthetics, Art against the Huns. He was also spurred on by an inner need to become at last the hero of his mother, that proud, tyrannical Pole who had chivalric ancestors going back to Ryurik, the first king and legislator of Russia. "Count Guillaume Albert Wladimir Alexandre Apollinaire de Kostrowitzsky" his service record read; he wondered at times if he were not another Napoleon, starting out like that Corsican in the artillery; and he hoped that the war would finally bring about the liberation of Poland and the return of his titled estates (letters to Lou). He also joined the armed forces to impress a new love, a convent-bred party girl like his mother who happened to be a member of one of the most illustrious houses in Europe, with the same name as a famous ancestress, Louise de Coligny, daughter of Admiral Coligny, wife of Prince William the Silent. To climax his joy, he found that she was also Juliette in person.

The extraordinary ladder of erotic love they climbed together in the space of a few months is described in minute detail in the numerous poems and more than two hundred letters he sent her from his basic training camp and the front; suffice it to say here that their erotic range was remarkably wide, unconsciously incestuous, and included sodomy, one of the ultimate stages of sexual liberation for Apollinaire as it had been for de Sade. Heterosexual sodomy, accompanied by essential flagellation—binding the two eternities (this time compared to Xerxes and the sea) together by the whip—was a supreme triumph to him of "pure and perverse love" "mythic, carnal, absolute," a way through the valley of the shadow of death to life (she did not quite understand but was quite willing to play along with it).[30] He had said in his prefaces to erotic classics that love sought to destroy dualism, that there could not be two freedoms. Now as Lou was a microcosm of the female principle, the archetype of Helen, Mary Magdalene, and Messaline (letters of 18 December 1914 and 3 February 1915), and as he was a microcosm of all creation, "the head of creation" (letter of 5 May 1915), so their union was godlike and sacred and contained everything in the universe. He was the flagellating sun (letter of 27 January 1915), she the Marvelous Rose (Poem 11); "Vice never enters into sublime loves" (Poem 14).

Yet he soon found the defect in the absolutely free woman when she moved on to other male microcosms; and he pathetically repeated after she had gone his ideas on the essential importance of the couple (letter of 25 April 1915). She had been a rebound from Marie Laurencin; now a young Algerian English teacher took *her* place and rose to the rank of ideal goddess, phantom of clouds, and mother of letters and poems. Apollinaire created Madeleine almost entirely out of his own imagination and her letters (he had met her only briefly on a train), just as he was doing everything in his power to create aesthetic significance for the war; but he never found another woman who so well embodied his philosophy of Eros Transcendent as his Lady Ashley, the Lady who was known as Lou.

Nevertheless, he wrote a volume of letters to Madeleine from the front—later published by her under the title of *Tendre comme le souvenir* (Tender as memory)—in which he made her his "Roselys" (Rose-lily), his Mary Magdalene ("Madeleine" in French), his Eve, his slave, in short, his fiancée. Reality, after a visit on leave to her home in Oran and after his head wound in March 1916, inevitably dispelled the mirage—and the marriage. His uncharacteristic and dishonorable abandonment of her was a great sorrow to him, perhaps recorded as "the secret grief" in the beautiful poem of *Calligrammes* "Tristesse d'une étoile" ("Sorrow of a Star"); and he never fully recovered either from his wound or from his loss of Lou, even in new love and marriage (1918) to Jacqueline Kolb, *la jolie rousse* (the pretty redhead) of the last poem in *Calligrammes*. As usual, he took out his own inadequacies on his women: his final writings are full of bitter misogyny, from the transvestism of his stories ("Les Epingles" [The pins], "La Suite de Cendrillon ou le Rat et les six lézards" [Cinderella continued or the rat and the six lizards], "L'Aventurière" [The adventuress], etc.) to the paranoiac denunciations of *La Femme assise* in which even his new mistress and future spouse, Jacqueline, pictured therein as "Corail," is not spared. A final pessimistic if more rational attitude can be found in his last play, *Couleur du temps* (Color of the weather), produced a month after his death, in December 1918.

Couleur du temps is a résumé of the dark side of his philosophy on love. It picks up for the last time his first positivistic trinity, History, Science (Mathematics), and Philosophy, and allegorizes it in the three key personages of the play, Van Diemen the rich man, Ansaldin the scientist, and Nyctor the poet (scene 1). Escaping from reality, represented by the terrible beauty and suffering of war as personified by a mother and a young woman weeping over the death of a soldier, they flee to the Antarctic against the poet's better instincts and there immolate each other over the figure of a beautiful woman frozen in ice. The play ends on the ironic comments of the dead soldier's fiancée and mother contrasting their hero's sacrificial struggle for life with the egotistical and idealistic battle for a phantom peace and beauty.

In 1914 he had been excited by his discovery of Rimsky-Korsakov's *Golden Coquerel* as danced by the Ballets Russes; in 1918 he called it a subversive revolutionary work that showed that sexuality was the strongest force in life, transcending patriotism and religion (*Europe nouvelle,* 24 August). Thematically, the ancient Russian legend is similar to *Couleur du temps:* a king, a magician, and the king's two sons, trying to forestall war, kill each other for love of a phantom Oriental beauty. Apollinaire's play is a modern, science fiction account of the fatal implications of the romantic pursuit of the Ideal: the last act sums up a number of icebound romantic and symbolist quests from Mary Shelley's *Frankenstein* and Poe's *Gordon Pym* to Rimbaud's "Being Beauteous" and Gide's *Voyage d'Urien.* Yet his polemical intent of proposing a different kind of love to take its place, one committed to duty, to procreation, and to France (the fiancée and the mother) is belied by the prosaic flatness of the play's tone, and the discouragement felt in many of the lines ("Farewell farewell all must die"). With *La Femme assise* one of Apollinaire's most pessimistic works, it is modern and realistic in its prophetic doubts about science's ability to save the world from catastrophe and its prophetic advocacy of a form of realpolitik; but its disparity in tone and idea and the contrast between its fantasy plot and its prosaic dialogue are jarring to the reader and keep it from being a successful work of art. Nevertheless, as a revelation of the underside of his symbolist and modernist philosophy—the Anteros side—and as a counterpart to the prolific optimism of *Les Mamelles de Tirésias*, produced the year before, the play is a tribute to the poet's intellectual integrity. The more characteristic philosophy of *Les Mamelles* predominates in his total ethos, however, and provides the basis for the three successful manifestoes of revolutionary aestheticism written at the end of his life, "La Victoire" ("Victory"), "Les Collines" ("The Hills"), and "La Jolie Rousse" ("The Pretty Redhead") (discussed below).

In summary, Apollinaire's New Woman rose full-blown out of his positivistic pantheism and his early idealism. The biological separation of the sexes paralleled the division of the world into anima and animus, Ariadne and Dionysus, the Lady and her Knight, the Madonna and Christ. His lifelong quest could be termed the desire and the pursuit of the whole; he knew like modern psychologists and theologians "the eschatological proposition that mankind will not put aside its sickness and its discontent until it is able to abolish every dualism."[31] Eros was the connecting link between the two separate eternities of man and woman, "love which fills like light / All the solid space between the stars and planets" ("Poème lu au mariage d'André Salmon"). When, as it recurrently happened, Eros turned into Anteros and led the poet to a woman of straw, he substituted for her such other animae of his inner vision as Revolution, Nature, Memory, the Muse, the Madonna, Eve, Will, Desire *(Volupté),* and the Modern World—or, in his nihilistic, onanistic works, himself, Lilith, the Bitch-Goddess, the Sirens, or a fatal illusion. Eros was also Apollo, Orpheus, Dionysus, and Pan; their Psyche was Ariadne-Juliette, an illusory twin image, a guide and an inspiration, Eagle, Mole, and Panther. Their marvelous child was Art. Historically, Pan's symbolism went all the way from Theocritus's god of noonday rutting (used by Apollinaire in "Un monstre de Lyon") to the Platonic Celestial Face Itself, the incarnation of the Word, the Orphic Whole (Abbé d'Aubignac, *Satyres)*. Apollinaire made the shepherd-god into the creative spirit of the universe, piping now sphinxes, women, and stars, now paintings and words into new worlds.[32] His own flock of words, "following into the myrtle groves / Eros and Anteros in tears" ("La Victoire") could change the faces of children and renew the universe:

> La parole est soudaine et c'est un Dieu qui
> tremble

....
La Victoire avant tout sera
De bien voir au loin
De tout voir
De près
Et que tout ait un nom nouveau
("La Victoire")

(The word is sudden and it is a trembling god / . . . / Victory above all will be / To see well from afar / To see all / Nearby / And may all have a new name)

The New Poet: Ideas of 1914–18

Apollinaire's lyrical acceptance of World War I and his role in it as an artillery sergeant and infantry lieutenant was in keeping with his character and ideas. He had foreseen a blood purge of nations since his adolescence; he knew the dangers of the antipoetic forces loose in the technological age; and he had felt early in his life the world's need for the hegemony of French art to save it from barbarism. Also French humor and joie de vivre: early in the war he wrote his friend Jean Mollet, "It's important to stay upbeat *(Il faut être gai),* without that, everything is lost *(tout est foutu)"* (letter of 15 January 1915). He was always one to be in the forefront of every movement he endorsed. His early poetry had been among the most Byzantine and Decadent, his anarchistic tracts the most violent, his anticlerical stories the most satirical, his Rhenish lyrics the most romantic, his pornographic writings the most outrageous, his symbolism the most messianic, his futurism the most destructive, and his "poèmes-conversations" the most modern of our time; it was natural that his war poetry was to be the most enthusiastic. He had always known the secret of giving himself totally to a cause; and his main weapon, in war as in peace, was his personal example, his myth. The shift from errant poet to knight-errant poet was correspondingly easy. The soldier had been a recurrent symbol of poetic adventure in *Alcools,* and the simplified and intensified life in wartime, with its easy blacks and whites and great surface reserves of emotion waiting to be exploited, gave extra significance to his favorite verbs *sing, dance, look, love, weep,* and *die.* He knew that mere photographic reporting of love and life grew charged with emotion when it came from under a bombardment on the front; his hundreds of poetic dispatches to friends and periodicals used the simplified, impressionistic cosmopolitanism of his prewar muse to keep up with exploding events.

In letters to Lou, Madeleine, and a literary pen pal, Jeanne-Yves Blanc, he discussed the new aesthetic to come out of the war. Fernand Fleuret (who had written three-line short stories for newspapers), Blaise Cendrars, and he, three poets who had adopted a simplified telegraphic syntax to mirror external reality, constituted the only trinity in French poetry that had "true talent and lyricism" (letter to Lou, 7 January 1915). Literature was moving back to the principles of language, he said, taste and classical restraint were changing rapidly and returning to *life* which was the governing principle of art (letters to Madeleine, 1 July, 3 August 1915; letter to Jeanne-Yves Blanc, 30 October 1915). Who were the great forgetters, he asked, the Christopher Columbuses who could *forget* a continent in order to make even greater discoveries? He was certainly one himself, "the Don Juan of the thousand and three comets," on a cosmographic search for new forces ("Toujours" ["Always"]). Out of the poet's mental explorations would arise an epic muse that would be neither one of esoteric symbolism nor of imagistic impressionism, but rather one of aesthetic humanism mirroring a secular religion of honor, duty, and heroism (Jeanne-Yves Blanc, 19 November; Madeleine, 20 May, 1 July 1915).

Most of his war poems incorporate these ideas and testify to his exuberant, if oversimplified, picture of himself as a troubadour, crusading knight, and lover, singing war's marvels to his loves, his *amors de lonh,* and his friends on the home front. At their best, in "La Nuit d'avril 1915" ("April Night 1915"), for example, they present a unique appreciation of life and love in the most harrowing situations:

> Le ciel est étoilé par les obus des Boches
> La forêt merveilleuse où je vis donne un bal
> La mitrailleuse joue un air à triple-croches
> Mais avez-vous le mot
>   Eh! oui le mot fatal
> Aux créneaux Aux créneaux Laissez là les
>   pioches
> ....
> Ulysse que de jours pour rentrer dans Ithaque
> Couche-toi sur la paille et songe un beau

remords
Qui pur effet de l'art soit aphrodisiaque . . .

(The heavens are starred by the shells of the Boche / The marvelous wood
where I live throws a ball / The machine gun plays a demisemiquaver air /
But did you get the word / Yes! the fatal word / To the battlements to
the battlements leave your shovels there /. . . / Ulysses how long to get
back to Ithaca / Lie down on the straw and dream a fine remorse / Which
pure effect of art is aphrodisiac . . .)

At their worst, they comprise the excessively conceptual, patriotic
war poetry of forgotten anthologies:

Prends mes vers ô ma France Avenir Multitude
Chantez ce que je chante un chant pur le
        prélude
Des chants sacrés que la beauté de notre temps
Saura vous inspirer plus purs plus éclatants
Que ceux que je m'efforce à moduler ce soir
En l'honneur de l'Honneur la beauté du Devoir
        ("Chant de l'honneur" ["Honor's Hymn"])

(Take my verses O my France Future Multitude / Sing what I sing a pure
chant the prelude / Of the sacred hymns the beauty of our time / Will
inspire you with more pure sublime / Than those that this evening I am
trying to sing / In honor of Honor and the beauty of Duty)

It is ironic that Apollinaire's cynical aesthetic of *Les Onze Mille
Verges* (unintentionally rediscovered in *La Femme assise*) would have
served him better to portray war in terms that we more readily
accept as accurate after almost a century of genocidal wars. Occasionally, however, he let down his guard and let slip a few lines
that avoid the weight of war's ulterior motives, as in "Peu de chose"
(Not much), cited here in full:

Combien qu'on a pu en tuer
Ma foi
C'est drôle que ça ne vous fasse rien
Ma foi
Une tablette de chocolat aux Boches
Ma foi Feu

Un camembert pour le logis aux Boches
Ma foi Feu
Chaque fois que tu dis feu! le mot se change
    en acier qui éclate là-bas
Ma foi
Abritez-vous
Ma foi
Kra
Ils répondent les salauds
Drôle de langage ma foi

(How many you can kill / By God / Funny you don't feel anything / By
God / A chocolate bar for the Boche / By God Fire / A Camembert cheese
for the Boche's house / By God Fire / Every time you say fire! the word
changes out there into flying steel / By God / Take shelter / By God /
Kra / They're answering back the dirty / Funny language by God)

Especially after he joined the infantry from the artillery did he
become aware that the war was no medieval joust between Saint
Guillaume and the Dragon. The following fragment (cited in full),
an inadvertent cry of distress out of the bloody trenches, is more
valuable as poetry and truth than much formal rhetoric:

Endurcis-toi vieux coeur entends les cris
    perçants
Que poussent les blessés au loin agonisants
Hommes poux de la terre ô vermine tenace

(Harden yourself old heart to the piercing cries / The wounded make out
there in their agonies / Men lice of the earth O vermin tenacious)

The war poems of *Calligrammes* and the poems to Lou and Madeleine, therefore, constitute no epic *Iliad* or *Song of Roland,* a form
of literature that will probably never return; but they do make up
a remarkable modern romance of war. Apollinaire was closely acquainted with the Freudian connections between desire and battle,
the relation between love and hate and the phallic release of artillery
fire; and he finally broke his vow of chastity to take advantage of
the erotic opportunities that are one of the major baits of recruiting
sergeants. Living for the most part like the Marquis de Sade through
a period of enforced abstinence, he released his pent-up desires in

a flood of erotic letters and poems that may be regarded as one of
the most extraordinary war records in literature. Here is an example,
written from the front to Madeleine, the young virgin he knew only
by correspondence:

> Ma bouche aura des ardeurs de géhenne
> Ma bouche te sera un enfer de douceur
> Les anges de ma bouche trôneront dans ton
> > coeur
> Ma bouche sera crucifiée
> Et ta bouche sera la barre horizontale de la
> > croix
> Et quelle bouche sera la barre
> > verticale de cette croix
> O bouche verticale de mon amour
> Les soldats de ma bouche prendront d'assaut
> > tes entrailles
> Les prêtres de ma bouche encenseront ta beauté
> > dans son temple
> Ton corps s'agitera comme une région pendant
> > un tremblement de terre
> Tes yeux seront alors chargés de tout l'amour
> > qui s'est amassé dans les regards de
> > l'humanité depuis qu'elle existe
> Mon amour ma bouche sera une armée contre toi
> ("Quatrième poème secret" [Fourth secret poem])

(My mouth will have the ardors of Gehenna / My mouth to you will be
a hell of sweetness / The angels of my mouth will reign in your heart /
My mouth will be crucified / And your mouth will be the horizontal bar
of the cross / And what mouth will be the vertical bar of that cross / O
vertical mouth of my love / The soldiers of my mouth will storm and take
your entrails / The priests of my mouth will sense your beauty in its
temple / Your body will toss like a region during an earthquake / Your
eyes will then be full of all the love that has accumulated in the eyes
of humanity since it began / My love my mouth will be an army against
you . . .)

His dream of the New City of the future was equally aphrodisiacal-
paradisiacal. A whole new civilization, he prophesied, with a new
humanity would rise phoenix-like out of the ashes of France. It
would constitute a multiplication of Eros, a more Dionysian dance
even than the one he danced in Paris in the spring of 1914[33] or
with Lou at the beginning of the war in Nice and Nîmes. There

would be an increase in sensuous enjoyments, voluptuousness, bacchic games, and fleshly perfection.[34] The world would drive with more speed and dynamism into new ranges of experience; explorers would move into the abysses of earth and sky; and mankind would find "all the joys":

> . . . Femmes Jeux Usines Commerce
> Industrie Agriculture Métal
> Feu Cristal Vitesse . . .
>   ("Guerre" ["War"])

(Women Games Factories Commerce / Industry Agriculture Metal / Fire Crystal Speed)

He, the poet, would be the supreme architect of this new world simply by inventing it in his mind—just as an ancient poet by inventing Icarus invented airplanes:

> C'est moi qui commence cette chose des siècles
>   à venir
> Ce sera plus long à réaliser que non la fable
>   d'Icare volant
>
> Je lègue à l'avenir l'histoire de Guillaume
>   Apollinaire
> Qui fut à la guerre et sut être partout . . .
> ("Merveille de la guerre" ["Wonder of War"])

(It is I who begin this thing of the future ages / It will be longer to realize than was the fable of flying Icarus / / I bequeath to the future the history of Guillaume Apollinaire / Who was at the war and was able to be everywhere)

He would replace Christianity—Christ having lived and died in vain, since He had failed to bring peace to the world—with his soldier-poet's religion of pagan love and, especially, the new Beauty, consisting of "Grace Virtue Courage Honor which are / Nothing but the same Beauty" ("Chant de l'honneur").

Back in Paris after being wounded in the head early in 1916, he continued to sketch out his vision of the future utopia in his poems.

Apocalyptic elevation as in "Le Brasier" would raise the rest of the
world to the poet's heights:

> . . . il y a encore là-bas un brasier
> Où l'on abat des étoiles toutes fumantes
> Et ceux qui les rallument vous demandent
> De vous hausser jusqu'à ces flammes sublimes
> Et de flamber aussi
>
> O public
> Soyez la torche inextinguible du feu nouveau
>   (prologue to *Les Mamelles de Tirésias*)

(. . . there is still a brazier up there / Where they are shooting down
smoking stars / And those who rekindle them demand of you / To raise
yourselves up to those transcendent flames / And flame in kind / / O
public / Be the inextinguishable torch of the new fire)

The tombs had already been opened by the war in a great resurrection
("A l'Italie"); a beast resembling Leviathan or the Dragon-Antichrist
of Revelation would appear in the heavens bringing with it "things
so subtly new that they will fill space . . . as if the sky began to
speak a thousand different tongues" ("Profondeurs" [Depths]). The
Lucifer of the Past was being shot down by the Saint Michael of
the Future in a dogfight of airplanes over Paris ("Les Collines");
man was flying higher now than eagles, and a fabulous merchant
of prodigious stature and unbelievable opulence was displaying extraordinary wares. Gigantic shepherds were abroad, driving great
word-browsing flocks of men; and the poet felt in himself new beings
of great dexterity bringing forth a new universe ("La Petite Auto"
["The Little Car"].[35]
    The messianic poet was even more carefully defined in the critical
writing of 1916–18. Man's new faith would be in himself and in
his species rather than in God (*Mercure de France*, 1 November 1915),
and his new religion of will, duty, and honor would take the place
of the old superstitions: "Religions promised rewards in the other
world, sociologists promise individuals happiness in this one; we
must suppress all that so that men henceforth find happiness only
in themselves through the satisfaction of duty accomplished and
honor safe-guarded. We shall arrive at this through education without weakness or error . . ." (*La Femme assise*). The poet would be

a member of the free elite as before, but he would have to be
exceptionally steadfast before the increasing danger of the reactionary
democracies of the future ordering men about in "great docile
flocks."[36] Moreover, he was at a new disadvantage, having fallen
behind the scientist in progress and influence. In fact, scientists
had forged so far ahead that "mathematicians have the right to say
that their dreams, their preoccupations surpass by a hundred cubits
the crawling imagination of poets." Just as the poet's ancestors
invented Icarus—and as Apollinaire himself invented a kind of
androgenesis in *Les Mamelles de Tirésias*—the poet must *will* the
truths of the future:

> Those who imagined the fable of Icarus . . . will find others. They
> will carry you along alive and awake into the closed, nocturnal world of
> dreams. Into the universes palpitating ineffably over our heads. Into those
> universes closer and farther from us which gravitate at the same point of
> infinity as the one we carry in ourselves.
>
> *(L'Esprit nouveau et les poètes* [The new spirit and the poets])

> [Thérèse's] husband [in *Les Mamelles*] relies completely on will. And as a
> matter of fact, we won't know the limits of will for a long time to come.
> Will is the most powerful lever for a nation as for an individual, and we
> couldn't possibly overdevelop its boldness. *(Sic,* June 1917).

Thus he must *prophesy,* prophesy being nothing more than the clair-
voyant perception of mankind's possibilities. Fortunately, on his
side he has the discoveries of the past to guide him, the artistic
masterpieces and, particularly, the great ethical patrimony of France,
its classical order, morality, duty, honor, and patriotism. These
virtues will orient him in his reasoned yet adventurous, *free* explorations into the future and the unknown. Terrible suffering and
pain will be his lot on this road of self-sacrifice and martyrdom
before the uncomprehending antipathy of the world; but his reward
will be the joyful reality of the future. "The poet is one who discovers
new joys, however painful they may be to endure" *(L'Esprit nouveau
et les poètes).*

What would be the poet's new techniques? Here Apollinaire's
muse moves farther away from the absolute aestheticism of 1908
and becomes a herald of the antiart of the dadaists and the surrealists.
He had tentatively suggested the possibility of this surrealistic marvelous, this nonaesthetic creation which would reconcile the artist

with the people, while writing in 1913 of the art of Marcel Duchamp. Now he speaks more fully of unaesthetic poetic exploration of reality and virtue *(bonté)* for the sake of pure reality, truth without art. The new "art" *"is not a decorative art, nor is it an impressionist art"* (Apollinaire's emphasis); its artists are not only men of beauty, they are also and primarily men of truth. The world has seen the end of dilettantism *(Sic,* October 1916). The artist would use, as he was beginning to do in 1913–14, all the genres, all the arts, and all the machines—like the phonograph and the film projector— in his effort to include in his great synthesis "the entire world, its noises and appearances, thought and human language, song, dance, all arts and all artifices." Inevitably it would be *surprising* to the old world, still living in the past. It will be far from naturalism and naturalism's deceitful photography of a slice of life *("trompe l'oeil")*. It will be rather what he called in 1914 *surnaturalisme* (supernaturalism) and what he christens in 1917 *surréalisme* ("superrealism" or *surrealism),* that is to say, a *translation* of reality—and he gives as his favorite example the early poet, who, when he wanted to imitate walking, invented the wheel. If this translation is more truthful than beautiful, still it may yet bring about a new beauty ("who would dare to say that, for those who are worthy of joy, what is new is not beautiful?"). It will contain in advance the new universe of joy, lyricism, knowledge, and virtue. In the final manifesto of *Calligrammes,* "La Jolie Rousse," Apollinaire ringingly speaks for himself and for his poet-companions as he describes this new universe to the traditionalists, the partisans of *order:*

> . . . Nous voulons vous donner de vastes et
> d'étranges domaines
> Où le mystère en fleurs s'offre à qui veut le
> cueillir
> Il y a là des feux nouveaux des couleurs
> jamais vues
> Mille phantasmes impondérables
> Auxquels il faut donner de la réalité
> Nous voulons explorer la bonté contrée énorme
> où tout se tait
> Il y a aussi le temps qu'on peut chasser ou
> faire revenir
> Pitié pour nous qui combattons toujours aux
> frontières

> De l'illimité et de l'avenir
> Pitié pour nos erreurs pitié pour nos péchés . . .

(We wish to give you vast and foreign domains / Where mystery in flower is offered to him who would pick it / There are new fires colors never seen / A thousand imponderable phantasms / To which we must give reality / We want to explore virtue that enormous country where all is still / We can also pursue or bring back time / Pity for us who are always fighting on the frontiers of limitlessness and the future / Pity for our errors pity for our sins . . .)

He is under the sign of his final Muse, a graceful red-headed goddess of reason (Jacqueline):

> O Soleil c'est le temps de la Raison ardent
> Et j'attends
> Pour la suivre toujours la forme noble at
> douce
> Qu'elle prend afin que je l'aime seulement
> Elle vient et m'attire ainsi qu'un fer
> l'aimant
> Elle a l'aspect charmant
> D'une adorable rousse
> ("La Jolie Rousse")

(O Sun it's the time of ardent Reason / And I await / To follow her forever the noble tender form / She assumes so I can love her only / She comes and attracts me as an iron the magnet / She has the charming appearance / Of a pretty redhead)

"Les Collines" ("The Hills")

A hill was the most appropriate symbol Apollinaire found for the superior poet, the prophet who sees farther than others into the worlds of order and adventure, the past and the future. A hill himself, he spoke down to humanity and summed up his lifetime aesthetic, orienting it toward the new reality:

> Certains hommes sont des collines
> Qui s'élèvent d'entre les hommes
> Et voient au loin tout l'avenir
> Mieux que s'il était le présent

Plus net que s'il était passé
....

Je dis ce qu'est au vrai la vie
Seul je pouvais chanter ainsi
Mes chants tombent comme des graines
Taisez-vous tous vous qui chantez
Ne mêlez pas l'ivraie au blé
      ("Les Collines," stanzas 6, 18)

(Certain men are hills / Who rise above men and see / The future from afar / Better than the present / Clearer than the past / . . . / I say what life truly is / Only I could sing like this / My songs fall like seeds / Keep quiet you who sing / Don't mix the tares and wheat)

With "Les Fiançailles" one of his two major prophetic poems, "Les Collines" may be mentioning the experience of its predecessor and similarly placing itself under Picasso's aegis in two hermetic stanzas (like many other critics, Apollinaire habitually used terms relating to depths and abysses when referring to Picasso's paintings):

Une autre fois je mendiais
L'on ne me donna qu'une flamme
Dont je fus brûlé jusqu'aux lèvres
Et je ne pus dire merci
Torche que rien ne peut éteindre

Où donc es-tu ô mon ami
Qui rentrais si bien en toi-même
Qu'un abîme seul est resté
Où je me suis jeté moi-même
Jusqu'aux profondeurs incolores
      (stanzas 30,31)

(Another time I begged / But received only a flame / Which burned me to the lips / I couldn't speak my thanks / Torch inextinguishable / / Where are you then my friend / Who turned so far in yourself / That only a gulf remained / In which I have thrown myself / Down to the colorless depths)

Again as in the 1908 poems he sacrifices his past—which now includes his young manhood—to the future; and he foresees the end of the old beauty, which he terms "that of proportions." The

following stanza, which is reminiscent of the pure, immobile beauty
at the end of *Couleur du temps,* is perhaps a picture of the death of
the legendary beauty sought by the symbolists:

> Un vaisseau s'en vint dans le port
> Un grand navire pavoisé
> Mais nous n'y trouvâmes personne
> Qu'une femme belle et vermeille
> Elle y gisait assassinée
>   (stanza 29)

(A vessel arrived in port / A great pavilioned ship / But the only soul we
found / Was a beautiful lady in red / Lying assassinated there)[37]

"Les Collines" resumes the experience of "Le Brasier":

> Bien souvent j'ai plané si haut
> Si haut qu'adieu toutes les choses
> Les étrangetés les fantômes
>   (stanza 20)

(Very often I have soared so high / So high farewell all things / Phantoms
and phantasies)

and that of early Decadent poems:

> Et je ne veux plus admirer
> Ce garçon qui mime l'effroi
>   (stanza 20)

(No longer will I admire / That boy who mimics fear)

to pass beyond:

> Le bal tournoie au fond du temps
> J'ai tué le beau chef d'orchestre
> Et je pèle pour mes amis
> L'orange dont la saveur est
> Un merveilleux feu d'artifice
>   (stanza 38)

(The dance in the depths whirls on / I have killed the fine orchestra leader / And I am peeling for my friends / The orange of which the savor / Is a marvelous fireworks)

The poet has a Rimbaud-like self-sufficiency

> Je m'arrête pour regarder
> Sur la pelouse incandescente
> Un serpent erre c'est moi-même
> Qui suis la flûte dont je joue
> Et le fouet qui châtie les autres
> (stanza 24)

(I stop to watch / On the incandescent lawn / A serpent glide it is myself / Who am the flute I play / And the whip which punishes others)

As in his last critical works, he speaks of semi-scientific explorations into the subconscious, into the powers of will and the meaning of suffering, all for the sake of new prodigies and a new virtue:

> On cherchera dans l'homme même
> Beaucoup plus qu'on n'y a cherché
> On scrutera sa volonté
> Et quelle force naîtra d'elle
> Sans machine et sans instrument
> . . . .
>
> Habituez-vous comme moi
> A ces prodiges que j'annonce
> A la bonté qui va régner
> A la souffrance que j'endure
> Et vous connaîtrez l'avenir
> (stanzas 15, 34)

(We will seek in man himself / Much more than has ever been sought / We will scrutinize his will / And its power born without / Machine or instrument / . . . / Accustom yourselves like me / To the prodigies I announce / To virtue about to reign / To the suffering I endure / You will know the future too)

At the end of the poem, using the magic talisman of poetry, he conjures up a few of those prodigies himself, little secrets that bring all the arts together and embody a *surprising* reality:

Un chapeau haut de forme est sur
Une table chargée de fruits
Les gants sont morts près d'une pomme
Une dame se tord le cou
Auprès d'un monsieur qui s'avale
                              (stanza 37)

(A top hat sits upon / A table covered with fruit / By an apple the gloves
are dead / A lady wrings her neck / Near a man swallowing himself)

He discovers a final trinity, a slave (in the manuscript, an emperor),
a car driver, and an ascending lady in an elevator, and he concludes
with his most universal symbols, the male flame and the female
rose:

Des bras d'or supportent la vie
Pénétrez le secret doré
Tout n'est qu'une flamme rapide
Que fleurit la rose adorable
Et d'où monte un parfum exquis
                              (stanza 45)

(Golden arms support life / Penetrate the golden secret / All is a rapid
flame / Flowered by the adorable rose / From which arises an exquisite
perfume)

Prometheus in an airplane, he has brought a torch to the poet of
the future; he can die content:

Je me suis enfin détaché
De toutes choses naturelles
Je peux mourir mais non pécher
Et ce qu'on n'a jamais touché
Je l'ai touché je l'ai palpé

Et j'ai scruté tout ce que nul
Ne peut en rien imaginer
Et j'ai soupesé maintes fois
Même la vie impondérable
Je peux mourir en souriant
                              (stanzas 18, 19)

(I have finally detached myself / From all things natural / I can die but cannot sin / And that which has never been touched / I have touched O I have fondled / / And I have scrutinized more / Than can possibly be conceived / Many times I have weighed / Imponderable life itself / I can die with a smile)

Jacqueline Apollinaire had these last two stanzas engraved on his tomb at the Père Lachaise cemetery in Paris.

Epilogue

The world of suffering, secular morality, and truth foreseen by Apollinaire has come into existence since his death. The surrealists, denouncing the "assassinated" poet's faith in art and his patriotism while praising his revolutionary explorations into modernism, the dream, and the past, chose the realities of the subconscious and international morality over the old symbolist beauty; and the social consciousness of modern literature has coincided with the collectivization of men "in docile flocks" following World War I. Science has indeed outdistanced art and taken remarkable voyages into truth; and the fact that Apollinaire's new age of lyrical joy has not yet resulted from the voyages of both science and art is perhaps due to a present-day lack of his supreme faith in the divinity of the individual and in the individual's creative externalizations through art.

Apollinaire's own voyages into life and art, however, resulted in works that partly combat these tendencies with their successful conciliation of beauty and truth, the individual and society, the erotic male and female, Orpheus, Empedocles, Mary, Christ, Kropotkin, and the modern, civic-minded citizen. Their synthesis of the mythic, the Hegelian, and the Freudian dialectics in a creative vision of aesthetic and social progress that would release humanity from its psychic and political repressions and send it off on the trail of the solar Eros-Christ-Pan-Creator-Poet has been a quiet but ubiquitous influence on the world's intellectual integrity since the publication of *Alcools* in 1913. Before 1918, his poems were used as revolutionary tracts in Russia, Germany, Hungary, and Poland; since his death, they have spread over the world in hundreds of translations and appreciations, until, after World War II, his dream of being read by an American black boxer, a Chinese empress, a German journalist, a Spanish painter, an Italian peasant, and an English officer in India (letter to Jeanne-Yves Blanc, 19 November 1915) has come close to actuality. Max Jacob once predicted that our century would be known as "the century of Apollinaire"; and in truth, at the centenary of his birth in 1980, celebrations and colloquia were held in towns and cities throughout the world, including Edinburgh, Warsaw, Brussels, Bari, Oxford, Nice, Belgrade, Rome, Paris, Tokyo, Madrid, Kyoto, Nagoya, New York, San Francisco, Fukuoka, Geneva, and Santa Barbara. His works are continually being translated into all the major languages; scholars pour over and argue about the meaning of every line in every major poem; and nations dispute the facts of his birth and ancestry just as he predicted they would in the first chapter of "Le Poète assassiné." And everywhere they go his works carry the same tidings of a cultural, intellectual millennium about to break forth with a new, transcendent individual creating the future in freedom and love. Bringing a sensitive appreciation of beauty to a chaotic age of anxiety, welding together nymphs and airplanes, roses and electricity, Babylon, Rome, Leningrad, Paris, Tokyo, and New York, they constitute the enchanted "castle of air" of a modern Merlin; it behooves their readers to build this castle in reality, carefully, with science and art, over the precipice of universal destruction.

In the beginning was the Word, said Apollinaire, that is to say, Poetry; if we do not travel toward it in the future we are lost. He knew that scientism in itself, like technological progress and democracy, is harmful to poets, as it is to all men; he said as much in "Orphée," *Couleur du temps,* and "Le Poète assassiné." But it is because he recognized the potential of science and democracy—as he recognized their poetic, anthropomorphic origins—that he has become an important prophet of our times. At the end of his life, in "Les Collines," he sang of the possibility of a renaissance of Aphrodite and the gods, born once again from the poet's vision of matter, of the machine:

> Ordre des temps si les machines
> Se prenaient enfin à penser
> Sur les plages de pierreries
> Des vagues d'or se briseraient
> L'écume serait mère encore
> (stanza 8)

(Sign of the times if machines / Should finally begin to think / On the beaches of precious stones / Waves of gold would break / The foam would be mother again)

The poet who invented Icarus invented the airplane; other poets like Lucian, Cyrano de Bergerac, and Jules Verne invented the rocket and the voyage to the moon; who in an age of space stations and computers could maintain that Apollinaire's vision was unrealistic?

> Moins haut que l'homme vont les aigles
> C'est lui qui fait la joie des mers
> Comme il dissipe dans les airs
> L'ombre et les spleens vertigineux
> Par où l'esprit rejoint le songe
>
> (stanza 9)

(Higher than eagles goes man / He makes the sea's joy / As he dissipates in air / Shadow and dizzy spleen / Where mind rejoins the dream)

Glossary of References

A great deal of research into Apollinaire's vast network of literary references has been going on since 1950. Unfortunately, much of what has been discovered is scattered through dozens of scholarly articles and books and is thus inaccessible to the average reader. In an effort to provide a basic map of this fascinating and often little-known territory, I offer the following glossary of the more obscure references and words that have been traced to date by myself and my colleagues. They are from the main creative works *Le Bestiaire ou Cortège d'Orphée (Best), L'Enchanteur pourrissant (Ench), Onirocritique, L'Hérésiarque et cie, Alcools, Calligrammes, Le Poète assassiné (P Ass)*, and *Les Mamelles de Tirésias (Mamelles)*. For the most part, they are references that do not appear in principal French and English encyclopedias or dictionaries. In order to be as brief as possible, I have included only the aspects of the references that are relevant to Apollinaire's work. Uncertain or ambiguous references are marked (?). Lack of space prevents stating the full sources; however, the last names of the discoverers are placed in parentheses after the references. They are Willard Bohn, Madeleine Boisson, LeRoy C. Breunig, Jean Burgos, Jean-Claude Chevalier, Robert Couffignal, Margaret Davies, Claude Debon, Michel Décaudin, Marie-Jeanne Durry, Lionel Follet, Antoine Fongaro, Anne Hyde Greet, Ian Lockerbie, Pascal Pia, Maurice Piron, Marc Poupon, Philippe Renaud, André Rouveyre, Georges Schmits, Roger Shattuck, and Raymond Warnier.

It will come as no surprise to Apollinaire's readers that many of the references are erotic. Apollinaire believed that all life, death, and art proceeded from Eros; life was Love, and Love was "not only French art but Art itself, universal art" *(Chroniques,* 26 January 1911). Poetry in its basic sense meant *creation* to him and was by definition an orphic externalization of the erotic unity of the universe found within himself: it constituted, therefore, a basic pun between His creative Word and its created world. His poems are therefore complex, highly organized puns, pantheistic microcosms of the total reality; and they are filled with erotic wordplay designed to draw the reader into that reality. I have included these words in the knowledge that most of the terms are common enough in a literary heritage that includes Aristophanes, Rabelais, and Shakespeare; and I sincerely believe that, as Apollinaire wrote in *Les Diables amoureux* (The amorous devils), they could shock only cads and pedants.

A

abelmosch "abelmosk" *(P Ass* 7). Plant used for perfume (Debon).

abigeat (P Ass 7). Roman crime of stealing a large domestic animal (Debon).

Above Bar Street (Matelot d'Amsterdam). Main commercial street of South-hampton in the Old Port.

Advocat in fame vatem dici "he advocates in times of famine that they name a divine" *(Sacrilège).* Sixteenth-century punning phrase (Boisson).

aémère (Ermite, Juif latin). Saints *aémères* are saints without saints' days; Apollinaire also used the term to apply to African sculpture *(Mercure de France,* 1 April 1917, *Anecdotiques).*

agate (Passant, Zone). Stone with portraits of kings and gods in medieval lapidaries; pun on testicle (see *Saint-Vit).*

Agla (Montre, Que faire?). Magic word in occult formulae, from initial letters of Hebrew phrase *Athab gabor leolam Adonaï,* "You are powerful and eternal, Lord" (Debon).

alcancie (Larron, Roi-Lune). "Alcancia" (Sp.), a round vessel thrown at festivals in Spain "at the time of the Moors" according to Apollinaire *(Chroniques,* 7 May 1910); symbol of women's bodies.

Aldavid (Toucher). "Offspring of David" (Arab.); Messiah.

Alkmaar (Matelot d'Amsterdam). City in Holland.

alvé (Otmika). Sweet pastry, like Turkish *halva,* made of nuts and honey (Debon).

Amblève (Ench, Que vlo-ve?). River near Stavelot, Belgium, with mussel pearls (Christian Fettweis, Marcel Thiry).

amandes de pomme de pin. "Pine-cone seeds" *(Larron)* erotic symbol.

âme. "Soul" *(Ench, Larron),* round in some Pythagorean, Gnostic beliefs (e.g., in Hermes Trismegistus); see poem *Passion* of Apoll.; see *licorne.*

améthyste (Passant, Simon Mage, Zone). Symbol of the divinity, of Cruci-fixion, in medieval lapidaries, cabalistic works.

amour socratique (Ench, Larron) amor socraticus. "Socratic love," homosexual love to the ancients; see *Socrate.*

amie de Justin Prérogue. "Mistress of J. P." *(Serviette),* Fernande Olivier; see *Justin Prérogue.*

Amphion (Amphion faux messie, Brasier). Greek builder of Thebes to the strain of his lyre, symbol of the demiurgic artist; see *Orphée.*

ancolie. "Ancoly" *(Clotilde),* flower of melancholy (Her.).

anémone (Clotilde, Fiançailles). Traditional Flower of sickness, abandon, of Venus and Adonis; literally, "windflower" (Greet).

ange. "Angel" *(Porte),* species of Mediterranean fish.

Antéros (Victoire). Anteros, twin brother of Eros, symbol of the death of love, impotence, and/or homosexuality, sometimes associated with Thanatos and Judas.

Apollonius de Thyane (Ench, Passant, Zone). Apollonius of Tyana, Pythagorean philosopher, rival of Christ, famous for chastity, mysterious disappearance; see *gymnosophites, pantaure.*

apôtre. "Apostle" *(Un soir).* Judas Iscariot, who hanged himself on a fig tree in folklore, was associated with Anteros in fin de siècle works.

arc-en-ciel. "Rainbow" *(CMA, Grâce exilée),* probably phallic symbol (Fongaro).

arc-en-terre. "Earthbow" *(De la batterie de tir),* archaic term for rainbow in wet grass, dew (Debon).

Archelaus (Ench). Enchanter in OF work *Amadis de Gaule.*

Arcture (Clair de lune). Star of occult power under which Apollinaire was born; pun on *arc,* "bow," phallic symbol; see *arc-en-ciel.*

Ardabure (Ench). Ardaburius, chief of militia at Antioch in 459 A.D.

Argyraspides. "With silver shields" *(CMA),* elite guard of Alexander, "immortal" because always remained at same number (40).

Ariane. "Ariadne" *(Arbre, Musicien de Saint-Merry),* name for prostitute (see *taupe)* and lover to Apollinaire, perhaps because of symbolist interest in labyrinths of love; also archetypal woman; see *mériennes, Musicien.*

armes. "Weapons" *(P Ass 4, Arthur roi passé),* traditional pun on phallus.

arrêtez cocher. "Stop, coachman" *(Lettre-Océan),* beginning of bawdy song (Fongaro).

arveye (Que vlo-ve?). "Au revoir" in Wall. (Piron).

asticot. "Maggot" *(Il y a),* traditional phallic symbol.

attentive. "Attentive woman" *(Un soir, Lul de Faltenin, Zone),* loving woman; prostitute; perhaps also the sea (mother) in *Lul de Faltenin.*

Attys (Vent nocturne, Giton, Histoire d'une famille). Son and lover of the mother goddess Cybele, symbol of the aroused male (see *débraillé).*

aubépine. "Hawthorne" *(Ench, Merlin),* traditionally, plant over Merlin's tomb.

Aubry-le-Boucher. "Aubry-the-Butcher" *(Musicien),* street in section of Saint-Merry *(q.v.)* famous for its barricades in popular uprisings (1830, 1832, 1834, 1848, 1851).

B

babo (Que vlo-ve?). "Baby," "simpleton" (Wall.) (Piron).

bacelle (Que vlo-ve?). "Girl" (Wall.) (Piron).

baiser florentin. "Florentine kiss" *(CMA, Larron)* lingual kiss (It.) often anal.

baller. "To dance" *(Ench, Merlin, Passant, Histoire d'une famille, Otmika, Rose de H, Que vlo-ve?),* traditional slang for "make love" (eighteenth century).

bandelettes noires et blanches. "Black and white bands" *(Larron)* Babylonian, Hebrew talismans.

barcarols (CMA). "Boatmen" (It. *barcaroli)* (Durry).

bâton. "Staff" *(Salomé),* attribute of John the Baptist in early Church iconography (Couffignal); phallic symbol *(bâton pastorale* in *D'un monstre).*

Bavière. "Bavaria" *(P Ass* 7), country satirically associated with syphilis because of OF pun on *baver,* "sweat out (in barbers' baths)" (Pia).

bec de gaz. "Gas jet" *(Un soir, Fiançailles),* phallic symbol; see *fausse oronge.*

Befana (Giov Moroni). Italian good fairy of Epiphany, from *Epiphania.*

bègue. "Stutterer" *(Larron),* Moses (from Ex. 4:10).

Beheime (P Ass 15). Hebrew for "cow" (note of Apollinaire).

belle mais noire, la. "The comely but black one" *(Ench, Larron),* the Shulamite, from Song of Solomon 1:5; the black Virgin; Cybele, Isis, etc. (?)

Belo (Roi-Lune). Antilles sailor, pure-blood Negro (Pia).

Belphégor (Larron). Pagan god, sometimes Priapus (Durry); god often associated with the sun and erotic, scatological rites.

bergère. "Shepherdess" *(Zone),* nineteenth-century name for Eiffel Tower, since it was situated on a *berge* ("bank") of the Seine and looked female.

Bé-Rieux (CMA). Probably from Provençal word *bérius,* "heretics" (J.-P. Chambon).

besace. "Double bag" *(Larron),* erotic symbol.

bobosses (Soupirs du servant). Military slang for infantrymen.

boiteuse. "Limping woman" *(Ench, Hôtels),* traditionally an erotic woman; see *La Vallière.*

Bôma (Musicien). Capital of Belgian Congo, place of a Catholic military school for native boys.

bonnet à poil. "Hairy hat" *(Que vlo-ve?),* slang for tall grenadier's hat; also for female pubes.

bouche de Dieu. "Mouth of God" *(Jolie Rousse, Simon Mage),* Sidra, the Angel of Order in cabalistic angelology (cf. *Quatrième Poème Secret).*

bouton de rose. "Rosebud" *(Annie),* slang for menses.

boyaude (Histoire d'une famille). Lyonese patois for "girl" (Debon).

bran. "Bran" *(Arthur roi passé roi future),* slang for excrement.

brasier. "Brazier" *(Brasier, Mamelles),* symbol of religious martyrdom (Her.); creative locus to Apollinaire; traditional metaphor for vulva.

brouet. "Broth" *(Larron),* food of Spartans.

brûler le dur (Lettre-Océan). "To hook a ride on a train" (slang).

bruyère. "Heather" *(Adieu, Ench),* prophetic "plant of double sight" in French folklore; good luck charm (see letter to Lou, 26 July 1915); magic plant to druids (Pliny); symbol of purity to Greeks, Romans, Celts; see *selage.*

C

Calais (CMA). Town of fourteenth-century incident involving heroic French hostages; subject of famous Rodin statue *Les Bourgeois de Calais.*

calcophane. "Chalcophanite" *(P Ass* 12), marvelous stone, reputed to clarify the voice (Debon).

calligramme (Calligrammes). Neologism formed in 1917 by Apollinaire (Debon).

capiston. "Captain" *(Saillant),* slang for *capitaine* in World War I.

Câpresse (Fenêtres). Daughter of a black and a mulatto (Debon).

Carabosse (CMA). Wicked fairy in French tales.

cas. "Case" *(Cas du brigadier masqué),* pun on male member (It. *cazzo); one* of Apollinaire's pseudonyms was *Germain Amplecas.*

cénobite. "Coenobite, monk" *(Du coton),* a popular sign on trenches during World War I was LES CENOBITES TRANQUILLES, a triple pun on *laissez nos bites tranquilles,* "Leave our pricks alone" (Debon).

centaures (Brasier). Centaurs, born of Ixion *(q.v.)* and cloud in shape of Hera; erotic symbol of human-divine poetry, prophecy.

chabin, chabine (Fenêtres, Roi-Lune). Antilles mulatto (Pia).

Chancesse (Que vlo-ve?). Tschantchesse, Wall. for *Françoise* (Piron).

chanson d'amour. "Song of love" *(Automne),* Eichendorff's *Das Zerbrochene Ringlein,* "The Broken Ring" (E. M. Wolf).

chansonnettes farcies. "Stuffed songs" *(Ench),* songs with Latin mixed in (Debon).

Chantre. "Cantor, choir leader" *(Chantre),* undoubtedly Apollinaire himself, master of the male and female forces of the world; see *cordeau, trompette marine.*

Chapalu (Ench) Capalu, Chappulu, Cath Paluc, Cath Palug, Kapalu. Monster cat, enemy of King Arthur; with cat's head, dragon's feet, horse's body, lion's tail, in romance *Bataille Loquifer* (Gaston Paris).

chape. "Cope" *(Larron, Merlin),* ecclesiastical cape; term of blazonry, two rectilinear triangles with isosceles triangle between (Durry); see *triangle.*

Chariot d'enfant. "Child's wagon" *(Chant de l'honneur),* from classic Indian play, *The Toy Cart.*

chat. "Cat" *(Mamelles* 2.7), pun on slang for vulva; see *souris.*

châtaignes. "Chestnuts" *(Rhénane),* traditional funereal fruit of All Saints' Day (folklore); heart with swords in it (Décaudin); see *sept épées.*

Chatou (Lettre-Océan). Suburb of Paris where Apollinaire's mother lived.

chauve-souris. "Bat" *(Ench),* vampire, lesbian to Apollinaire (bats menstruate, according to Remy de Gourmont); perfect, angelic animal created by Christ in Arab legend.

Chef du Signe de l'Automne. "Chief of the Sign of Autumn" *(Signe),* the angel Torquaret, the *Caput signi Autumni* of the *Heptameron* (1788) of Pierre d'Aban (Pol-P. Gossiaux).

chérubin. "Cherubim" *(Ench, Bestiaire, Rose de H),* winged steers in Jewish *Haggadah,* Assyrian myths.

chevalier de cuivre. "Copper knight" *(Ench)*, often castle guard in medieval romances.

chevaux de frise (Chevaux de frise). World War I term for barbed wire.

Che vuoi (A travers l'Europe). "What do you want?" (It.), greeting of devil in Jacques Cazotte's *Le Diable amoureux*.

chibriape (CMA). Neologism of Apollinaire from *chibre* and *priape*, French terms for phallus.

chien. "Dog" *(Cortège, Larron)*, diabolical companion of Cornelius Agrippa in tradition; in "Larron" symbol of masturbation, of Diogenes the Cynic (Gk. "dog"; see poem *Vae Soli).*

chirimoya (Lettre-Océan). Sweet Mexican fruit, like a custard-apple (Bohn).

Chichina (Favorite). Françoise in Italian (Pia).

cigale. "Cicada, grasshopper" *(Aussi bien que les cigales)*, soldiers' term for hopping shell fragments that "piss" out earth.

cinyre. "Cinnor, kinnor" *(Larron)*, Greek, Hebrew harp.

citron. "Lemon" *(Brasier, Fiançailles)*, Mary's fruit; ex-voto, lover's heart.

cloches. "Bells" *(Cloches)*, bells of Oberpleis in Rhineland (Décaudin).

Clotilde (Clotilde). Nickname for Marie Laurencin. (?)

coco (Arbre). Soft licorice drink (Greet).

cogourdes. "Yams" *(P Ass* 8), "stupid people" in slang (Debon).

colchique. "Saffron" *(Colchiques)*, poisonous flower, used by Medea; see *filles de leurs filles.*

colombe poignardée. "Poignarded dove" *(Colombe poignardée, Refus de la colombe)*, a Philippine dove with red spot on breast (André Rouveyre); erotic symbol.

colombes. "Doves" *(Chevaux de frise)*, symbols of Madeleine's breasts.

concorde. "Concord" *(Liens)*, pun on *con-corde*, "vulva-penis"; see *cordeau.*

connin. "Bunny" *(Best)*, traditional euphemism for vulva.

corbeau. "Raven" *(Ench, Vend)*, scavenger; with eagle, bird of Gallic gods (see *Lugu).*

cordeau. "String" *(Chantre)*, pun on *cor d'eau*, "water trumpet," and probably *corps d'eau*, "water body"; a measuring string; the single string *(corde)* of the trumpet marine; phallic symbol (see *Chantre, concorde, trompette marine).*

cornu. "Horny" *(CMA)*, same erotic pun in French slang as in English.

Cosaques Zaporogues. "Zaporogian Cossacks" *(CMA)*, Christian warriors of the Ukraine asked by Turkish Sultan *(q.v.)* to join his army in seventeenth-century according to legend; their violent epistolary refusal became famous.

Costantzing (Favorite). *Costantino*, name of Apollinaire's father (Pia).

couteau punique. "Punic knife" *(Larron)*, euphemism for "untrustworthy phallus."

Cox-City (Cox-City). Pun on *Cock City* or *Cocks City* (see *Horn*).

coye, coyon (Que vlo-ve?). Wall. for *couille*, slang for "testicle" and "stupid ass, coward" (Piron).

cramignon (Que vlo-ve?). Serpentine Wall. dance with song (Piron).

crâne d'Adam. "Adam's skull" *(Zone),* said to be buried at Golgotha, "the place of the skull" (Couffignal).

crapaud. "Toad" *(Echelon),* slang for a German explosive (Debon).

crapaute (P Ass 2, Que vlo-ve?). "Girl friend, fiancée" in Wall. (Piron).

crapoussin. "Little toad" *(Echelon),* small German mortar (Debon).

Croniamantal (P Ass). "Croniamental" in manuscript; from *Cronos (?) Craniomental (?).* *Cronia* is the Latin form of the Greek for *saturnalia.* Marie Laurencin confided that Apollinaire derived the name from *Cro Magnon* and *Neanderthal,* thereby vaunting the Stone-age rigidity of his phallus.

ctéïs (Roi-lune). Greek word meaning "comb," "seashell," and "vulva." Perhaps the comb in the "Orkenise" section of *Ench* has last meaning (Boisson).

cucuphe. "Cucupha" *(Ermite),* medieval medical bonnet worn by patient.

cyclope. "Cyclops" *(Ench),* slang for phallus; also anus (in poem *L'Attente*).

cyprès. "Cypress" *(CMA, Fiançailles),* funereal, phallic tree; tree of King Charming, the *oiseau bleu (q.v.).*

D

Dame-Abonde (Arbre). Principal good fairy in French folklore.

dard. "Dart, ray, sting" *(Clair de lune),* phallic symbol.

dauphin. "Dolphin" *(Best, Emigrant, Larron),* animal of Apollo; classical symbol of joy; phallic symbol.

débraillé. "Indecently dressed" *(Vent nocturne, Histoire d'une famille, Roi-lune),* used consistently by Apollinaire for "sexually aroused."

demoiselle. "Damsel, damselfly" *(Ench),* "dragonfly" in French provincial dialect; "lesbian" in French slang; cf. *Poèmes à Lou, LII.*

dendrophores (CMA). Roman tree-carriers, usually slaves or poor people, in spring festivals (Piron); see *pin.*

dernier venu ferme la porte, le. "The last comer closes the door" *(CMA),* seventeenth-century saying, meaning "he who trifles misses his chance."

Désirade (Brasier, CMA). Island in Antilles; first land Columbus found on second voyage.

diable. "Devil" *(Émigrant, Ench),* a cuckold to Apollinaire (horned); see *cornu, diablesse, Lilith.*

diablesse. "She-devil" *(Ench),* lover of dragonfly to Apollinaire (see *demoiselle, Lilith*).

Diamante (Ermite). Name from symbolist poetry (e.g., in Mendès's *Lieds de France*).

doge (Emigrant). Venetian magistrate who annually wed the sea in Renaissance; symbol of suicide by drowning to Apollinaire.

double orgueil. "Double pride" *(Lul de Faltenin)*, probably reference to testicles; see *otelles*.

douanier. "Customs officer" *(Arbre)*, nickname for painter Henri Rousseau.

doubler. "To double" *(Larron)*, in slang "to copulate."

Drikes (P Ass 16). Deformation of *Dreckig* "dirty," German name (Durry); see *Marizibill*.

druides. "Druids" *(Ench)*, refugees in Forest of Broceliande in ancient tales; had powers of shape-shifting.

E

Eau de vie. "Brandy, water of life, *aqua vita*": first title of *Alcools;* perhaps chosen partly for its erotic pun *eau de vit* ("water of phallus, sperm").

écrivisse. "Crayfish" *(Bestiaire)*, symbol of inconstancy (Her.)

Edesse (Larron). Edessa, first Christian city of Mesopotamia; Jesus invited to live there (see *roi d'Edesse); city of first miraculous portrait of Christ.

églantine. "Wild rose, eglantine" *(Fiançailles)*, Mary's flower; see *rose*.

égypan. "Aegipan" *(Ench, CMA)*, small satyr; demon to Middle Ages.

Elie. "Elias, Elijah" *(Ench, Passant, Zone)*, immortal Hebrew prophet, to return with Enoch *(q.v.)* at the end of the world; one of two olive trees of Rev. 11:4.

éliésaïte (Heresiarch). An Elkesaite, follower of Elxai, a Middle Eastern sage who believed that the Divine Spirit manifested itself successively in Adam, Enoch, Noah, Abraham, Isaac, Jacob, Moses, and Jesus (Décaudin); ancient believer that Holy Ghost was female (Debon).

Elinor (Ench, Sacrilège). Fairy mistress of Gauvain, mother of Giglan (from *Histoire de Giglan); first name of the Viscountess of Milhau.

Empédocle (Ench). Empedocles, pre-Socratic philosopher much admired by Nietzsche, Gourmont, and Apollinaire; said to have leaped in crater of Etna because of a woman (thus "Volcanique"); immortal in other legends.

Enoch (Ench, Passant, Zone). Immortal Hebrew prophet, to return at time of Antichrist with Elijah (see *Élie);* olive tree.

ensongés (Sapins). Archaic for "dreaming" or "worried" (Debon).

épervier. "Falcon" *(Automne Malade, Échelon)*, bird associated with fairies in folklore, medieval romance; symbol of sun, Ra, Horus, Apollo, Pluto.

épurge. "Spurge" *(Fiançailles)*, plant used by beggars to make artificial wounds.

équevilles (Histoire d'une famille). Lyonese jargon for "junk" (Pia).

ermite. "Hermit" *(Ermite)*, ninth Tarot card, carries staff and lantern; a prototype for the early Apollinaire; see *papesse*.

Ernest (CMA). Probably a symbol of impotence, castration, and/or homosexuality, from Apollinaire's (and Oscar Wilde's) friend Ernest La Jeunesse who was a kind of Herma: he had a high voice and, as a well-known *boulevardier*, sat by the side of the road (see *Hermès*).

Escavalon (Ench). Arthurian city common in Old French romances (Burgos).

étoile de six branches. "Six-branched star" *(Zone)*, Star of Solomon, David, Christ; Greek cross or star; chrismon; Hebrew hexalpha; see Rev. 22:16.

Etoile du Bénin. "Benin star" *(Du coton)*, official colonial military decoration (Greet, Lockerbie).

Euripos (Voyageur). The Euripus, a narrow strait in the Aegean Sea, famous for its changing tides.

Eviene (Ench). Variation of *Viviane (q.v.)* from Old French *Aivienne*.

F

fantôme de nuées. "Phantom of clouds" *(Fantôme de nuées, Roi-lune)*, Hera in cloud shape, mother of Centaurs *(q.v.)*; the poetic vision to Apollinaire; see *Ixion*.

Faltenin (Lul de F). Phallus (from *phallum tenens*) (René Louis); see *Lul*.

far tiz (Madeleine). "To give the fig" (Arab.) (Chevalier).

Farwaschen Ponim (P Ass 15). "Dirty mouth" (Heb.); note of Apollinaire.

fausse oronge. "False agaric, amanita" *(Un soir)*, poisonous, phallic mushroom, reddish spotted with white; forbidden plant in Garden of Eden.

fauste (CMA). "Favored, favorable" (Lat. *faustus*).

fèces. "Feces" *(Onirocritique)*, pun on *fesses*, "buttocks"; see *oignons, pards*.

Fenêtres. "Windows" *(Fenêtres)*, title of orphic paintings by Robert Delaunay.

fenouil. "Fennel" *(Ench, Otmika, Salomé)*, traditional metaphor for body hair.

Ferdine (Zone). Mulatto prostitute who dies of syphilis in Effe Geache's pornographic novel *Une nuit d'orgies à St. Pierre* (Pia).

feuillard. "Leafy branch" *(Ench, Vendémiaire, Lul de Faltenin, P Ass 12, Victoire)*, provincial term (Burgos), often phallic in Apollinaire; see *loulab*.

fèves. "Beans" *(Ench, Larron)*, vegetable shunned by Pythagoreans; ancient symbol of testicles (Follet).

figue, figuier. "Fig, fig tree" *(Larron)*, phallic tree with vulvic fruit.

filles de leurs filles. "Daughters (whores) of their daughters (whores)" *(Colchiques)*, adaptation of German local names for autumn saffron, from fact that the poisonous plant flowers in autumn, leafs and fructifies in spring; see *colchique*.

fleur de la passion. "Passion flower" *(Ermite, Fiançailles)*, erotic symbol (also called *passiflore*).

fleurs. "Flowers" *(Signe)*, pun on common French term for menstruation.

fleur de lys qui meurt au Vatican. "Fleur de lys which dies at the Vatican" *(Vendémiaire, A l'Italie)*, probably a reference to the downfall of Gallicanism after the Vatican Council of 1870; also the separation of church and state in France in 1905.

flûte. "Flute" (*Poème lu au mariage, Musicien de Saint-Merry*), traditional phallic symbol, instrument of Pan, Eros, Pied Piper. André Salmon was married at Saint-Merry (*q.v.*).

fontaine. "Fountain" (*Lundi rue Christine, Musicien, P Ass* 12), traditional metaphor for vulva; in *Lundi rue Christine,* with venereal disease; see *quinte.*

fopoïte (P Ass 12). Neologism, from *faux poète* "false poet" (Pia).

forêt. "Forest" (*Ench, PA, Alcools, Calligrammes, passim*), frequently a womb symbol for Apollinaire; see *jardin, mer, verger.*

fornarine (Ermite, Passant). Erotic woman to Apollinaire; neologism from name of Raphael's mistress, La Fornarina (It. "the baker's wife").

Fortunatus (Passant). Character in popular fifteenth-century German novel with magic purse and hat.

fraises. "Strawberries" (*Mamelles* 2.7), traditional name for female nipples.

Frajle (Otmika). "Miss" (*Fraulein*) in Hungarian (Warnier).

Frankenstein, Eulenbourg, Jacob Ernst, Durkheim (Roi-lune). Royal attendants at the court of Ludwig II (*q.v.*) several of whom were involved in the famous homosexual trial of 1910.

Frau Sorge (Femmes). "Madame Care" (Ger.), title of poem by Heine (Durry); name in Goethe's *Faust,* II.

fricassée. "Fricassee" (*Que vlo-ve?*), Wall. term for bacon omelette (Piron).

furet. "Ferret" (*Voyageur*), used for phallus in erotic writings; see *hérisson.*

G

garde républicaine (Musicien). Name given to *garde de Paris* in 1848; it suppressed uprising of 1851; barracks near Saint-Merry (Poupon).

gaulé. "Shaken, hit with a pole" (*Signe*), in slang, "cheated" (Poupon); see *noyer.*

Gauvain (Ench). Arthurian sun-night (*Perceval,* prose *Lancelot*); *chevalier des demoiselles* "ladies' knight" in *Méraugis;* searcher for Merlin in *Vulgate Merlin, Brut*) (Gaston Paris).

gazelle (CMA). Companion of Shakuntala (see *Sacontale*), hunted by King Dushyanta in first act of Kalidasa's play.

genévrier. "Juniper tree" (*Maison des morts*), tree symbolic of protection and refuge (Her.).

gerce (Lettre-Océan). French slang for "girl" (pejorative) (Schmits).

gibelin (CMA). Neologism from *gibel,* "mountain" in Arabic; *Mont Gibel* was medieval term for Mount Etna, place of Vulcan's forge, Morgane.

Giovanni Moroni (Giov Moroni). Apollinaire at Rome (Décaudin) with his foster parents (Davies); see *Moroni.*

giroflée. "Gilly-flower" (*Fiançailles*), a cruciform or cross-shaped flower.

giroflier. "Clove tree" *(CMA)*, tree symbolic of Christ's Crucifixion (cloves-nails).

gnou. "Gnu" *(Larron)*, Chaldean *rimi*, sacred antelope-buffalo, symbol of power. (?)

gône (Histoire d'une famille). Lyonnese patois for "child" (Debon).

Grattez-vous si ça vous démange. "Scratch yourself if it itches" *(Mamelles* 2.7), slang for "masturbate" or "make love" *(ça* is slang for penis).

grenade. "Pomegranate, grenade" *(Larron, Grenadines repentantes)*, traditional female erotic symbol.

gros. "Fat," from *gros cul*, "fat ass" *(A l'Italie)* is soldiers' name for tobacco.

grotte. "Grotto" *(Ench, Lul)*, locus of Christ, Merlin, Sirens, Thaïs in legend; erotic symbol.

grusiner (Que vlo-ve?). "Sing" in Wall. (Piron).

v' grusiner one saquoué (Que vlo-ve?). "Fix you" (literally "sing you something") (Wall.) (Piron).

guivre. "Wyvern" *(Ench)*, fabulous beast turned into princess by kiss in romance *Bel Inconnu;* common emblem in Her.

gurabié (Otmika). A round butter cake (Debon).

G.V.C. (Venu de Dieuse) Gardes des Voies et des Communications. Civil railroad and road crossing guards during the war.

gymnosophites. "Gymnosophists" *(Ench)*, Indian sages, hosts of Apollonius of Tyana *(q.v.).*

H

haleine tiède. "Warm breath" *(Lul de F)*, traditional poisonous breath of Sirens; erotic symbol along with *bouche muette.*

Hambourg (Best). Home of famous animal dealer Karl Hagenbeck.

Hanoten ne Kamoth bagoim tholahoth baleoumim (Synagogue). "He gives vengeance to the nations, punishment to peoples" (Hebrew, from Psalm 149) (Breunig).

hareng. "Herring" *(P Ass* 8), slang for "pimp"; phallic symbol; see *huître.*

hareng saur. "Kippered herring" *(A travers l'Europe)*, detail from Chagall's paintings; possibly Marie Laurencin's German fiancé (see *maison ronde, Rotsoge).*

Haute-Rue. "High Street" *(Marizibill)*, Hohe-Strasse, street in Cologne frequented by prostitutes in 1901 (Décaudin).

Hélène (Ench, Que vlo-ve?). Wife of Menelaus, quite old when abducted by Paris according to cock Pythagorus, a character in Lucian's *The Dream.*

hématidrose. "Hematidrosis" *(Ermite)*, bloody sweat (medical term); Christ's sweat in Garden of Olives; symbol of menstruation to Apollinaire; cf. *Poèmes à Lou,* XLI.

hérisson. "Hedgehog" *(Voyageur)*, traditional slang for vulva; see *furet.*

Hermès (CMA, Que vlo-ve?). Greek god, trickster, messenger, thief; phallic roadside idol, a Herma, castrated in famous incident (René Louis);

term for fin de siècle magus (from Hermes Trismagistus). See *Ernest.* (?)

Hésus (Ench). Esus, god of Gallic trinity with Taranis, Teutatès *(q.v.)*.

hibou. "Owl" *(Ench, Ermite, Bestiaire)*, bird of Minerva, Lilith *(q.v.)*, symbol of Christ in Edgar Quinet's *Ahasuérus.*

Hijo de la Cingada. "Son of a whore" *(Lettre-Océan)*, Latin-American obscenity (Bohn).

hilare. "Mirthful" *(Merlin)*, "benevolent" when related to moon, Diana.

Horn, Willy (Roi-lune). English name chosen for erotic pun (and perhaps for Apollinaire's first name, Wilhelm), like other names Amblerod, Miss Ole *(Chirugie esthétique)*, Roger *(Les Exploits d'un jeune Don Juan)*, and Cox (see *Cox-City*).

houhou (Lettre-Océan). Sound of boat whistle *(sirène);* seventeenth-century term for prostitute (see poem *L'Anguille);* see *sirène.*

huître. "Oyster" *(P Ass 8)*, common symbol for vulva; see *hareng, hareng saur.*

I

ibis (Best). Sacred bird, eater of corpses, mummified by Egyptians; pun on Latin for "you will go" (cf. Hugo's poem *Ibo)* (Durry).

Infirme divinisé (Infirme divinisé). The transcendent phallus according to psychiatrist critic Anne Clancier; see *Musicien.*

înel, înelle (Histoire d'une famille, Danseuse, Rose de H). Archaic term for "agile, lively" (Debon).

IOD (Onirocritique). The Yod, first letter of the Hebrew tetragram forming the name Yaveh; in Gourmont's *Lilith*, "male, God, and Phallus, axis of the world and axis of the Spirit" (Burgos).

Isabelle Lefaucheux (P Ass 11). Character in Rétif's *M. Nicolas* (Pia).

Ixion (Brasier, Vend, Roi-lune). King in Greek myth who embraced a cloud in the form of Hera, engendered centaurs *(q.v.)*, and was crucified on a wheel in the sky for his presumption; symbol to Apollinaire of poet embracing his vision to create poetry; see *fantôme de nuées.*

J

Jacques (Lettre-Océan). Jacques Dyssord, who ran newspaper in Tunis (Bohn).

jardin marin. "Marine garden" *(Larron, Emigrant, Voyageur)*, symbol of womanhood, the mother, the vulva.

Jean-Baptiste. See *bâton, mouches, Saint-Jean.*

jeu de la grande oie. "Game of the great goose" *(Ermite)*, coitus (from seventeenth-century French slang for foreplay, *jeu de la petite oie).*

Juan Aldama (Lettre-Océan). Postage stamp of Mexican patriot (Bohn).

Justin Prérogue (Serviette). Picasso, who had only one napkin when living in Montmartre with Fernande Olivier.

K

Kadisch. "Kaddish" (*Juif latin*), Jewish funeral prayer (Debon).

khaliandra (Otmika). Phallic dance at the end of wedding festivals in the Ukraine.

kief (Lundi rue Christine). Tunisian word for hashish.

kolo (Danseuse, Otmika). "Round dance," common group of Serbian folk dances; *Arschtanz,* "dance of the derrière," according to Apollinaire's German source; see *postkotznida.*

kordax, cordace "cordax" (*P Ass* 12). Obscene dance in ancient Greek comedy.

L

labrint (Que vlo-ve?). "Labyrinth"; *o labrint* "in a fix" (Wall.) (Piron).

Lac Lomond (Ench). Scottish lake borrowed from medieval romance *Le Roman de Brut* (which only mentions sixty islands however) (Burgos).

Lacouf (P Ass 11, *Mamelles).* Proper name based on provincial French slang for derrière, *la couffe* "the basket."

laps. "Lapse [as of time]" (*Merlin*), forced apostasy (Durry); *laps d'amour* pun on *lacs d'amour,* term of blazonry.

lard. "Bacon, fat" (*Mamelles,* 1.1), traditional erotic slang for prostitute ("un lard") and for male member; here also a pun on *l'art,* "art."

larron. "Thief" (*Larron*), Jesus Christ (see Rev. 3:3, 16:15); an orthodox, puritanical Christian; Apollinaire himself in the eyes of some critics (e.g., Durry).

larron de gauche. "Thief on the left" (*Larron*), traditionally, Gestas, the impenitent thief of the Passion.

laurier. "Laurel" (*Cortège, Fiançailles, P Ass*), bitter-tasting plant sacred to Apollo, Orpheus, poets; pun on name Laurencin.

La Vallière (Hôtels). Pious, limping mistress of Louis XIV; see *boiteuse.*

Léonard Delaisse (Serviette). Mécislas Golberg, who died of tuberculosis in 1907.

Léviathan (Ench, P Ass 17, *Synagogue).* Talmudic beast to be killed by God, eaten by faithful at end of world (Breunig).

liberté (Fenêtres). Name of Parisian newspaper; see *temps.*

licorne. "Unicorn" (*CMA, Ermite, Larron*), the flesh (phallic); the soul; zodiac sign of Virgin under which Apollinaire was born; see *triangle isocèle.*

lien. "Link" (*Liens*), the "link between all lovers" is the phallus; see *concorde, Pont Mirabeau, pontifes.*

ligure. "Ligurian" (*Larron*), "musical" to Apollinaire (from Celtic; see letter to Lou, 25 December 1914). Also probably a Latinism from *ligurio,* "to lick," and thus "caressing" with erotic implications (*aller en Ligure* "to go to Liguria," was an erotic term for "perform cunnilingus").

Lilith (Ench, Ermite, P Ass 7, 15). "Owl" (Heb.; see Isaiah 34:14); first mother, disobedient wife of Adam, wife of Beelzebub, lives in Red

Sea, howls (folklore); symbol of menstruation, lesbianism, sterility to Apollinaire; see *diable, diablesse, Mer Rouge, Naama.*

Linde (Ench). Lindus, city of roses on Isle of Rhodes, first inhabited by Telchins (Burgos); city in which Apollonius of Tyana *(q.v.)* disappeared.

Loreley (Loreley). Adaptation from Clemens Brentano's "Loreley."

Lorie (Ench, Ermite, Colombe poignardée). Fairy love of Gawain in *Rigomer;* love of Apollinaire (?).

lotte. "Burbot" *(Fenêtres),* sacred fish of Tanit, goddess of moon, figures in Flaubert's *Salammbô;* see story *Le Cubisme culinaire.*

loulab. "Leafy branch" in Hebrew *(Synagogue),* traditional object in Jewish rites, probably with a phallic origin; see *feuillard.*

Ludwig II (Passant, CMA, Roi-lune). "Mad King Louis" of Bavaria, "the moon King," Wagner lover, admirer of Louis XIV, homosexual, had himself pulled in boat by swans in moonlight, drowned in Starnberger Sea. Cult figure to symbolists (e.g., Paul Verlaine) because of his love of art.

Lugu (Ench). Lug or Lugus, Gallic Mercury or Apollo; "crow" (Celtic; the site of Lyon, *Lugudunum,* was said to have been first indicated by crows).

Luitpold (CMA). Regent of Bavaria 1886–1912, "tutor" of mad regent Othon and King Ludwig II *(q.v.).*

Lul (Carte postale, CMA, Lul de F). Phallic symbol (Flemish for "pipe," "phallus"); pseudonym of Apollinaire; see *Faltenin.* (?)

lune. "Moon" often symbol for the derrière in Apollinaire (e.g., in *Clair de lune, Que vlo-ve?, Ermite, Roi-lune)* or a woman's breast *(Onirocritique, P Ass* 9); see *miel, Rosemonde, Roi-lune.*

Lydiennes. "Lydian women" *(Larron),* women in ancient Asia Minor who earned their dowries through prostitution, thus they have "Ligurian" ("caressing") voices (see *ligure).*

M

Macarée (P Ass). "Happy," feminine name from Rétif's *M. Nicholas* (Pia).

maclotte (Ench, Marie). "Big head" or "tadpole" in Wall. dialect; Wall. folk dance; religious festival dance; Marie Laurencin skipping rope (Décaudin).

Madoine (Ench). Fairy at castle of Morgane le Faye (q.v.), mistress, enchantress of Laris in story *Claris et Laris.*

main coupées. "Cut-off hands" *(Marie, Rhénane d'automne, Signe),* dead leaves, like those of oaks in Stavelot, Belgium (Décaudin) (women with amputated hands are often associated with trees in European folklore).

Main de Massiges. "Massiges's Hand" *(Désir)* name of French plateau; system of German defenses (a *main)* near town Massiges in World War I (Debon).

Maison des morts. "House of the dead" *(Maison des morts),* open morgue in

Munich's old North Cemetary visited by Apollinaire in 1902 (Décaudin).

maison ronde. "Round house" *(A travers l'Europe),* famous old building *la Ruche* ("the beehive") in Montparnasse, place of Chagall's studio in 1914 (Greet); also probably an erotic allusion to Marie Laurencin (see *hareng saur, Rotsoge).*

malefaim (Serviette). Archaic: "hungry rage" (Debon).

Malourène (CMA). Perhaps neologism from *mâle ou reine* ("male or queen") or *malheur reine* ("queen misfortune"). (?)

mamzelle à vinde (P Ass 1). "Woman for sale" in Wall. (Piron).

mappemonde. "Map of the world" (map in two connected hemispheres, like a figure eight on its side) *(Giton),* traditional slang for derrière.

Mara (Otmika). "Mary" (Slav) (Warnier).

Marco (Otmika). From Marco Kraljevic, Slavic folk hero (Warnier). (?)

Mareye (Colombe poignardée). Marie Dubois, Apollinaire's Belgian love in 1899.

marguérite. "Daisy" *(CMA),* flower of game "she loves me, she loves me not."

Marizibill (Cox-City, Marizibill, P Ass 16). "Mary-Sybil" *(Marie Sibyll),* popular name at Cologne; see *Drikkes, Haute-Rue.*

M. D. (A travers l'Europe). Either Maurice Denis or Marcel Duchamp, both artist friends of Apollinaire.

mec à la mie de pain. "Crummy guy, pimp" *(Lundi rue Christine),* common slang for small-time hoodlum, insignificant individual.

Médaillon toujours fermé. "Locket still closed": the title Apollinaire gave to the first seven poems in the *Lueurs de tirs* section of *Calligrammes,* referring to his lost love Marie Laurencin; pun on *médaillon,* "vulva" or "anus" in French slang.

Meicabl (P Ass 15). "Devil" (Heb.); note of Apollinaire.

menhir (Ench). Phallic god in European folklore, nineteenth-century archaeology.

merde de pape. "Pope's excrement" *(Ench),* from traditional Breton riddle, "What is the rarest thing in the world?"

mériennes (Musicien). Women from the Saint-Merry quarter in Paris; see *mordonnantes.*

Merlin (Ench, Merlin, P Ass). In history an epileptic Celtic bard, prophet; in mythology an archetypal figure like Prometheus, Orpheus, Hercules; in Arthurian legend the son of a priestess, son of a virgin and a devil or serpent, son of Satan, is baptized, immortal, teaches and loves Morgane *(q.v.),* teaches Viviane *(q.v.)* to make springs (cf. *P Ass* 12), is lover of 100-year-old woman in Richard's *Prophéties de Merlin,* is enchanted, entombed by Viviane, goes to Jerusalem in *Robert de Borron,* goes to Rome in *Livre d'Artus,* is the Antichrist, a divine prophet; in Edgar Quinet's "Merlin l'enchanteur" the son of Satan, represents French genius, humanity, marries Nature-Viviane, engenders son, destroys Hell, leads nations to freedom (Hésart de la Villemarqué).

Mer Rouge "Red Sea" *(CMA, Ench, Larron, P Ass* 7). Home of Lilith *(q.v.);* symbol of sterility, menstruation to Apollinaire; *Poèmes à Lou, XLI.*

mesure du doigt. "Finger size" *(Venu de Dieuze),* Lou's ring size; visual pun on letter Q, pronounced *cul,* "ass" (Fongaro).

Métive. "Mulatto woman" *(Zone),* perhaps an allusion to Marie Laurencin, who was reputed to be of Creole extraction.

Mia (Colombe poignardée, P Ass 8). Love of Apollinaire at Monaco. (?)

miel. "Honey" *(Clair de lune),* euphemism by antithesis for *merde,* "shit," in French slang (note American term, "honeywagon"); see *rayon de lune.*

mirliton. "Little flute" *(A travers l'Europe),* reference to Marie Laurencin's toy flute (Poupon); often an erotic symbol in French erotica.

moine de Heisterbach (Sacrilège, P Ass 12). Miraculous sleeper in legend of Heisterbacensis Caesarius.

mordonnantes (Musicien), adj. Neologism from *mort donnantes,* "death-givers," referring to "the little death" *(la petite mort)* of prostitutes (Poupon); see *Ariane, Pâquette, Musicien, Saint-Merry.*

Morgane le Faye (Ench, Merlin, P Ass 11, *Giov Moroni).* Enchantress, traditionally young and beautiful but old and ugly to Apollinaire, temptress of knights in her castle Sans Retour on Mount Gibel (Etna); student, mistress of Merlin; dispenser of mirages *(fata morgana);* symbol of lust, death, night, art to Apollinaire; see *Merlin, vieille femme.*

Moriane (Ench, P Ass 1). Mauritania, Africa, country of the Moors in medieval romances *Brut, Morien,* etc. (Gaston Paris).

morue. "Cod" *(Mamelles* 2.3), pun on common slang for "prostitute."

Moroni (Giov Moroni). Leading Mormon angel; see *Giovanni Moroni.*

mouches. "Flies" *(Ench, Musicien, Santé, Tourbillon de mouches),* sterility symbols, lesbians to Apollinaire (cf. prose poem *Pablo Picasso);* see *quinconces, Saint-Jean.*

mouches de la Saint-Jean. "Flies of Saint John Day" *(CMA),* fireflies (called *mouches de Saint-Jean* in Belgian folklore); see *Saint-Jean.*

mouches ganiques (Best, Que vlo-ve?). Invisible flies used by Lapp sorcerers to torment evil doers; from Norwegian *ganne,* "to hex."

mouqu' dans d'huile, enn'. "A fly in oil" *(Venu de Dieuse),* northern French patois for a failure, a "sad sack" (Debon).

mouton. "Sheep" *(Lettre-Océan),* probably a bottle of Mouton wine (Bohn).

murènes. "Muraenas" *(CMA),* species of eels to which Vedius Pollon, a Roman gastronome, fed slaves according to Pliny, Seneca, Tertullian, etc., also Victor Hugo (Piron), Karl Marx, and Gustave Moreau.

Musicien (Musicien de Saint-Merry). Phallic god like Priapus, Dionysos, Eros, Pan, and/or the phallus itself, a Pied Piper figure in an ancient quarter of Paris famous for its many prostitutes. Apollinaire was a tour guide in the quarter in 1913; see *Ariane, Aubry-le-Boucher, flûte, mériennes, mordonnantes, Pâquette, Saint-Merry*.

myrtaie (Onirocritique, Victoire). Neologism for "myrtle grove" (Debon).

myrthe. "Myrtle" *(Maison des morts, Victoire)*, plant of Limbo, of Venus.

N

Naama, Lilith, Aguereth, Manala (P Ass 15). Demon mothers, dominated by Solomon, governesses of four seasons in Hebrew lore (Couffignal).

nageur. "Swimmer" *(CMA, Lul de F, Vend)*, lover, poet; Apollinaire.

Nancéenne. "Woman from Nancy" *(2e canonnier conducteur)* prostitute, subject of bawdy World War I ballad sung to tune of reveille.

navire pavoisé. "Pavilioned ship" *(Collines)*, magic, unmanned boat of folklore, medieval romance, symbolist poetry; see works *Le Printemps* and *Onirocritique*.

noir et blanc. "Black and white" *(Emigrant, Larron)*, ancient Oriental color talismans; see *bandelettes*.

noms six par six. "Names six by six" *(Vend)*, number of names of Apollinaire, Croniamantal.

Noubosse (CMA). Neologism of Apollinaire for pudendum (Lawler, Davies) or for phallus (Fongaro); from *faire la nouba* and *se donner une bosse* "to go on a spree" (Greet); from Latin *nubo, nubere*, "to marry" (Follet).

noyer. "Walnut tree" *(Signe, Simultanéités)*, blazon of persecuted innocence (Her.); phallic, cursed tree to nineteenth-century mythologists (e.g., Gubernatis).

O

oblong (Cortège, Larron, Lul de F). Shape of light, fire, vision; of Apollinaire's face; possibly derives from "the golden section" in art.

oignon. "Onion" *(Onirocritique)*, slang for derrière; see *fèces, pards*.

oiseau bleu. "Blue bird" *(Fiançailles, Tzigane, Un oiseau chante)*, Roi Charmant ("King Charming") changed into bird *couleur du temps* ("color of the weather") in story *L'Oiseau bleu* by Mme d'Aulnoy; see *cyprès, Truitonne*.

oiseau de Bénin "Benin bird" *(P Ass)*. Apollinaire's name for Picasso, from an African sculpture from that country.

oiseau de la quintaine. "Quintain bird" *(Fiançailles)*, phoenix; phallus; cock in religious feast-day jousts in Germany; Christ; see *quintaine*.

oiseau tranquille. "Tranquil bird" *(Cortège)*, one of several footless birds that nest in mid-air according to Oriental, medieval tales (bird of paradise, hummingbird, etc.). (?)

oiseau gemmipares. "Gemmiparous birds" *(Larron)* birds born of buds, issued from fruit in medieval travel literature, cabalistic writings; "birds who make pearls" to Durry (?); see *GA* 4, 116ff.

oke (Otmika). Turkish weight, equivalent to 1,280 grams.

olivier. "Olive tree" *(Ench)*, tree of Minerva; see *Elie, Enoch*.

ombre du soleil. "Shadow of the sun" *(Photographie)*, from *ombre de soleil*, term of Her. (?)

onirocritique. "Interpretation of dreams" *(Onirocritique)*, archaic term.

or du rhin. "Rhine gold" *(Nuit rhénane, Roi-lune)*, title of Wagnerian opera, favorite of Ludwig II of Bavaria *(q.v.)*.

orient. "Orient" *(Palais)*, pun on the East and the "orient" of a pearl; symbolist term for instinctive self; reference to *aller en orient*, "to go to the Orient," slang for fellatio.

Orkenise (Ench). Arthurian town visited by Perceval, Lancelot, etc. (Burgos).

Orphée (Best, Larron, Poème lu au mariage). Orpheus, symbol of poet martyred (beheaded) by women; occult, messianic figure (rose again in Orphic mysteries); disciple of Dionysus; traditionally the first pederast *(Larron)*; major symbol along with Amphion *(q.v.)* of the divine creator, prophet, magician, and patron of the arts who moves all nature to his lyre.

orphelin. "Orphan" *(Vend, Voyageur)*. Adjective for "disinherited," "abandoned," "deprived" (archaic).

otelle (Lul de F). Blazon in shape of peeled almond, spear head, cicatrized (raised) wound (Poupon); erotic symbol to Apollinaire; see *double orgueil*.

oua-oua (Fenêtres). "Wawa," Canadian Indian name for Canada Goose.

P

pad (Lettre-Océan). From Spanish for "father," "padre" (Schmits).

padalobre (P Ass 11). Slang for "porter" (Debon).

pahule (P Ass 1). Wall. for "calm," "peaceful" (Piron).

pain. "Bread" *(Ench, Ermite, Larron, P Ass 1, Sacrilège, Vend, Zone)*, symbol of the flesh (testicles in *L'Ermite*), resurrection, Christ, hospitality.

palais. "Palace, palet" *(Palais)*, female erotic symbol.

Pâline (CMA). Name of sword, perhaps neologism from *pâle* and *câline* (James Lawler).

Pallas (Larron). Goddess of femininity, reason, geometry; name from Greek for "virgin," "maiden"; see *triangle*.

Pan (Un monstre de Lyons, Ench, CMA, Brasier, Musicien [?], Chant du horizon). Shepherd of flock of sphinx *(q.v.)*, symbol of poetry, art, love, death, and the life force to Apollinaire; god of noonday rutting; see *pâtre*.

panéthnique (Cas du brigadier). Neologism, "all-peopled" (Debon).

pantaure (Larron). Old French spelling of the *Pantarbe*, a magical magnetic stone shown to Apollonius of Tyana *(q.v.)* in India (Philostratus, 3:46).

panthère (CMA, Chevaux de frise). Traditional term for seductive woman or prostitute, related to Pan by some etymologists.

paon pythagorique. "Pythagorean peacock" *(Larron)*, bird of Pythagoras's transmigration.

papesse. "Popess" *(Cox-City, Ermite)*, the legendary ninth-century antipopess Joan, second Tarot card, a seated woman (see *Ermite);* a Catholic woman; pope's mistress; courtesan. (?)

Pâquette (CMA, Musicien). Traditional name in French folklore for pretty, available peasant girl (e.g., in *Candide)*.

pard. "Feline" *(Onirocritique)*, from Latin for "farter," from flatulent reputation of cat family; see *fèces, oignon*.

pasquéïe (P Ass 1). Wall. folksong (Piron).

pâtre. "Shepherd" *(Brasier, P Ass 10)*, Pan *(q.v.);* Picasso in *P Ass.*

Peau-rouge. "Redskin" *(Fantôme de nuées)*, American Indian; Latin Quarter bohemian (see *Flâneur des deux rives*, chap. 1).

pêcher. "Peach tree" *(Larron)*, the forbidden tree of Eden according to Gourmont *(Lilith);* pun on *péché*, "sin" (Poupon).

pédauque. "Goose-footed" *(P Ass 15)* (Debon).

pendé. "Five" *(Otmika)*, insult, from Greek meaning "take all five" (Debon).

péket (Que vlo-ve?). Cheap brandy, gin in Wall. (Piron).

pendeco (Lettre-Océan). Sic for *pendejo*, "pubic hair" (Sp.), Latin-American obscenity (Bohn).

pentacle (Brasier). Five-sided astral figure, man, the microcosm-macrocosm, Pan, God, in magic; see *quinconces*.

perruque à canon. "Wig for a cannon" *(SP)*, perhaps camouflage; probably pubic hair, from bawdy song with refrain *perruque à morpion*, "wig for lice" (Fongaro).

petit frère. "Little brother" *(P Ass 11)*, common European euphemism for penis.

pétomane (P Ass 11). Term for professional farter, popular at carnivals at the turn of the century (from *péter*, "to fart"); see *vents*.

Phantase (dedication of *L'Hérésiarque et cie*). Son of Sleep in Greek myth, personification of bizarre imagination (Décaudin).

phénix. "Phoenix" *(CMA, Zone)*, symbol of poetic, erotic renewal, death-birth to Apollinaire; Christ in medieval bestiaries; flew to pyre accompanied by world's birds in Latin legends; see *oiseau de la quintaine*.

Pie X (Infaillibilité, Zone). Pius X, the antimodern pope (1903–14).

pierre d'un coq. "Cock's stone" *(Larron)*, the *alectorian* or *cock's stone*, found in cock's maw; a *bezoar* or amulet in ancient times often worn on necklace; virility symbol, aphrodisiac; see *Tanagre*.

pierre fitte (P Ass 12). From Latin *petra ficta*, "planted stone" (Debon).

pigeonnier. "Pigeon loft" *(Loin du pigeonnier),* Apollinaire's nickname for his apartment in Latin Quarter.

pihi (Fenêtres, Zone). Fabulous Chinese bird with one eye, one wing, flew in couples, male to right, female to left (Décaudin).

pimpan (Que vlo-ve?). Slang for sexual intercourse.

pimus (Porte). Legendary Chinese fish with one eye, one fin, swims in mixed couples (Décaudin).

pin. "Pine" *(Vent nocturne),* tree of Atys into which he was metamorphosed, carried in spring fertility festivals; phallic symbol; see *dendrophores.*

pipe, pipeau. "Pipe" *(Mamelles* 2.7), slang for phallus.

pissala (Giton). Provençal garlic sauce (Debon).

Plandrong (Giton). Local term for bad person, rascal, tramp (Debon).

Polydamne (Ench). Wife of Egyptian Thoon, taught Helen *(q.v.)* how to make *nepenthe.*

pont des Reviens-t'en. "Bridge of Return" *(CMA),* opposite of *pont de Nul Retour,* "Bridge of No Return," of medieval romance (term invented by Apollinaire ?).

Pont Mirabeau. "Mirabeau Bridge" *(Pont Mirabeau),* bridge in Paris near apartments of Apollinaire and Marie Laurencin in Auteuil; erotic symbol: Apollinaire edited the erotic works of Count Mirabeau (1749–91).

pontifes. "Pontifs" *(Liens),* "bridge-builders" (from Lat.); see *lien.*

Port-Aviation (Zone). Airport at Javisy-sur-Orge south of Paris in 1912 (Warnier).

porte. "Door" *(Porte, Marizibill, Lettre-Océan, Voyageur),* often erotic symbol of woman, the beloved, the mother of Apollinaire.

postkotznika (Otmika). Kind of *kolo (q.v.)* often accompanied by licentious and seditious songs.

pouhons (Petite auto). Wall. word for mineral springs (Piron).

probloque (Lundi rue Christine). French slang for "proprietor, landlady."

Psylles (Collines). The Psylli, African people who perished battling the South Wind when it dried up their reservoirs (Heroditus); snake charmers, diviners to ancients.

puiseurs d'eau. "Water drawers" *(Larron),* Chaldean priests who used water from sacred Euphrates for divining.

pupille de mon oeil. "Pupil of my eye" *(Fiancée posthume, Zone),* term of endearment (same as "apple of my eye") from Deut. 32:10.

pyrauste (CMA). "Fire-lighter," moth that lives in fire on Cyprus (Pliny).

Q

quadruple triangle (Simon Mage). Cabalistic talisman (as △ or ⊠); early Greek nimbus for Christ; symbol of absolute divinity in Christian iconography.

quarantaine (Fiançailles). "Age of forty" (Durry), "forty in number" (Davies); period of mourning (Debon); "quarantine"; "Lent." (?)

quarante de Sébaste. "Forty of Sebastus" *(CMA),* sainted Christian soldiers frozen and burned by Romans in Asia Minor in fourth century (Holy Day: March 9).

Quélus (Roi-lune). Homosexual companion of Henri III.

quenouille. "Distaff" *(Palais, CMA),* phallic symbol.

quinconce. "Quincunx" *(Ench, Salomé),* magic five-starred pattern, associated with erotic death dances of flies, Salome *(q.v.)* by Apollonaire; see *mouches, pentacle.*

quintaine (Fiançailles). The quintain or jousting target, sometimes a ring; female erotic symbol; see *oiseau de la quintaine.*

quinte major (Lundi rue Christine). Equivalent of a royal flush in a card game; popular term for a hard slap in the face (Debon); *quinte* can also be a coughing spasm, a fifth in music, syphilis, and slang for the vulva (Eng. *coynte,* from OF *quince* or *quinte).* (?)

quinze signes du jugement dernier, les. "The fifteen signs of the Last Judgment" *(Ench, Passant),* early Christian and medieval list of fifteen miraculous happenings at end of the world, earthquakes, burning oceans, etc. (Bede, Saint Augustine, etc.).

quiot' (Venu de Dieuze). M' *quiot' fille* is northern French patois for "my little girl" (Debon).

queue. "Tail" *(Eventail de saveurs),* common slang for phallus; here it becomes attached to a bird, *oiseau,* the maidenhead (Fonteyne).

quoniam (P Ass 1). Medieval term for genitalia, as Apollinaire states, but for *female* genitalia; is this an error or, as Renaud believes, a reference to Croniamantal's female appellations (?).

R

rampioule (Que vlo-ve?). "Bindweed" in Wall. (Piron).

rayon de lune. "Moon ray" *(Clair de lune),* pun on *rayon de miel,* "honeycomb," and the *raie* or cleft of the buttocks (see *roseraie;* in letter to Lou of 13 May 1915, Apollinaire speaks of a whip made of *rayons de lune);* see *lune, miel, rose des vents.*

R. D. (Tour). Robert Delaunay, orphic painter of the Eiffel Tower; see *Fenêtres.*

rimbambelle ursuline. "Ursuline procession" *(Cortège),* Saint Ursula and her 11,000 virgin companions said to have been massacred by the Huns in Cologne in either the third or fifth century.

rival (Lul de F, Merlin et la vieille femme). Pun: both "rival" and "fellow dweller on the same bank" (OF).

robe sans couture. "Seamless robe" *(Ermite)* from John 19:23.

roi d'Edesse. "King of Edessa" *(Larron),* Abgar V "The Black" (7 B.C.–

50 A.D.) considered first Christian king by ancients; invited Jesus to Edessa *(q.v.)* according to fourth-century legend.

Roi-lune. "Moon king" (see *Ludwig II, lune*).

rois mages de Cologne. "Magi of Cologne" *(Cortège, Ench, Rose de H)*, relics of Three Wise Men said to be in Cologne Cathedral, also church of Hildesheim.

romarin. "Rosemary" *(Maison des morts, Rhénane d'automne)*, funeral flower; flower of remembrance.

Rosalie (A l'Italie). Soldiers' name for bayonet in World War I.

roseau. "Reed" *(Larron)*, mock scepter given to Jesus (Matthew 27:29); Christian symbol of humility.

rose des vents. "Rose of the winds" *(Clair de lune, Merlin)*, navigator's compass; the yellow moon; derrière (cf. *"ton derrière de miel et de lumière"* in *Tendre comme le souvenir*, 26 November 1915), a fin de siècle pun; see *lune, miel, roseraie*.

Rosemonde (Best, Palais, Rosemonde). Rosamond Clifford, "the Rose of the World," mistress of Henry II of England, said to have dwelt in a labyrinthine palace at Woodstock and to have been killed by the jealous queen, Eleanor of Aquitaine; pun on Dutch for "rosy mouth," (Greet) and German for "rosy moon" (Poupon); see *lune*.

roseraie. "Rose garden" *(Palais)*, pun on *raie rose*, "rosy cleft" (of buttocks) and *rayon de lune (q.v.)*.

rose sans épines. "Rose without thorns" *(Merlin et la vieille femme)*, common medieval term for Virgin Mary.

Rotsoge (À travers l'Europe). "Red wake" or "red trail" (Ger.), perhaps a nickname for artist Marc Chagall; probably also a reference to menstruation (cf. end of *Ench*); see *hareng saur, maison ronde*.

Roue. "Wheel" *(Tour)*, huge Ferris wheel near Eiffel Tower before World War I.

roux. "Russet" *(Histoire d'une famille, Larron, Un soir, Marizibill, Zone, P Ass 8)*, color of King David's and Christ's hair in Byzantine art, Hebrew prophecies, apocalyptic works, etc. (Couffignal); traditional color of evil Jew's hair (diabolical) in Mysteries, Shakespeare, Marlowe, etc.

Roy. "King" *(Lettre-Océan)*, pun on Apollinaire's friend Pierre Roy (Bohn).

rue St-Isidore (Lettre-Océan). Former red-light district in Havana (Bohn).

S

sac à malice. "Trick sack" *(Echelon)* magician's bag, slang for army pouch (Debon).

Sacontale. "Guarded by birds" *(CMA)* Shakuntala, Indian queen, heroine of Kaladasa's fifth-century play of the same name; see *gazelle*.

Sacré nom de Dieu quelle allure. "Holy name of God, what speed" *(2e canonnier conducteur)*, refrain of soldiers' song *L'Hôtel-Dieu*.

Sainte-Fabeau (CMA, Onirocritique). Invented name for sword, probably from *beau phallus* (Davies) or *fabo,* provincial word meaning "bean, phallus" (Fongaro); in any case, a phallic saint.

Saint-Jean, la (CMA). 24 June, the nativity day of Saint John the Baptist, when fires, fireworks, firebrands are lighted; see *mouches de la Saint-Jean.*

Saint-Merry (Musicien de Saint-Merry). Twelfth-century church, picturesque quarter of Paris well-known for its prostitutes; see *Musicien, Ariane, Pâquette.*

Saint-Vit. "Holy Face {*Vis*}" *(Passant, Zone),* the Prague cathedral; Apollinaire implies a pun on *Vit,* "phallus," especially because he was first baptised in the church of Saint Vito at Rome; see *agate, Eau de vie.*

Salomé (Danseuse, Salomé). Salome, favorite symbol of immortal fatal woman to nineteenth-century authors; same as *Hérodiade;* died in river with head on plate of ice in medieval legend and in seventh-century Apocrypha *(Letter of Herod).*

sardine (P Ass 17). Fish big enough at Marseilles to block harbor according to boast of Marseillais (Roger Shattuck).

Schinderhannes (P Ass 11, Schinderhannes). Famous eighteenth-century robber, enemy of Jews, hanged in 1803 (Décaudin); his companions included Jacob Porn, the Bible lover Benzel, and his mistress, the sixteen-year-old violinist Juliette Blaesius (Durry).

sciomancie (Sur les prophéties, Départ de l'ombre). Divination by spirits of the dead (note pun on *ombres,* "shadows/spirits") (Debon).

scorpions (Ench). Animals that sting themselves to death when ringed with fire (Migne, *Encycl.).*

scurriles (Larron). "Scurrilities, rowdy jokes" (archaic), traditional in Roman triumphs.

sel. "Salt" *(Larron),* traditional symbol of hospitality.

selage (P Ass 10, Ench). Selago, magic plant of druids (Pliny); see *bruyère.*

sept épées. "Seven swords" *(CMA),* swords piercing Mary's or Christ's heart in Christian tradition (from Luke 2:35), see *châtaigne.*

sept femmes. "Seven women" *(Nuit rhénane),* the seven bathers of a Rhine legend of Oberwesel combined with legends of green-haired nixies (Décaudin).

serpents qui s'entr'aiment. "Serpents making love" *(Larron),* basic creation myth (Indian, Greek [Zeus and Persephone], Druidic, etc.); homosexuals ("sixty-nine"); Tiresias's serpents. (?)

Sicile (Vend). Sicily, place of disastrous earthquake of 28 December 1908.

signe du troisième mois. "Sign of third month" *(Fiançailles),* Virgo the Virgin, zodiac sign of third month of summer under which Apollinaire was born.

silence (Larron). Harpocrates, sometimes an erotic god (Durry).

singe. "Monkey" *(Du coton)* soldiers' term for tin of beef; also shell (Debon).

sirènes (CMA, Fiançailles, Emigrant, Ench, Lettre-Océan, Vend, Zone). Sirens, woman-birds, enchantresses of the Strait of Messina; erotic women, prostitutes in French slang; "boat whistles"; see *haleine, houhou.*

sixième sens. "Sixth sense" *(Fiançailles),* traditionally, sexual love.

Socrate (Ench, Larron). Socrates, symbol of homosexual love to Apollinaire (see *Chroniques,* 4 May 1911); see *amour socratique.*

soleil dansant. "Dancing sun" *(Merlin, Fiançailles),* common European belief that the sun dances on Easter Day.

Soleils. "Suns" *(Fenêtres),* pun on name for a species of shellfish (Renaud).

sol hawai (Que vlo-ve?). "Sur le pouce"—literally "sur le boyau"—"on the run" in Wall. (Piron).

songe matinal. "Morning dream" *(Ench, Hérésiarque, Juif latin),* dream that is always veracious, according to Apollinaire; see first version of *Juif latin.*

souris. "Mouse" *(Dame, Mamelles* 2.7), pun on woman, prostitute, vulva (slang).

SP (SP). Initials for *Secteur Postal* at the war (Debon).

sphinx (Brasier, Ench, Couleur du temps). Female symbol of erotic wisdom, commits suicide when her riddles are guessed (Apollinaire puns on "little death" or orgasm); "prostitute" in Latin slang; in *Larron,* the male, Egyption sphinx; see *Pan.*

sphingerie. "Place of sphinxes" *(Brasier)* neologism; perhaps a brothel. (?)

statues suant. "Statues sweating" *(Larron),* phenomenon noted by Cicero, etc.

stupre (Hérésiarque, Roi-lune). Latinism (from *stuprum),* "rape of a virgin."

Suger (Musicienne). Twelfth-century abbot, lived near Saint-Merry, influenced Gothic style (e.g., Notre Dame cathedral).

Sultan (CMA). Turkish Sultan, either Mohammed IV (1642–91) or Ahmed III (1673–1736); see *Cosaques.*

surmarine (Voyageur). Neologism, opposite of submarine (Debon).

svastica (Ench, Saillant). Sun symbol; sign of fertility, happiness (Boisson); in novel *La Fin de Babylone,* it is tattooed on the pubis of fertile women.

synagogue (Synagogue). Building at Unkel near Honnef in Rhineland (Breunig).

T

tacot (Du coton). Soldiers' slang for brandy.

Tanagre (Larron). Tanagra, former Spartan town famous for its fighting cocks; see *pierre d'un coq.*

Taranis la femelle. "Taranis the female" *(Ench)* member of Gallic trinity with Esus (Hésus), Teutatis *(q.v.)* according to Lucan, thus female god to some nineteenth-century Celtic scholars (e.g., John Rhys); Gallic Jupiter, Thor.

taupe. "Mole" *(Arbre),* common slang for "prostitute."

taureau. "Bull" *(Larron),* virile male force; Mithra (Durry); Marduk, Baal, Dionysus, etc. (?)

Tchatcha (Que vlo-ve?). Wall. word for blueberry marmalade (Piron).

témoins. "Witnesses" *(Roi-lune),* testicles, translation of Latin *testes.*

temps. "Times" *(Fenêtres),* Parisian newspaper; see *liberté.*

Tenso (Otmika). "Anthony" in Bulgarian; note of Apollinaire.

Téremtété (Otmika). "Made by the Devil" (Hung.) (Warnier).

Teutatès (Ench). Gallic Jupiter, Mars, Mercury, or Pluto; see *Hésus, Taranis.*

Tircis (Montre). Classical name of shepherd; pun on *tire six,* copulate six times; perhaps also pun on *l'heure du berger,* "the hour of the shepherd," the trysting hour.

todis à vinde (P Ass 1). "Always for sale" in Wall. (Piron).

toison d'or. "Golden fleece" *(Bestiaire),* traditional erotic term for pubic hair.

tranchée. "Trench" *(Cas du brigadier masqué),* soldiers' slang for vulva.

tremblement de terre. "Earthquake" *(Lettre-Océan),* earthquake on French Riviera in spring of 1887.

Trèves (Vend). Trier, ancient capital of Gaul (see letter to Lou, 2 May 1915).

triade. "Triad" *(Larron),* reference to the Christian trinity.

triangle isocèle. "Isosceles triangle" *(Larron),* female erotic symbol (cf. "Deuxième poème secret"); symbol of Pallas *(q.v.);* symbol of reason, geometry (Durry); see *chape.* Apollinaire's logo was the head of a unicorn in an isosceles triangle with the inscription *J'émerveille,* "I marvel."

trismégiste (Best, Crépuscule, Vend). "Thrice powerful," popular epithet among symbolists, occultists, etc. (from Hermes Trismagistus).

Tristouse (P Ass). Woman's name from medieval romance, opposite of *Joyeuse.*

trompette marine. "Trumpet marine" *(Chantre),* name both for a large musical instrument with one string and a large Mediterranean conch; symbol of the female forces of the universe; see *Chantre.*

Troudla (Veille). Euphemism for *trou du cul,* "ass hole"; from erotic song, *Trou du cul, champignon, tabatière (champignon,* "mushroom," and *tabatière,* "tobacco pouch," are French slang for phallus and derrière).

Truie. "Sow" *(Ermite, Du coton),* traditional word for prostitute; name of sector on battle front in World War I, called by field telephone (Debon).

Truitonne (Histoire d'une famille). Ugly, evil princess in Mme d'Aulnoy's story *L'Oiseau bleu;* see *oiseau bleu.*

Tseilom Kop (P Ass 15). "Baptized head" (Heb. invective); note of Apollinaire.

Tyolet (Ench). Hero of Breton lay of same name, has gift of calling animals by whistling.

Tyndarides (Brasier). Castor and Pollux, sons of Zeus and Leda.

U

Urgande la méconnue. "Urganda the unrecognized" *(Ench)*, sorceress in *Amadis de Gaul* (see prefatory poem to Cervantes's *Don Quixote*).

V

Vendémiaire (Vend). "Vintage month," September in French Revolution calendar.

vague. "Wave" *(Du coton)*, a gas attack (Debon).

vase. "Vase" *(Larron)*, traditional metaphor for vulva.

veilleuse. "Night light" *(Palais)*, symbolist metaphor for moon (Follet).

vents. "Winds" *(Merlin)*, various kinds of cosmic flatulence (see *pard, pétomane, rose des vents, haleine tiède*). It is likely that the *cadences plagales*, "plagal cadences," in *Le Larron* also fall into this category. According to friend André Salmon, Apollinaire was accomplished farter.

Ventre affamé n'a pas d'oreilles. "Hungry stomach has no ears" *(Palais)*, traditional proverb, also erotic reference to parallel proverb "Pine raide [stiff prick] n'a pas d'oreilles."

verger. "Orchard" *(Ench, Larron, Ermite, Onirocritique, Fiançailles)*, ideal, erotic gardens related to Eden, Elysium, Golden Age, Avalon, Hesperides, etc., found throughout Apollinaire's writings; see *jardin marin*.

vêtue. "Clothed woman" *(Un soir)*, word for heretic in thirteenth-century France; Eve; Annie Playden. (?)

vieil ange. "Old angel" *(Ermite)*, angel in Luke 22:43 (Couffignal).

vieille femme. "Old woman" *(Merlin)*, personification of Memosyne, Greek form of Memory, who conceived the Nine Muses from Zeus; Morgane le Faye *(q.v.)* to some critics (Merlin loved both an old woman and Morgane in Old French romances).

Vierselin Tigoboth (P Ass 2). "Grumpy your-basket's-dripping" in Wall. dialect (Piron).

vieux Rhin. "Old Rhine" *(Synagogue)*, Father Rhine of German legend (Pierre Orecchioni).

villa (Annie). Probably erotic symbol; see *bouton de rose, palais*.

vin de Chypre. "Cyprus wine" *(Palais)*, Eucharistic wine and erotic symbol in Apollinaire (Cyprus is isle of Venus); from *botrus cypri*, symbol of Christ, from Latin translation of Song of Solomon 1:12–13 (Follet).

Viperdoc (P Ass 1). Ukrainian insult, "born farting" (not "born of a fart" as Apollinaire mistranslates).

Viviane (Ench, Merlin). Viviane, Niniane, Aivienne, Eviène, the Lady of the Lake, who enchanted, entombed Merlin in OF romances.

Vulcain (CMA). Symbol of cuckold, of masturbation, husband of Venus who deceived him with Mars; the first phallic sword in *CMA* is therefore an *arme de Vulcain*, "Vulcan's weapon," a cuckold's penis in popular use.

X

Xexaèdres (Loin du pigeonnier). Apollinaire's spelling of *hexaèdres* (hexahedrals), perhaps to imitate the *x*'s of the barbed wire on their (six-sided?) rolls (Debon).

Y

Yette (Colombe poignardée, P Ass 9). Mariette, perhaps one of Apollinaire's first loves (Décaudin).

Ypiranga (Lettre-Océan). German ship, brought arms to Mexican revolutionists, was stopped by American marines at Vera Cruz (Bohn).

Z

Zamir (Brasier). Shamir, fabulous worm or stone used by Solomon to cut stone for Temple of Jerusalem (Jewish-Arabic folklore, *Talmud*).

Zélotide (Ermite, P Ass 3). Name for Boccaccio's *Fiammetta* (James Lawler); name common to characters in eighteenth-century French novels.

Zone (Fumées, Zone). Area around Paris, ended at Avenue des Ternes in 1912 (Durry); term for plane in orphic paintings; name (in plural) of a projected review of Apollinaire (Naömi Onimus-Blumenkranz); name of region in Alsace; military terrain.

Zun (Lettre-Océan). Henri Barzun, with whom Apollinaire quarreled in 1914 (Schmits).

Notes and References

Chronology of Alcools

1. Possible dates: 1905, 1906, and 1908, when Apollinaire took trips to Holland (Michel Décaudin, "Apollinaire en Belgique après Stavelot" *(Que vlo-ve?,* (January–March, 1987): 3–10]). I have placed the poem in the 1908 period because of its optimistic symbolism and because it bears some resemblance in theme and imagery to Gustave Kahn's story about Holland, "Au jardin, en passant, Jacob vola une rose" (Passing by a garden, Jacob stole a rose) which Apollinaire read and admired in the summer of 1908 *(Phalange,* 15 November 1908).

2. Marie Laurencin wrote in her memoirs that she loved French queens and heroines, beginning with Sainte-Clotilde *(Le Carnet des nuits* [Geneva: Cailler, 1956], 17). She herself was an anonymous poet like the nineteenth-century "Clotilde de Surville" whose poems were in Apollinaire's library. "Clotilde" resembles certain poems of the 1911–12 period (for example, "Marie," "Cors de chasse," and "Le Pont Mirabeau") in prosody and symbolism. All these reasons, plus the fact that it seems to refer to the end of Apollinaire's liaison with Marie, have caused me to place it here among the poems of the Marie cycle.

Chapter One: Christ and Antichrist

1. This reading is supported by a suppressed line from the manuscript, "Thou must put Hell and darkness *(ombre)* in thy voice" (Michel Décaudin, *Le Dossier d' "Alcools"* [Paris: Lettres Modernes, 1965], 197).

2. Suggested by Robert Couffignal in his *L'Inspiration biblique dans l'oeuvre d'Apollinaire* (Paris: Lettres Modernes, 1966), 138.

3. Couffignal; see *roux* in Glossary.

4. *Intransigeant,* 25 January 1910. See poem "Lettre-Océan" *(Calligrammes)* and Camille Flammarion, *La Fin du monde* (Paris: E. Flammarion, 1894), 197.

5. Saint Jerome seems to have been a favorite of Apollinaire. Among many references to him, two are of special interest:

[Speaking of the importance of the belt in dancing:] "The dance has always been considered one of Satan's pomps by Church Fathers, completely unjustly in my opinion—and in this connection I shall recall that Saint

Jerome, who was an authority on the subject, used to place the power of the fallen angel close to the belt."

(La Grâce et le maintien français, 57).

[Speaking against Charles-Henry Hirsch] "In reality, everything that has to do with poetry irritates M. Charles-Henry Hirsch. He would like to imitate the angel who beat Saint Jerome because he read a work of poetry"

(Phalange, 15 March 1908).

6. Ms. of *Le Poète assassiné* (in *Oeuvres en prose).* Although Apollinaire told Madeleine that he lost the manuscript of *La Gloire de l'olive* (letter of 14 September 1915), a great part of the work can easily be reconstructed from crossed-out sections on the ms. What he lost, therefore, may have been an amplified copy of the original.

7. See letter dated 1899 by A. Toussaint-Luca in his *Guillaume Apollinaire* (Paris: Editions du Rocher, 1954), 27–28.

8. Maurice Le Blond, *Le Théâtre héroïque et social, conférence prononcée au Collège d'esthétique moderne, le 11 mai 1901* (Paris: Stock, n. d.).

9. Madeleine Boisson in discussion at Stavelot, August 1984.

10. Stanza 16 ("The bearded water drawers . . .") was in part taken from M. Karppe's article "Mélanges assyriologiques et bibliques" *(Journal Asiatique* 10 [July–August 1897]), the black-and-white bands from pp. 83–84 and the water drawers from p. 78. Karppe also discusses a line from Psalm 11 on the Red Sea crossing: "The sea saw it and fled" (Apollinaire has the sea "open like an eye" in stanza 15), the Chaldean *rimi* or sacred buffalo-antelope (Apollinaire's gnu?) and the symbolism of Jehovah as fire and the sun. The main point of the article is to show that the Pentateuch comes from Chaldean belief and custom. On the other hand, the reference to the fourth-century legend of King Abgar the Black inviting Jesus to come to Edessa and cure him of leprosy comes from the *Journal Asiatique* of September–October 1891, and its article "Histoire politique, religieuse et littéraire d'Edesse," chapter 5.

11. Toussaint-Luca, 28.

12. Apollinaire copied the angels and their qualities from Moïse Schwab's *Vocabulaire de l'angelologie* (Paris: C. Klincksieck, 1897); see my article on this source and others in *GA* 4 (1965), 68–77. Couffignal gives a list of the biblical sources, 25–26.

13. L. Turgan, *Histoire de l'aviation* (Paris: L. Geisler, 1909); Baeder and Dubouchet, *Dictionnaire illustré de la navigation aérienne* (Paris: Librairie Aéronautique, 1913); etc.

14. L. A. Paton, *Les Prophéties de Merlin* (New York: Heath, 1927), 2:192ff.

15. Michel Décaudin, "Compléments à un dossier," *GA* 1 (1962), 58.

Chapter Two: The Death of the Sun

1. Pascal Pia, *Apollinaire par lui-même* (Paris: Seuil, 1954), 30.
2. *Tendre comme le souvenir,* 22 July 1915. Picasso also boasted of this power.
3. The legend of the king who coveted his daughter when informed he could marry only someone who resembled her dead mother probably provided the name *Tristouse* to "Le Poète assassiné"; the king's daughter cut off her hands in order to terminate the resemblance and changed her name from Joyeuse to Tristouse (Hermann Suchier, *La Manekine* [Paris: 1884], Vol. 1, introduction). Perrault and the Grimms printed versions of this tale, and Apollinaire referred to it in the second chapter of *L'Enchanteur pourrissant.* The *manekine* or "girl with the cut-off hands" is found throughout European folklore and in symbolist literature, and is often associated with trees (she sits in them). Her hands, therefore, make natural symbols for autumn leaves, an image Apollinaire uses in "Automne Rhénane," "Signe," and "Marie."
4. Françoise Dininman's thorough and perceptive thesis of 1980, *Du merveilleux au mythe personnel; merveilleux, scénario initiatique et mythe personnel dans les contes d'Apollinaire,* gives an exhaustive breakdown of this process; my comments in this section owe a great deal to her perceptive analyses.
5. Dininman, 258–99.
6. "Anteros arrives at first, that brother of love who resembles him, but he soon flees to leave place for the little born-blind boy who rules us all" (article in *La Phalange,* 15 July 1908, p. 82). According to Greek myth, both Eros and Anteros were born of the adulterous union of Ares and Aphrodite. Anteros turns up again toward the end of Apollinaire's life, in the poem "La Victoire" *(Calligrammes).* In the Athenian tale of Meles and Timagoras, noted by Apollinaire in Bibliothèque nationale ms. Fr. Nouv, Acq. 16280–106 *(Que vlo-ve?* [October–December 1984], 3), Anteros is a symbol of homosexuality. Judas has been traditionally associated with Anteros (and Thanatos); for an interesting discussion of this association in the works of Aubrey Beardsley, see Ewa Kuryluk's *Judas and Salome in the Cave of Sex* (Evanston, Ill.: Northwestern University Press, 1987), 265–68.
7. L. C. Breunig, "Le Roman du mal-aimé," *La Table Ronde,* September 1952; see also Breunig's general study *Guillaume Apollinaire* (New York: Columbia University Press, 1969). The whole poem was probably composed over the years between 1903 and 1907, and it is probable that the hermetic "seven swords" sequence (stanzas 42–48) was written towards the end of that period, at a time when Apollinaire was celebrating the symbolists and Mallarmé.
8. Many of these sources were cited by Apollinaire himself in his 1904 article on Anatole France's novel *Thaïs (Mercure de France,* July).

9. Apollinaire's source for the letter was the *Kryptadia,* a nine-volume collection of erotic and scatological folklore published privately by leading (and anonymous) ethnologists; see my discussion of this work in *Petit glossaire des mots libres d'Apollinaire* (1975), 21–22, 50–51.

10. Madeleine Boisson, "Apollinaire et Hugo," *Que vlo-ve?* (April–September 1983): 8.

11. An example close to this poem: "I took [Annie] to one of those gin palaces at the end of the street which was flaming like the perfidious signal lights of ship wreckers in the middle of the blackness of mystery. Annie was in the service of a clergyman" (Georges Darien, *Le Voleur,* 1898, chapter 8).

12. Michel Décaudin, *Dossier,* 171.

13. The term *sirène moderne* is used for *prostitute* in the preface of a book Apollinaire catalogued in his *Enfer de la Bibliothèque nationale, La Masturbomonie ou Jouissance solitaire.*

14. René Louis, "Encore 'Lul de Faltenin,' " *Flâneur des deux rives* 2 (June 1954), 11. See Glossary.

15. L. C. Breunig, "Lul de Faltenin," *Revue des sciences humaines* (October–December 1956):401–12.

16. Madeleine Boisson, in "Orphée et anti-Orphée dans l'oeuvre d'Apollinaire" *(GA* 9: 32–33) makes a strong case for Butes who, in spite of Orpheus's rival song, jumped ship to join the Sirens and was finally rescued by Aphrodite.

17. *Reliques of Ancient English Poetry,* edited by Thomas Percy (1847), 2:156, stanza 6, 11. 21–24. Marc Poupon states that Apollinaire probably translated the stanza from Herder's German translation, "Die schöne Rosemunde," found in his library.

18. See André Rouveyre, *Amour et poésie en Apollinaire* (Paris: Seuil, 1955), 183–186; Lionel Follet and Marc Poupon, *Lecture de "Palais" d'Apollinaire* (Paris: Lettres Modernes, 1972); and my *Glossaire des mots libres d'Apollinaire* (Sewanee, Tennessee: privately printed, 1975), 69.

19. *Oeuvres en prose,* 1213.

20. *Revue Littéraire de Paris et de Champagne* (February–September 1906) (cited in full by Décaudin, *Dossier,* 230).

21. Décaudin, *Dossier,* 205.

22. Décaudin, *Dossier,* 202.

Chapter Three: The Phoenix

1. Charles Maurras, *Barbarie et poésie* (Paris: Nouvelle librarie nationale, 1925); reprint of article of 21 July 1901.

2. Gwendolyn Bays, *The Orphic Vision, Seer Poets from Novalis to Rimbaud* (Lincoln: University of Nebraska Press, 1964), chapter 1.

3. *Les Diables amoureux,* 75 (from introduction to *L'Oeuvre de Crébillon le fils,* 1911).

4. Peter Read, "Apollinaire *libertaire:* Anarchism, Symbolism and Poetry," *Forum for Modern Language Studies,* 21, no. 3 (July 1985): 239–56. Professor Read cites as a main example of Apollinaire's anarchism his poem on René Dalize's death, "Je suis la vie [I am life]," yet the poet's attitude on this occasion may have been more the result of his praise for an unregenerate anarchist (he had earlier included some of Dalize's anarchist writings in his *Soirées de Paris*) than out of personal conviction.

5. For example, he is mentioned as being seen at one in the years just before the war in Jeanne Humbert's *Sous la cagoule* (Paris: Lutèce, n.d.).

6. See Willard Bohn, "Apollinaire's Reign in Spain," *Symposium,* 35, no 3 (Fall 1981): 186–214, for a thorough discussion of Apollinaire's interest in Spain and his important influence on modern Spanish literature; his reply to the inquiry is printed in the *Oeuvres complètes* (Paris: Balland-Lecat, 1965–66), 3: 896–97.

7. *La Grande France* (April 1903): 244.

8. Erich Meyer, "La Poésie française contemporaine" (January, April 1903). Pierre Caizergues has shown that Apollinaire's celebration of Fernand Gregh's humanism at this time was not without self-interest; he was hoping that Gregh would help him get into the *Revue de France* ("Pascal Hédégat et l'humanisme de Fernand Gregh," *Les Cahiers de Varsovie* 11 [1984]:25–38).

9. The leftist press, including the *Européen,* had been full of such stories, and the accounts of atrocities by Leo Tolstoy were much heeded. Apollinaire wrote exultantly to René Dalize in June 1904, "The Russians are getting beaten like old carpets," and in *Le Festin d'Esope,* he scolded "ignorant pacifist groups" for spreading pro-Russian propaganda.

10. Noëmi Onimus-Blumenkranz, *Apollinaire témoin des peintres de son temps, thèse pour l'école du Louvre* (unpublished thesis, 1960), 124–28. This is the first critical work to analyze in detail Apollinaire's crusade for a synthesis of the plastic arts.

11. L. C. Breunig, and J. C. Chevalier, critical edition of *Les Peintres cubistes* (Paris: Hermann, 1965), introduction.

12. L. C. Breunig, *"Apollinaire et le cubisme,"* GA 1 (Spring 1962):19. My translation.

13. Marcel Adéma, *Apollinaire,* trans. Denise Folliot (New York: Grove Press, 1955), 154.

14. *Les Peintres cubistes,* chapter 1; first printed in a catalog to a fauvist exposition in June 1908 (in *Chroniques,* 56–58).

15. *La Phalange* (August 1908):162, (January 1909):640; *Pan* (October 1908):260.

16. *Peintres cubistes,* chapter 1; "Jean Royère"; *Phalange* (August 1908):161.

17. *Vers et Prose* (June–July–August 1908):124; *Phalange* (January 1909):640, (September 1908):63.

18. "Henri Matisse," 103–7; *Phalange* (April 1909):910.

19. *Le Dernier Cahier de Mécislas Golberg* (Paris: "l'Abbaye," 1908), 220–23, reviewed in *Phalange* (March 1908).

20. *Peintres cubistes,* chapter 1; "Jean Royère"; letter to Toussaint-Luca, 1908; *Chroniques,* 11 May 1910, 96–97.

21. *Phalange* (August 1908):161.

22. Quoted by Christopher Gray in his *Cubist Aesthetic Theories* (London: Oxford Press, 1953).

23. *Peintres cubistes,* chapter 1.

24. "Jean Royère"; *Peintres cubistes,* chapter 1.

25. *Phalange* (November 1908):463; *Chroniques* (1 May 1908):51.

26. Some friends of Apollinaire were planning to start an agricultural community, a "Confrérie amphionienne," which "will see the New City rise stone by stone to the sound of lutes" and which will bring about the end of the "old corrupt world." André Mary, writing this to Fernand Fleuret, warns him, "not a word to Apollinaire about my idea of a congregation. He would sabotage it and would commit indiscretions" (letter reproduced in J. de Saint-Jorre, *Fernand Fleuret et ses amis* [Coutances: Imprimerie P. Bellée, 1959], 86–87). Apollinaire was nevertheless in accord with the idea of a mystical confederation of artist-activists, as is revealed in the last section of "Les Fiançailles." He became friends with several unanimists, members of the Abbaye congregation.

27. "Jean Royère"; *Phalange* (April 1909):154; *Poésie symboliste,* 180.

28. Letter to Toussaint-Luca, 1908; Adéma, *Guillaume Apollinaire, le mal-aimé* (Paris: Plon, 1952), 94; *Phalange* (April 1909):910; *Peintres cubistes,* chapter 1.

29. *Chroniques* (1908–9), 54, 59, 62.

30. *Phalange* (November 1908):463; "André Salmon"; "Jean Royère"; "Henri Matisse"; *Chroniques* (November 1908):60.

31. Georges Braque later told art historian Henry Hope that he always saw Picasso's *Demoiselles d'Avignon* as a huge fire (Henry Hope, lecture at Indiana University, 7 November 1987).

32. See L. C. Breunig, "Apollinaire et le cubisme," and Michel Décaudin, *La Crise des valeurs symbolistes* (Toulouse: Privat Editeur, 1960). Charles Morice emphasized the divine mission and the autonomous creation of the poet in his influential symbolist manifesto *La Littérature de tout à l'heure* (1889), and Albert Aurier and Edouard Schuré, philosophers of the Nabi movement, had revealed to the artists their Platonic and Pythagorean mission. Orpheus, Ixion, and the flame were used everywhere as symbols;

see, for example, the *Ixion* (1903) of Fagus, Golberg's *Lettres à Alexis* (1904), and Remy de Gourmont's "Théâtre muet" in *Le Pèlerin de silence* (1896).

33. *Chroniques,* 146, 265, 272 (1911–13); see also 253 (30 June 1912) and *Peintres cubistes,* chapter 7. According to Georges Hilaire in *Derain* (Geneva: P. Cailler, 1959), 42, Apollinaire introduced Derain to Picasso. Derain was present at the genesis of *Les Demoiselles* and had been an admirer of African Art since 1901. His "conversion" took place in 1905 and consisted of a new, "divine" conception of light without shadow in which colors became all-important (Gaston Diehl, *Derain* [New York: Crown, 1964]). Apollinaire wrote in 1912, "Today all shadow has disappeared" *(Chroniques,* 211). Fire was one of the fauvists' main symbols.

34. See Derain's *Lettres à Vlaminck* (Paris: Flammarion, 1955) in which he describes his search for the absolute, his reactions to Nietzsche, his solitude, his early anarchism (which "destroyed the world every night to reconstruct it every morning"), and his disgust with women and humanity. He pictures the latter in 1907 as voluntarily committing suicide.

35. *Les Marges* (May 1909).

36. Cf. the second chapter of *L'Enchanteur pourrissant,* where the sphinxes follow the shepherd-god and are probably prostitutes, administering *la petite mort* to themselves when their erotic riddles are solved. In chapter 10 of "Le Poète assassiné" Picasso is portrayed as a shepherd with a flock of paintings, while in "Le Musicien de Saint-Merry," a Phallus-Pan-Dionysus figure leads a flock of prostitutes to the stars. For Apollinaire's Pan symbolism see chapter 5, section 3, of the present study.

37. Also for humor, as the poem about All Saints' Day, "Rhénane d'automne," dedicated to an old school friend *Toussaint*-Luca (Allsaint-Luca).

38. Adéma, *Apollinaire,* 104; Gertrude Stein also reports that Picasso's beginnings of cubism were discouraging for Apollinaire *(Picasso* [Paris: Floury, 1938], 16). Again, it was probably more the painter's goals that influenced the poet than his actual practice. L. C. Breunig, in his excellent study of "Les Fiançailles," states flatly, *"Les Fiançailles* is Apollinaire's *Demoiselles d'Avignon" (Essays in French Literature* 1 no. 3 [November 1966]:1). This is particularly true thematically, in its erotic primitivism. In addition, "Le Brasier," originally part of the poem, ends like the *Demoiselles* in a *sphingerie,* a brothel. The devouring of the poet here should be compared to that in "Le Poète assassiné," chapter 10, where the she-wolves of distress (she-wolves, like sphinxes, were prostitutes in Latin) were waiting to devour him and Picasso "in order to build in the same place the New City."

39. This pun is also found in "Le Poète assassiné" (chapter 10), "Cortège," "Anvers," and, perhaps, "Arbre." Cf. the lyrical evocation of

Marie's tree-like paintings in the *Soirées de Paris* of 15 November 1913 (*Chroniques,* 332).

40. "Nabi," besides its usual meaning of "Prophet"—which included Jesus—was also given its Hebrew meaning of "Solomon's Temple" by members of the group (Caroline Boyle Turner, *Paul Sérusier* [Ann Arbor: University of Michigan Press, 1983], 36–37). They first met in the 1890s at Paul Ranson's apartment, which they called "Le Temple."

41. André Mary suggested *Confrérie amphionique, Confrérie amphionienne, Confrérie Apollonienne,* and *Confrèrerie* to Fernand Fleuret as names for their commune (J. de Saint-Jorre, *Fernand Fleuret et ses amis,* 86–87).

Chapter Four: The Traveler

1. *Le Figaro,* 5 December 1910.
2. Letter to Henri Martineau in *Le Divan,* June 1913, 267.
3. André Billy, *L'Evolution actuelle du roman* (Paris: L'Echo Bibliographique du Boulevard, 1911), 75.
4. "To have a bud on one's rosebush" (1. 11) is traditional slang for "to menstruate" (F. Vosselmann, *La Menstruation* [Paris: l'Expansion scientifique française, 1936], 74).
5. See my article "Un voyage à Ispahan" in *GA* 7, 82–88.
6. Ms. of "A la Santé" (*Dossier,* 212).
7. The main French discussion of the Greek and Roman history of this traditional genre was published by H. de la Ville de Mirmont in 1909 in "Le Παραχλαυσίθυρον dans la littérature latine"in *Philologie et linguistique. Mélanges offerts à Louis Havet par ses anciens élèves et ses amis* (Paris: L'Edition de Paris, 1909), 572–92.
8. Quoted by N. Calas in "The Rose and the Revolver," *Yale French Studies* (Fall–Winter 1948):111.
9. The two passages with the two sailors. The origin of this image may be a photograph of Guillaume and his brother in sailor suits (Décaudin, *Dossier,* 133) combined with a passage from Remy de Gourmont's *Un volcan en éruption* (1882) telling how two sisters were found in each other's arms at Pompey, the oldest of whom wore two iron rings and had fallen on her side, the youngest of whom wore her hair in a braid. A ms. of the poem reproduced in the catalogue of the Milan Apollinaire exposition of 1960 has a drawing in the margin of two stalwart French sailors accompanying lines about how if one dies in combat the other will commit suicide. In the ms. of "Les Fiançailles" there is the line "My true brothers are only mohammedan sailors" (Décaudin, *Dossier,* 207). A popular meaning of *matelot* (sailor) in nineteenth-century French was "close companion."
10. The Euripus is an estuary in Boetia famous for its changing tides. Apollinaire's line is an adaptation of the ancient proverb, "Man is a Eu-

ripus" *(Homo Euribus est*—Sylvain Maréchal, *Les Voyages de Pythagore* [Paris: Déterville], 6:125).

11. In May 1911 (Couffignal, *L'Inspiration biblique*, 148).

12. Note that this is not Christ, as many commentators have thought; he flew *after* Icarus, Enoch, and Elijah, whereas the twentieth century is the first real airplane. Apollinaire wrote a few months later, "We are going higher now and don't touch the ground any more" ("Le Musicien de Saint-Merry"). During the war he wrote about French criticism that it "had wings and soared gracefully beyond the Empyrean"—above prosaic German thought trapped like Ariadne in the labyrinth below (letter of 11 December 1916 to Francesco Meriano [*GA* 15, 148]).

13. "The night withdraws like a beautiful mulatto girl." Marie's frizzy hair made some believe that she was part Creole (she was illegitimate like Apollinaire) (Francis Steegmuller, *Apollinaire, Poet Among the Painters* [New York: Farrar, Straus, 1963], 160). This may explain the references to mulattoes in "Les Fiançailles" and "Les Fenêtres."

14. *Paris Journal*, 24 May 1914.

Chapter Five: The New City

1. Décaudin, *Dossier*, 224. Fagus, a friend of Apollinaire, published an almanac of poems in 1903 with some titles from the Revolutionary calendar, and Pierre Quillard used "Vendémiaire" as a title in *La Lyre héroïque et dolente* (1897). Peter Read notes that *Vendémiaire* had been the name of a Parisian anarchist paper ("Apollinaire *libertaire:* Anarchism, Symbolism and Poetry," *Forum for Modern Language Studies* [July 1985]:248).

2. Pierre Orecchioni, *Le Thème du Rhin dans l'inspiration de Guillaume Apollinaire* (Paris: Lettres Modernes, 1956), 120.

3. See Jacques Naville, "A propos d'une lettre de Guillaume Apollinaire à André Gide," *Mercure de France* (June 1957):120.

4. Printed in *La Table Ronde* of September 1952.

5. See a report on the conversation between the two poets regarding the deletion of punctuation in Reverdy's *Le Voleur de Talan* (Paris: Flammarion 1967), 165–67.

6. Roger Shattuck discusses this possible influence in his article on "Lettre-Océan" in *The Innocent Eye: On Modern Literature and the Arts* (New York: Washington Square Press, 1984), pointing out that Gide gave a public lecture on the work at the time. On the other hand, Apollinaire told Reverdy that *Un coup de dés* was "not the most agreeable to the eye, and what Mallarmé was trying to do was not apparent and required explanation" (Reverdy in reply pointed out that while Apollinaire's work appealed to the eye, Mallarmé's new syntax was of the mind) *(Le Voleur de Talan*, 166). Yet it is hard not to believe with Profesor Shattuck that

Apollinaire, always a great admirer of Mallarmé, was not extremely impressed by the work.

7. The two poets met in 1912, and the two poems are remarkably similar, with many almost-identical lines and situations. Cendrars said repeatedly that he wrote his poem in New York in April 1912, and critics usually date "Zone" the following summer, after Marie Laurencin had definitively left Apollinaire. Yet, in a more general way, Apollinaire had provided early influences on the poem that was to influence him in turn—which partly accounts for the shock of recognition and admiration that he felt when he first encountered it.

Both poems are narrated, seemingly spontaneously, in the first person by a sad, sick, and lonely poet walking through a big city from dusk to dawn, discussing the past, the poor, and refugees from society as he goes. Both poets evoke the powerful figure of Christ. Both speak of their exotic voyages; both describe Jewish ghettoes. Neither goes into a church as he desires. Cendrars sees immigrants in flop-houses; Apollinaire watches emigrants at the Saint Lazare Station. In "Pâques," Jewish women are "polluted" "at the back of bars"; in "Zone," they are "bloodless" at the back of shops. "Pâques" ends with a description of the rising sun as Christ's face "covered with spit"; "Zone" ends with the rising sun-Christ's cut throat.

Now most of the above subject matter had been used before 1912 by Apollinaire in poems and stories from "Le Passant de Prague" (1902) to "Les Fiançailles" (1908): emigrants, Jewish ghettoes, rambles through cities by night and day, churches, Christ's presence or absence, Christ as the sun, prostitutes, dirty streets, the poor, etc. He had used similar poetic techniques to those of "Pâques" in "La Chanson du mal-aimé" and "Les Fiançailles," poems much admired by Cendrars. The latter, on the other hand, had written nothing before "Pâques" but some unpublished manuscripts, articles, and the traditional love poems, *Séquences,* which contain none of its symbols, subjects, themes, or techniques. This is not to denigrate Cendrars's great poem, one of the authentic masterpieces of modern French literature. It merely happened that both poets were to a remarkable extent "on the same wave length" because of similarities in cosmopolitan experience, poetic goals, and common influences. An example of the latter was Remy de Gourmont's anthology of medieval mystico-erotic Latin poetry, *Le Latin mystique,* which is directly quoted throughout Cendrars's poem and which had provided several references for Apollinaire's early poetry (for example, *Cypri botrus*).

8. Roger Shattuck, *The Innocent Eye,* 311. Professor Shattuck and his students have successfully "performed" the work using choral techniques and audio-visual materials.

9. For an important discussion of this point, see Philippe Renaud's *Lecture d'Apollinaire*, 307ff.

10. Peter Read, "Apollinaire *libertaire* . . ." 249.

11. Félicien Fagus also combined the Ixion myth with a divine child-savior *(Ixion* [Paris: la Plume, 1903]).

12. *Chroniques*, 1 October 1910.

13. See article on Apollinaire's painting by Willard Bohn in *Que vlove?* (July–September 1987):24–25.

14. An important letter to Picasso of 4 September 1918, in which Apollinaire speaks of their joint classical preoccupations and their admiration for Pascal (Apollinaire was calling for poetic trips into the two infinities at this time), was printed in *Cahiers d'Art* (1947):142–43.

15. Pierre Caizergues, *Apollinaire journaliste* (Lille: Université 3, 1979) 1:597. The passage is obviously more in Apollinaire's language than in Picasso's; yet the two men were so close that it may be assumed that the poet correctly interpreted the less verbal reaction of the painter.

16. Jean-Claude Blachère, *Le Modèle nègre, aspects littéraires du mythe primitiviste au XXe siècle chez Apollinaire, Cendrars, et Tzara* (Dakar: Nouvelles Editions africaines, 1981), 47.

17. My translation of ms. 7460 at the Fonds Jacques Doucet, published by Katiä Samaltanos in her ground-breaking study *Apollinaire Catylist for Primitivism, Picabia, and Duchamp* (Ann Arbor: University of Michigan Research Press, 1984), 190.

18. Katiä Samaltanos discusses this work extensively and reproduces some of the photographs from it—as well as photographs of some of Apollinaire's own collection of African art.

19. Apollinaire's originality in advancing this important thesis is proved conclusively by Jean-Claude Blachère in *Le Modèle nègre.*

20. See the articles by Theodore Reff, "Themes of Love and Death in Picasso's Early Work" and Roland Penrose, "Beauty and the Monster," in *Picasso in Retrospect* (New York: Praeger, 1973) which show how Picasso, who painted himself as a Christ-harlequin figure in the first decade of the century, became interested in Mithraism in the 1930s and portrayed himself both as the Minotaur and the crucified bull (or matador) of the corrida. He once said that if his whole work were seen all together it would probably assume the form of a minotaur.

21. Robert Lebel, *Sur Marcel Duchamp* (Paris: Trianon, 1959); Samaltanos, *Apollinaire Catylist,* 36–37, 61–105.

22. When Apollinaire arrived at the front, he wrote Paul Guillaume on 15 April 1915, "Here I am entirely in the rank of man-target as in Chirico's portrait" *(Arts à Paris,* January 1923).

23. Willard Bohn, "Apollinaire and Chirico: The Making of the

Mannequins," *Comparative Literature* 27, no. 2 (Spring 1975):153–65. As Professor Bohn demonstrates, both poet and painter were influenced by Nietzsche's pairing of Ariadne and Dionysus, to the extent that seven paintings—half of Chirico's output in 1913—included Adriadne figures. Apollinaire mentioned Nietzsche's Ariadne (at Naxos) in the *Soirées de Paris* issue of May–April 1912 *(Chroniques,* 223); see *Ariane* in Glossary.

24. Jean-Claude Chevalier, *Alcools* (Paris: Lettres Modernes, 1970).

25. *Physique de l'amour* (Paris: Mercure de France, 1903). Louis Pergaud used this description in the second story of his *De goupil à Margot,* the book which in 1910 won out over *L'Hérésiarque et cie* for the Prix Goncourt.

26. Seen on visit of 9 November 1964.

27. His friend André Salmon wrote that he would abandon everything to follow a new fair face, and a few previously hidden affairs have turned up in recent years. Georges Gabory, who saw the original production of *Les Mamelles* in 1917 and met the playwright at the time, says that Apollinaire told him in all seriousness that a good way to repopulate France was to flood the market with erotic books with many illustrations so that male readers would get so excited that they would fail to use contraceptives! ("Document Apollinaire, ou la leçon d'écriture," *Kentucky Romance Quarterly* 14 [1967]:94).

28. Couffignal, *L'Inspiration biblique,* 67.

29. Apollinaire's Polish ancestors had participated in rebellions against the hated Russians, and the poet had been, like his colleagues on the socialist paper *L'Européen* but unlike the majority of the French, on the side of Japan in the Russo-Japanese War. Several of the episodes in the book were taken from journalistic reports of Russian atrocities.

30. Willard Bohn, *Lettres de Lou* (forthcoming in *Romance Quarterly*).

31. Norman O. Brown, *Life Against Death* (New York: Wesleyan University Press, 1959), 52.

32. Besides in *L'Enchanteur pourrissant,* "La Chanson du mal-aimé" (where there is a momentary echo of Plutarch's "Great Pan is dead!"), "Le Brasier," "Le Poète assassiné" (chapter 10), and "Le Musicien de Saint-Merry," Pan shows up in "Les Neuf Portes de ton corps," "Le Deuxième poème secret," and "Chant de l'horizon en Champagne." Apollinaire's great interest in group dances and processions relates to this archetype.

33. See article in the *Mercure de France* of 1 April 1914 *(Anecdotiques).*

34. "La Mandoline l'oeillet [carnation] et le bambou," "A l'Italie," "Guerre" [War]" *(Calligrammes).*

35. The noncalligramatic part of "La Petite Auto" was written after the return from the front, as were "Les Collines," "Ombre" ("Shadow"), "Merveille de la guerre," and "Chant de l'honneur" (at least in part).

Apollinaire occasionally disrupted the (mostly) chronological order of the poems in *Calligrammes* to give more balance and perspective to the book.

36. Introduction to *Les Fleurs du mal* (1917), printed in *Les Diables amoureux*, 259.

37. Red is a color often associated with the magic unmanned boats of folklore, romance, and symbolist poetry. In the *Huth Merlin,* for example, one of these boats is pavilioned with "drap de soie aussi vermeil comme une escrelate," and in Régnier's "La Galère," which probably was a source of Apollinaire's "Le Printemps," the galley has scarlet sails. Our poet's unmanned golden vessels at the end of *Onirocritique* (compare the golden ships in Mallarmé and Rimbaud) have scarlet sails.

Selected Bibliography

PRIMARY SOURCES

Books

Oeuvres complètes. Edited by Marcel Adéma and Michel Décaudin. 4 vols. with 4 supplementary vols. of facsimiles. Paris: Balland et Lucat, 1966. Brief notes, no index. Contains main works, correspondence, articles, reviews. Omits minor novels and plays, a great deal of journalistic criticism, much correspondence, and various lesser works published in the Pléiade editions.

Oeuvres en prose. Edited by Michel Décaudin. Bibliothèque de la Pléiade. Paris: Gallimard, 1977. Contains the prose works found in the *Oeuvres complètes* plus several stories, the novels *La Fin de Babylone* and *Les Trois Don Juan,* fragments of novels and plays, and the film script *La Bréhatine.* 408 pages of notes and variants. Extensive bibliography.

Oeuvres poétiques. Edited by Marcel Adéma and Michel Décaudin. Bibliothèque de la Pléiade. Paris: Gallimard, 1975. The standard edition of the poetic works and plays. Introduction by André Billy. Chronology of poet's life and published poetic works. Notes, bibliography, indexes.

Alcools, poèmes (1898–1913). Paris: Mercure de France, 1913. The original edition of Apollinaire's major work. There are two complete translations in English (bilingual), by William Meredith (New York: Doubleday, 1964) and by Anne Hyde Greet (Berkeley–Los Angeles: University of California Press, 1965). Both are annotated, the first by Francis Steegmuller, the second by Professor Greet.

Anecdotiques. Edited by Marcel Adéma. Paris: Gallimard, 1955. Column written for the *Mercure de France* from 1911 to 1918. Notes, useful index of names not included in the *Oeuvres complètes.*

A quelle heure un train partira-t-il pour Paris? Fontfroide: Bibliothèque artistique et littéraire, 1982. Edited by Willard Bohn. First publication of a manuscript written in July 1914, a remarkable presurrealist pantomime based on the poem "Le Musicien de Saint-Merry."

Apollinaire et La Démocratie sociale. Edited by Pierre Caizergues. Archives des lettres modernes, 101. Archives Guillaume Apollinaire, 1. Paris: Lettres Modernes, 1969. Texts of columns written for this socialist, anticlerical paper in 1909. Not included in *Oeuvres complètes*. Notes, commentary.

Apollinaire journaliste—les débuts et la formation du journaliste (1900–1909). Edited by Pierre Caizergues. Bibliothèque Guillaume Apollinaire, 11. Bibliothèque des lettres modernes, 30. Vol. 1, 1900–1906. Vol. 2, 1907–1909. Paris: Lettres Modernes, 1976. Articles and echoes, most of them unsigned, which Apollinaire contributed to reviews and journals; arranged chronologically with extensive commentary and notes. Many important texts for the history of modern art and literature.

Calligrammes; poèmes de la paix et de la guerre (1913–1916). Paris: Mercure de France, 1918. Translated as *Calligrammes* by Anne Hyde Greet, with preface by S. I. Lockerbie and commentary by Greet and Lockerbie. Berkeley-Los Angeles-London: University of California Press, 1980.

Chroniques d'art (1902–1918). Edited by L. C. Breunig. Paris: Gallimard, 1960. Translated by Susan Suleiman as *Apollinaire on Art: Essays and Reviews 1902–1918* with introduction by Breunig. New York: Viking, 1972. Contains most of the art criticism not published in *Méditations esthétiques: les peintres cubistes* or in *Apollinaire journaliste*. Notes, bibliography, index of names. Referred to as *Chroniques* in text and notes.

Les Diables amoureux. Edited by Michel Décaudin. Paris: Gallimard, 1964. Collection of prefaces to erotic classics by de Sade, Aretino, Mirabeau, etc., published between 1910 and 1918. Notes, no index.

L'Enchanteur pourrissant. Edited by Jean Burgos. Bibliothèque Guillaume Apollinaire, 6. Paris: Lettres Modernes, 1972. Critical edition; variants and bibliography.

L'Enfer de la Bibliothèque nationale. Paris: Mercure de France, 1913. The first catalogue of the erotic works at the French National Library. Brief, interesting notes written by Apollinaire and his collaborators Fernand Fleuret and Louis Perceau.

Les Exploits d'un jeune Don Juan. Paris: J. J. Pauvert, 1977. The first scholarly edition of this erotic novel, originally published clandestinely in 1911 and never acknowledged by Apollinaire. Preface by Michel Décaudin. Translated as *Memoirs of a Young Rakehell* in same volume as *The Debauched Hospodar (Les Onze Mille Verges)*. Los Angeles: Holloway House, 1967.

La Grâce et le maintien français. Paris: J. da Silva, 1901 (communicated by Mme Onimus-Blumenkranz). A study of the style and references of this dance manual signed J. Molina da Silva shows that it was partly written by Apollinaire, as he himself claimed in a letter of 1902.

Much of it was copied from classic manuals like Rameau's *Le Maître à danser* (1748). Of interest for a few literary allusions (for example, Apollinaire's first reference to Rimbaud), some humor, and personal anecdotes.

Lettres à Lou. Edited by Michel Décaudin. Paris: Gallimard, 1969. 220 letters sent to Louise de Coligny-Châtillon from September 1914 to January 1916. History and chronology of the Lou liaison; notes, photographs.

Méditations esthétiques: les peintres cubistes. Edited by L. C. Breunig and J. C. Chevalier. Paris: Herman, 1965. Critical edition of work commonly known (and first published) as *Les Peintres cubistes.* Translated as *The Cubist Painters; Aesthetic Meditations, 1913,* by Lionel Abel. 2d rev. ed. New York: Wittenborn, Schultz, 1962.

Les Onze Mille Verges. Paris: Pauvert, 1979. Preface by Michel Décaudin. The best edition of this much-published erotic work, which appeared anonymously in 1907 and was banned in France until the 1970s. Translated as *The Debauched Hospodar* in the same volume as *Memoirs of a Young Rakehell (Les Exploits d'un jeune Don Juan).* Los Angeles: Holloway House, 1967.

Poésies libres. Paris: Pauvert, 1978. As Michel Décaudin hints in the preface, only thirteen of these sixty-eight poems are definitely by Apollinaire ("Chapeau-tombeau," "696666 . . . 69," "Epithalame," "Petit balai," "Le Teint," "La Vaseline," "La Cathédrale de Prague," "La Confession," "Hercule et Omphale," "Pyrame et Thisbé," "Le Système métrique," "Les Jumeaux," and "Epigramme sur une poétesse normande"). The others are probably clever parodies written by Pascal Pia and friends in the 1920s.

Que faire? Edited by Noëmi Onimus-Blumenkranz. Paris: La Nouvelle Edition, 1950. Newspaper serial novel of 1901 partially ghost-written by Apollinaire. Notes by Mme Onimus-Blumenkranz; preface on Apollinaire and science fiction by Jean Marcenac.

Soldes, poèmes inédits de Guillaume Apollinaire. Edited by Gilbert Boudar, Pierre Caizergues, and Michel Décaudin. Fontfroide: Bibliothèque artistique & littéraire, 1985. Heretofore unpublished poems out of the manuscript collection of the Bibliothèque nationale, most of them written before 1903. Two *calligrammes.*

Le Théâtre italien. Paris: Michaud, 1910. A summary history and anthology of Italian drama; some translations done by Apollinaire.

Literary Periodicals Edited by Apollinaire

Le Festin d'Esope, November 1903–August 1904 (no May issue).
La Revue Immoraliste, April 1905.

Les Lettres Modernes, May 1905.
Les Soirées de Paris, February 1912–August 1914.

SECONDARY SOURCES

Books

Adéma, Marcel. *Guillaume Apollinaire.* 2d rev. ed. Paris: La Table Ronde, 1968. Principal biography. New edition, thoroughly revised with much new material added, of *Guillaume Apollinaire le mal-aimé* (Paris: Plon, 1952), translated by Denise Folliot as *Apollinaire* (New York: Grove Press, 1955).

Adéma, Marcel, and Michel Décaudin. *Album Apollinaire.* Albums de la Pléiade, 10. Paris: Gallimard, 1971. Major work of iconography, a chronological biography with one to five black-and-white illustrations per page.

Bates, Scott. *Petit glossaire des mots libres d'Apollinaire.* Sewanee, Tennessee: privately printed, 1975. Comprehensive list with commentary of terms and metaphors for sexual actions and parts of body in Apollinaire's writings.

Bergman, Par. *"Modernolatria" et "simultaneità."* Paris: Lettres Modernes, 1963. Basic study on Apollinaire and futurism.

Berry, David. *The Creative Vision of Guillaume Apollinaire, A Study of Imagination.* Saratoga, California: Anima Libri, 1982. Analysis of leading symbols and themes.

Billy, André. *Apollinaire vivant.* Paris: Editions de la Sirène, 1923. The leading critical work before 1950. Based on author's close friendship with Apollinaire.

———*Avec Apollinaire, souvenirs inédits.* Paris, Geneva: La Palantine, 1966. Additions to the above.

Blachère, Jean-Claude. *Le Modèle nègre, aspects littéraires du mythe primitiviste au XXe siècle chez Apollinaire, Cendrars, et Tzara.* Dakar: Nouvelles Editions africaines, 1981. The first third of this important study on African influences in modern poetry is the best analysis to date of Apollinaire and African black art; also a close analysis of poem "Les Soupirs d'un servant de Dakar."

Breunig, LeRoy C. *Guillaume Apollinaire.* Columbia Essays on Modern Writers, 46. New York: Columbia University Press, 1969. Short, balanced appraisal of the strengths and weaknesses of the poet.

Bohn, Willard. *The Aesthetics of Visual Poetry, 1914–1928.* Cambridge; New York: Cambridge University Press, 1986. Structures and semiotics of concrete poems showing the influence of futurist experiments and Apollinaire's *calligrammes* on Spanish and American poets.

―――. *Apollinaire et l'homme sans visage: création et évolution d'un motif moderne; Guillaume Apollinaire, Albert Savinio, Giorgio de Chirico, Francis Picabia, Marius de Zayas.* Avanguardie storiche, 8. Rome: Bulzoni, 1984. Comprehensive analysis of "Le Musicien de Saint-Merry" and the history of its significant influence on subsequent literature and art.

Cailler, Pierre. *Guillaume Apollinaire, documents iconographiques.* Geneva: Cailler, 1965. Photographs of Apollinaire, his family, his residences, a few drawings and mss., and his personal art collection.

Chevalier, Jean-Claude. *Alcools d'Apollinaire, essai d'analyse des formes poétiques.* Bibliothèque Guillaume Apollinaire, 3. Bibliothèque des lettres modernes, 17. Paris: Lettres Modernes, 1970. Thorough structuralist study of types of poetic discourse in *Alcools.*

Couffignal, Robert. *L'Inspiration biblique dans l'oeuvre de Guillaume Apollinaire.* Bibliothèque Guillaume Apollinaire, 2. Bibliothèque des lettres modernes, 8. Paris: Lettres Modernes, 1966. Examination of poet's attitudes towards catholicism and of more than 200 biblical references in his works.

Davies, Margaret. *Apollinaire.* London: Oliver and Boyd, 1964. Good critical study arranged on biographical lines.

Debon, Claude. *Guillaume Apollinaire après "Alcools."* Bibliothèque Guillaume Apollinaire, 12. Bibliothèque des lettres modernes, 31. Vol. 1, *Calligrammes; le poète et la guerre.* Vol. 2, *Les Fictions du moi du "Poète assassiné" à la "Femme assise."* Paris: Lettres modernes, 1981. Major study of the poetry (vol. 1) and prose (vol. 2) of the 1913–18 period.

Décaudin, Michel. *La Crise des valeurs symbolistes.* Toulouse: Privat, 1960. Comprehensive survey of French literary movements from 1895 to 1914.

―――. *Le Dossier d'Alcools.* Paris: Minard, 1965. Basic work on *Alcools.* Includes manuscripts, published versions of poems, biography of poet, critical study of genesis of *Alcools,* its publication and reception. Important notes, critical bibliography.

Durry, Marie-Jeanne. *Guillaume Apollinaire, Alcools.* 3 vols. Paris: Société d'éditions d'enseignement supérieur, 1956–65. Long study of *Alcools* based on author's Sorbonne course. Important biographical and critical insights, sources, analyses.

Faure-Favier, Louise. *Souvenirs sur Apollinaire.* Paris: B. Grasset, 1945. Letters, memoirs from post-*Alcools* period by a friend of Apollinaire and Marie Laurencin.

Fettweis, Christian. *Apollinaire en Ardenne.* Brussels: Henriquez, 1934.

Description of Apollinaire's stay in Stavelot, Belgium, in 1899, and his criminal departure. Influence of this stay on work.

Follet, Lionel, and Marc Poupon. *Lecture de "Palais" d'Apollinaire.* Archives Guillaume Apollinaire, 6. Archives des lettres modernes, 6. Paris: Lettres modernes, 1972. Excellent analysis, from a mythical-structural point of view, of "Palais" and other early poems in *Alcools.*

Hilgar, Marie-France and Anne Srabian de Fabry, eds. *Etudes autour d'Alcools.* Birmingham, Alabama: Summa Publications, 1985.

Jannini, P. A., ed. *Apollinaire et l'avanguardia.* Rome, Paris: Bulzoni, Nizet, 1984. Essays by Adéma, Burgos, Caizergues, Décaudin, Richter, et al.

————. *La Fortuna di Apollinaire in Italia.* Milano: Instituto Editoriale Cisalpino, 1959. Apollinaire and futurism, other Italian movements. Testimonies of Italian artist-friends of poet.

————. *Le Avanguardie letterarie nell'idea critica di Guillaume Apollinaire.* Rome: Bulzoni, 1971. Solidly documented overview of Apollinaire's attitudes towards selected members of the avant-garde.

Jean, Raymond. *La Poétique du désir; Nerval, Lautréamont, Apollinaire, Eluard.* Paris: Seuil, 1974. The four sections on Apollinaire contain a profound analysis of the writer's erotic exhibitionism.

Pia, Pascal. *Apollinaire par lui-même.* Paris: Seuil, 1954. A biography, with more literary analysis than Adéma's work on which it depends for many facts. Very readable, by a member of the Parisian Bohemia.

Renaud, Philippe. *Lecture d'Apollinaire.* Lausanne: L'Age d'homme, 1969. Synthesis of Orphic and Promethean themes in the poetry, discerning analysis of the transition (in *Ondes*) between the musicality of word in *Alcools* and the musicality of form in *Calligrammes.*

Rouveyre, André. *Amour et poésie d'Apollinaire.* Paris: Seuil, 1955. Semi-Freudian meditation by an associate and friend concerning a few poems and prose passages.

————. *Apollinaire.* Paris: Gallimard, 1945. Fascinating psychological analysis of Apollinaire's amorous proclivities.

Salmon, André. *Souvenirs sans fin.* 3 vols. Paris: Gallimard, 1955–61. Anecdotes and reminiscences by a close friend.

Samaltanos, Katiä. *Apollinaire, Catalyst for Primitivism, Picabia, and Duchamp.* Studies in the Fine Arts: The Avant-Garde, 45. Ann Arbor: University of Michigan Research Press, 1984. Apollinaire as a major influence on dadaism, surrealism, cult of African art, etc.

Shattuck, Roger. *The Banquet Years.* New York: Harcourt, Brace, 1955. Delightful journalistic and critical account of four artists, Henri Rousseau, Alfred Jarry, Eric Satie, and Guillaume Apollinaire, and their creative age.

Steegmuller, Francis. *Apollinaire, Poet among the Painters*. New York: Farrar, Strauss, 1963. Biography, emphasizing picturesque, cosmopolitan aspects of life. Many photographs.

Tournadre, Claude. *Les Critiques de notre temps et Apollinaire*. Les Critiques de notre temps, 5. Paris: Garnier, 1971. Anthology of excerpts of leading articles and books on Apollinaire. Bibliography.

Toussaint-Luca, A. *Guillaume Apollinaire, Souvenirs d'un ami*. Monaco: Editions du Rocher, 1954. Memoirs by a school friend, covering principally the period of adolescence.

Zoppi, Sergio. *Apollinaire teorico*. Testi e saggi di letteratura francese, 3. Naples: Edizioni scientifiche italiane, 1970. Chronological tracing of Apollinaire's philosophy of aesthetic humanism.

Ongoing Periodicals Devoted to Apollinaire Studies

Guillaume Apollinaire, La Revue des Lettres Modernes. Paris: Lettres Modernes, 1962 to present (referred to in notes as *GA*).

Que vlo-ve? Namur, Belgium: January 1973 to present.

Special Issues of Periodicals

Sic 37–39 (January–February 1919).

Vient de Paraître 24 (15 November 1923).

Images de Paris 49–50 (January–February 1924), 56–57 (September–October 1924).

L'Esprit Nouveau 26 (October 1924).

Les Marges 225–226 (February–March 1936).

Présence d'Apollinaire (22 December 1943–31 January 1944).

Rimes et Raisons (1946).

La Table Ronde 57 (September 1952).

Le Flâneur des Deux Rives 1–8 (March 1954–December 1955).

Revue des Sciences Humaines 84 (October–December 1956).

Savoir et Beauté 2–3 (1964).

Europe 451–452 (November–December 1966).

Essays in French Literature 17 (November 1980).

Cahiers du Musée Nationale d'Art Moderne 5–6 (1981).

Les Cahiers de Varsovie 11 (1984).

Index

Index

203